EXERCISES IN ENGLISH

☆ GRAMMAR FOR LIFE ☆

TEACHER'S EDITION

LEVEL G

LOYOLAPRESS.

CHICAGO

The Complete Grammar Program with Character

Enhancing Grammar with Grade-Level Science, Social Studies, Language Arts, and Character Education

- **Instruction** and **practice** in every area of modern grammar, usage, and mechanics help students build comprehensive, lifelong skills.

- **Grade-level science**, **social studies**, and **language arts** content reinforces learning in other subject areas.

- **Character education** enriches students' lives through profiles of multicultural role models.

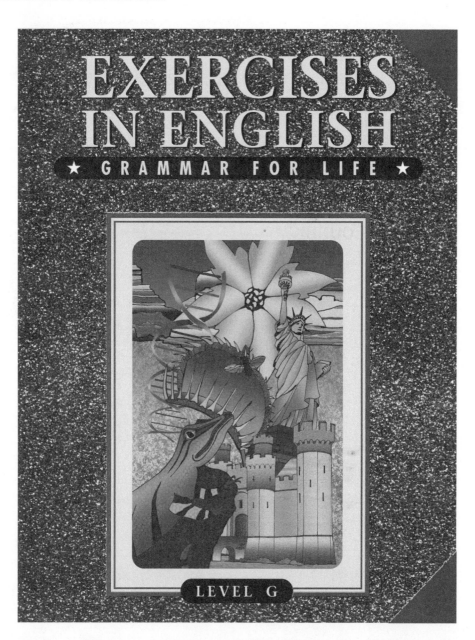

EXERCISES IN ENGLISH
★ GRAMMAR FOR LIFE ★

LEVEL G

A Six-Level Program

Carefully sequenced Student Editions for grades 3–8 provide thorough teaching of all modern grammar concepts.

Easy-to-use Teacher's Editions offer clear, concise answers to exercises.

Introductory Review section, starting at Level D, helps students get back on track at the beginning of the year.

Self-teaching student lessons optimize class time.

Section reviews offer regular assessment opportunities.

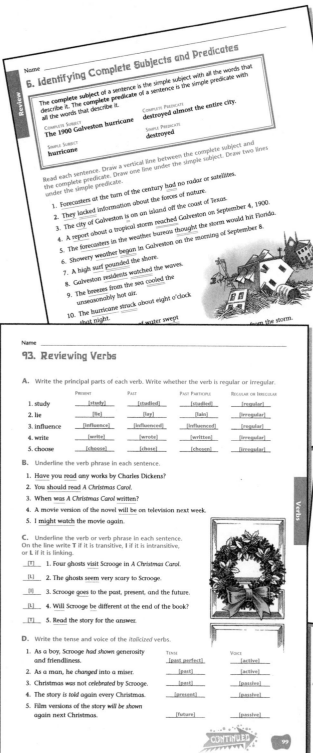

Review

Name _____

6. Identifying Complete Subjects and Predicates

The **complete subject** of a sentence is the simple subject with all the words that describe it. The **complete predicate** of a sentence is the simple predicate with all the words that describe it.

COMPLETE SUBJECT
The 1900 Galveston hurricane

COMPLETE PREDICATE
destroyed almost the entire city.

SIMPLE SUBJECT
hurricane

SIMPLE PREDICATE
destroyed

Read each sentence. Draw a vertical line between the complete subject and the complete predicate. Draw one line under the simple subject. Draw two lines under the simple predicate.

1. Forecasters at the turn of the century had no radar or satellites.
2. They lacked information about the forces of nature.
3. The city of Galveston is on an island off the coast of Texas.
4. A report about a tropical storm reached Galveston on September 4, 1900.
5. The forecasters in the weather bureau thought the storm would hit Florida.
6. Showery weather began in Galveston on the morning of September 8.
7. A high surf pounded the shore.
8. Galveston residents watched the waves.
9. The breezes from the sea cooled the unseasonably hot air.
10. The hurricane struck about eight o'clock that night.
... of water swept ... from the storm.

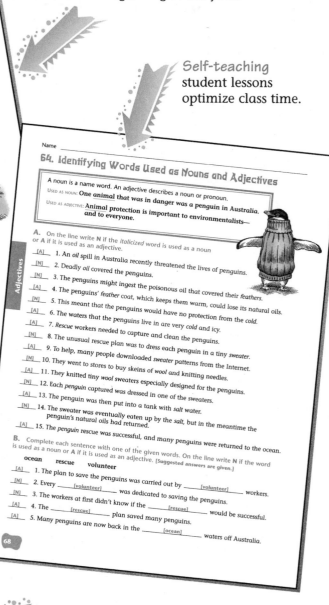

Name _____

64. Identifying Words Used as Nouns and Adjectives

A noun is a name word. An adjective describes a noun or pronoun.
USED AS NOUN: One **animal** that was in danger was a penguin in Australia.
USED AS ADJECTIVE: **Animal** protection is important to environmentalists— and to everyone.

A. On the line write **N** if the *italicized* word is used as a noun or **A** if it is used as an adjective.

[A] 1. An *oil* spill in Australia recently threatened the lives of penguins.
[N] 2. Deadly *oil* covered the penguins.
[N] 3. The penguins might ingest the poisonous oil that covered their *feathers*.
[A] 4. The penguins' *feather* coat, which keeps them warm, could lose its natural oils.
[N] 5. This meant that the penguins would have no protection from the *cold*.
[A] 6. The waters that the penguins live in are very *cold* and icy.
[A] 7. *Rescue* workers needed to capture and clean the penguins.
[N] 8. The unusual rescue plan was to dress each penguin in a tiny *sweater*.
[A] 9. To help, many people downloaded *sweater* patterns from the Internet.
[N] 10. They went to stores to buy skeins of *wool* and knitting needles.
[A] 11. They knitted tiny *wool* sweaters especially designed for the penguins.
[N] 12. Each *penguin* captured was dressed in one of the sweaters.
[A] 13. The *penguin* was then put into a tank with *salt* water.
[N] 14. The sweater was eventually eaten up by the *salt*, but in the meantime the penguin's natural oils had returned.
[A] 15. The *penguin* rescue was successful, and many penguins were returned to the ocean.

B. Complete each sentence with one of the given words. On the line write **N** if the word is used as a noun or **A** if it is used as an adjective. [Suggested answers are given.]

ocean   rescue   volunteer

[A] 1. The plan to save the penguins was carried out by ___[volunteer]___ workers.
[N] 2. Every ___[volunteer]___ was dedicated to saving the penguins.
[N] 3. The workers at first didn't know if the ___[rescue]___ would be successful.
[A] 4. The ___[rescue]___ plan saved many penguins.
[A] 5. Many penguins are now back in the ___[ocean]___ waters off Australia.

68

Adjectives

Name _____

93. Reviewing Verbs

A. Write the principal parts of each verb. Write whether the verb is regular or irregular.

	PRESENT	PAST	PAST PARTICIPLE	REGULAR OR IRREGULAR
1. study	[study]	[studied]	[studied]	[regular]
2. lie	[lie]	[lay]	[lain]	[irregular]
3. influence	[influence]	[influenced]	[influenced]	[regular]
4. write	[write]	[wrote]	[written]	[irregular]
5. choose	[choose]	[chose]	[chosen]	[irregular]

B. Underline the verb phrase in each sentence.

1. Have you read any works by Charles Dickens?
2. You should read A Christmas Carol.
3. When was A Christmas Carol written?
4. A movie version of the novel will be on television next week.
5. I might watch the movie again.

C. Underline the verb or verb phrase in each sentence. On the line write **T** if it is transitive, **I** if it is intransitive, or **L** if it is linking.

[T] 1. Four ghosts visit Scrooge in A Christmas Carol.
[L] 2. The ghosts seem very scary to Scrooge.
[I] 3. Scrooge goes to the past, present, and the future.
[L] 4. Will Scrooge be different at the end of the book?
[T] 5. Read the story for the answer.

D. Write the tense and voice of the *italicized* verbs.

	TENSE	VOICE
1. As a boy, Scrooge *had shown* generosity and friendliness.	[past perfect]	[active]
2. As a man, he *changed* into a miser.	[past]	[active]
3. Christmas *was* not *celebrated* by Scrooge.	[past]	[passive]
4. The story *is told* again every Christmas.	[present]	[passive]
5. Film versions of the story *will be shown* again next Christmas.	[future]	[passive]

Verbs

CONTINUED   99

TE4

Features that set us apart...

Clear definitions and examples
help students easily understand concepts.

38. Using Reflexive and Intensive Pronouns

A **reflexive pronoun** ends in *-self* or *-selves*. A reflexive pronoun is often the object of a verb or of a preposition. It refers to the same person, place, or thing as the subject of the sentence.

Walt Disney had confidence in himself and gained success.

When a reflexive pronoun is used as an appositive immediately after a noun or pronoun to show emphasis, it is called an **intensive pronoun**.

Walt Disney himself did much of the work on his films.

A. Underline the reflexive or intensive pronoun in each sentence. Circle the words it refers to.

1. Walt Disney made a name for himself as a producer of cartoon features.

Nouns

DIRECT OBJECT   APPOSITIVE
Many people have myopia, the inability to see things far away.

A. Underline the appositive in each sentence. Circle the noun it explains. Write **DO** over direct objects that have appositives.

1. The human eyeball houses the retina, a layer of nerve tissues with light receptors.
2. The eyeball has a sclera, a tough shell that covers the eyeball.
3. The eyeball contains vitreous humour, a jellylike liquid, to help it keep its shape.
4. The part that lets light pass through the eye is the cornea, a segment of the sclera.
5. Behind the cornea the eye has an iris, a set of muscles that open and close.
6. Light enters through the pupil, an opening at the center of the iris.
7. The retina contains rods and cones, the receptor cells.
8. Receptors send images to the optic nerve, the link between the eye and the brain.
9. Perceiving shapes and brightness is done by rods, light-sensitive cells.
10. Cones, light-sensitive cells of another type, perceive color and fine detail.
11. Thomas Young, an English physician, theorized the existence of color receptors in 1801.
12. Existence of the color receptors, the cones, finally was confirmed in the 1960s.
13. Lack of a set of cones explains color blindness, the inability to see red, green, or blue.
14. For example, people with protanopia, blindness to red, cannot distinguish red and green.

B. Use the phrase at the right as an appositive for each underlined object.

1. We can see light.   a kind of radiant energy
[We can see light, a kind of radiant energy.]

2. Light moves in waves.   an up-and-down motion
[Light moves in waves, an up-and-down motion.]

3. Light has its own wavelength.   the distance between the tops of two waves
[Light has its own wavelength, the distance between the tops of two waves.]

4. People use microwaves to cook food.   another kind of radiant energy
[People use microwaves, another kind of radiant energy, to cook food.]

5. Waves of different lengths form the light spectrum.   an array of six colors
[Waves of different lengths form the light spectrum, an array of six colors.]

Grade-level content
provides enrichment and reinforcement of what is being studied in science, social studies, and language arts.

Circle the abstract nouns. Underline the concrete nouns.

1. Maria Montessori (1870–1952) was a pioneer in the education of children.
2. Through her determination, Maria was the first woman in Italy to become a doctor.
3. The young doctor began to work with children and study their methods of learning.
4. Montessori worked in a poor area of Rome.
5. Her desire to help children was strong.
6. Maria even had workers cut down chairs and desks for the convenience of small children.
7. Her basic observation was that children have a great need to work toward goals.
8. Educators need to set the right environment so young learners can experiment independently.
9. The philosophy of Montessori was to present children with challenges.
10. There are many schools around the world that follow the principles of Montessori today.
11. In the classrooms you will see beads, blocks, and maps—all on low shelves.
12. In Montessori schools, children work with materials that have specific purposes.
13. One such material is the pink tower, which is made of ten pink blocks.
14. For success with a tower, the child starts with the largest block first.
15. The tower helps children learn the concept of size.

Maria Montessori used her knowledge to help others. Give an example of how you can use your talents to help others.

15

Character education lessons
offer students information on multicultural role models on a consistent basis.

4. On the statue's pedestal, visitors can read "The New Colossus," a poem by Emma Lazarus.
5. The Statue of Liberty gives people the promise of freedom and hope.

Try It Yourself
Write a paragraph about a famous monument in the United States. Be sure that you use capital letters and apostrophes correctly.

_____
_____
_____
_____

Check Your Own Work
Choose a piece of writing from your portfolio or journal, a work in progress, an assignment from another class, or a letter. Revise it, applying the skills you have reviewed. The checklist will help you.

✔ Have you capitalized all proper nouns?
✔ Have you used the correct forms of plurals?
✔ Have you used apostrophes in possessives correctly?

30

Writing in context
allows students to practice and use what they have learned.

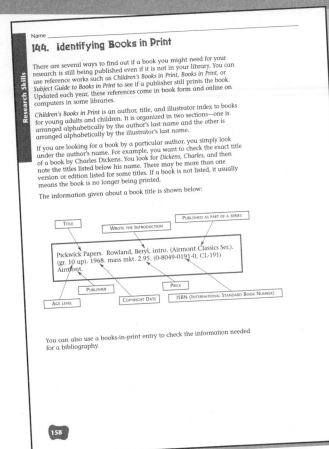

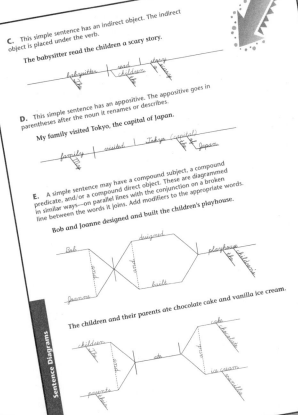

Research Skills section provides teaching and practice with tools such as the Internet and atlases. Students learn to combine grammar and writing in projects for other classes.

Handbook of Terms helps students refresh and expand their knowledge of grammar points.

Sentence Diagramming section, starting at Level D, helps students visually portray the parts of a sentence to better understand and remember concepts.

Plus

- **Flexible format** allows use of the books at multiple grade levels.

- **Perforated student pages** facilitate grading and inclusion in student portfolios.

- **Easy-to-grade exercises** are always divisible by five.

- **Sentence Analysis section** in the Teacher's Edition provides extra tools for daily oral grammar activities.

Exercises in English—Scope and Sequence

SENTENCES	C	D	E	F	G	H
The Four Kinds of Sentences	✔	✔	✔	✔	✔	✔
Subjects and Predicates	✔	✔	✔	✔	✔	✔
Simple Subjects and Predicates		✔		✔	✔	✔
Compound Subjects and Predicates		✔	✔	✔	✔	✔
Direct Objects		✔	✔	✔	✔	✔
Complete Subjects and Predicates			✔	✔	✔	✔
Natural and Inverted Order in Sentences			✔	✔	✔	✔
Indirect Objects				✔	✔	✔
Compound Sentences				✔	✔	✔
Complex Sentences					✔	✔
Compound Complex Sentences						✔
NOUNS	C	D	E	F	G	H
Proper and Common Nouns	✔	✔	✔	✔	✔	✔
Singular and Plural Nouns	✔	✔	✔	✔	✔	✔
Possessive Nouns	✔	✔	✔	✔	✔	✔
Nouns Used as Subjects		✔	✔	✔		
Nouns Used as Objects		✔	✔	✔	✔	✔
Nouns Used as Subject Complements			✔	✔	✔	
Nouns Used in Direct Address			✔	✔		
Nouns Used as Objects of Prepositions			✔	✔	✔	
Appositives				✔	✔	
Collective Nouns				✔	✔	✔
Concrete and Abstract Nouns				✔	✔	✔
Words Used as Nouns and Verbs				✔		✔
Nouns Used as Object Complements						✔
VERBS	C	D	E	F	G	H
Regular and Irregular Verbs	✔	✔	✔	✔	✔	✔
Present Tense	✔	✔	✔	✔	✔	✔
Progressive Tenses	✔	✔	✔	✔	✔	✔
Past Tense	✔	✔	✔	✔	✔	✔
Future Tenses	✔	✔	✔	✔	✔	✔
Action Verbs	✔	✔	✔			
Verbs of Being	✔	✔	✔			
Helping Verbs	✔	✔				
Forms of *Bring*	✔					
Forms of *Buy*	✔					

	C	D	E	F	G	H
Forms of *Come*	✔					
Forms of *Eat*	✔					
Forms of *Go*	✔		✔			
Forms of *See*	✔		✔			
Forms of *Sit* and *Set*	✔		✔	✔		
Forms of *Take*	✔		✔			
Forms of *Write*	✔					
Forms of *To Be*	✔	✔	✔			
Forms of *Begin*		✔				
Forms of *Break*		✔	✔			
Forms of *Choose*		✔	✔			
Forms of *Do*		✔				
Verb Phrases		✔	✔	✔	✔	
Intransitive Verbs (Linking Verbs)		✔	✔	✔	✔	✔
There Is and *There Are*		✔		✔	✔	
Subject-Verb Agreement			✔	✔	✔	✔
Transitive Verbs			✔	✔	✔	✔
Doesn't and *Don't*			✔	✔	✔	✔
Let and *Leave*			✔	✔		
Teach and *Learn*			✔			
Lie and *Lay*			✔	✔		
Rise and *Raise*			✔			
Perfect Tenses			✔	✔		
Words Used as Nouns and Verbs					✔	
Active and Passive Voice					✔	✔
Modal Auxiliary Verbs					✔	✔
You Are and *You Were*					✔	
Compound Tenses						✔
Emphatic Verb Forms						✔
PRONOUNS	C	D	E	F	G	H
Singular and Plural Pronouns	✔	✔	✔			
Subject Pronouns	✔	✔	✔	✔	✔	✔
Possessive Pronouns	✔	✔	✔	✔	✔	✔
I and *Me*	✔	✔				
Pronouns Used as Subject Complements	✔		✔	✔	✔	✔
Pronouns Used as Direct Objects		✔	✔	✔	✔	✔
The Person of Pronouns		✔	✔	✔		
The Gender of Pronouns			✔			
We and *Us*		✔				
Pronouns Used as Objects of Prepositions			✔	✔		

Pronouns Used in Contractions			✔	✔		
Reflexive Pronouns			✔	✔	✔	
Interrogative Pronouns				✔	✔	✔
Indefinite Pronouns				✔	✔	✔
Double Negatives				✔		
Pronouns Used as Indirect Objects					✔	✔
Who and *Whom*					✔	✔
Pronouns Used after *Than* and *As*					✔	✔
Relative Pronouns					✔	✔
Demonstrative Pronouns					✔	✔
Nothing and *Anything*					✔	
Pronouns Used as Objects of Prepositions					✔	✔
Intensive Pronouns			✔			✔

ADJECTIVES	C	D	E	F	G	H
Descriptive Adjectives	✔			✔	✔	
Adjectives That Tell How Many	✔	✔	✔	✔		
Indefinite and Definite Articles	✔	✔	✔	✔	✔	
Demonstrative Adjectives	✔	✔	✔	✔	✔	✔
Comparative Forms of Adjectives	✔	✔	✔	✔	✔	✔
Possessive Adjectives		✔	✔	✔		
Common and Proper Adjectives		✔	✔			✔
Good and *Bad*		✔				
The Position of Adjectives			✔	✔	✔	✔
Superlative Forms of Adjectives			✔	✔	✔	✔
Adjectives Used as Subject Complements				✔		
Words Used as Adjectives or Nouns				✔	✔	✔
Those and *Them*				✔		
Interrogative Adjectives				✔		
Fewer and *Less*					✔	

ADVERBS	C	D	E	F	G	H
Adverbs of Time	✔	✔	✔	✔		
Adverbs of Place	✔	✔	✔	✔		
Good and *Well*	✔	✔	✔			
Comparative Adverbs		✔	✔	✔	✔	✔
Adverbs of Manner		✔	✔	✔		
No, Not, and *Never*		✔	✔	✔		
Superlative Adverbs			✔	✔		
Real and *Very*			✔			
Their and *There*			✔	✔		
To, Too, and *Two*			✔	✔		

	C	D	E	F	G	H
Adverbs and Adjectives				✔	✔	✔
There, Their, and *They're*					✔	
Farther and *Further*					✔	✔
Interrogative Adverbs					✔	✔
Adverbial Nouns					✔	✔
As . . . As, So . . . As, and *Equally*						✔

PUNCTUATION, CAPITALIZATION, ABBREVIATIONS	C	D	E	F	G	H
End Punctuation	✔	✔	✔	✔	✔	✔
Periods after Abbreviations, Titles, and Initials	✔	✔				
Capital Letters	✔	✔	✔	✔	✔	
Titles of Books and Poems	✔		✔	✔	✔	
Commas Used in Direct Address	✔	✔	✔	✔		
Punctuation in Direct Quotations	✔	✔	✔	✔		
Apostrophes		✔	✔			
Commas after *Yes* and *No*		✔	✔	✔		
Commas Separating Words in a Series		✔	✔	✔		
Commas after Parts of a Letter			✔	✔		
Commas in Dates and Addresses			✔	✔		
Commas in Geographical Names			✔			
Commas Used with Appositives				✔		
Commas Used in Compound Sentences				✔		
Semicolons and Colons				✔	✔	✔
Apostrophes, Hyphens, and Dashes				✔	✔	✔
Commas and Semicolons						✔

PREPOSITIONS, CONJUNCTIONS, INTERJECTIONS	C	D	E	F	G	H
Prepositions and Prepositional Phrases			✔	✔	✔	✔
Interjections			✔	✔	✔	✔
Between and *Among*			✔	✔		
From and *Off*			✔			
Adjectival Phrases			✔			
Adverbial Phrases			✔			
Coordinate Conjunctions			✔			
Words Used as Prepositions and Adverbs				✔	✔	✔
At and *To*				✔		
Beside and *Besides, In* and *Into*				✔		
Coordinate and Correlative Conjunctions					✔	
Conjunctive Adverbs					✔	

	C	D	E	F	G	H
Subordinate Conjunctions					✔	✔
Without and *Unless, Like, As,* and *As If*					✔	✔
PHRASES, CLAUSES	C	D	E	F	G	H
Adjectival Phrases				✔	✔	
Adverbial Phrases				✔	✔	
Adjectival Clauses					✔	✔
Adverbial Clauses					✔	✔
Restrictive and Nonrestrictive Clauses					✔	
Noun Clauses						✔
PARTICIPLES, GERUNDS, INFINITIVES	C	D	E	F	G	H
Participles						✔
Dangling Participles						✔
Gerunds						✔
Infinitives						✔
Hidden and Split Infinitives						✔
WORD STUDY SKILLS	C	D	E	F	G	H
Synonyms	✔	✔	✔	✔		
Antonyms	✔	✔				
Homophones	✔	✔	✔			
Contractions	✔	✔				
Compound Words		✔				
PARAGRAPH SKILLS	C	D	E	F	G	H
Using Colorful Adjectives	✔		✔			
Combining Subjects, Verbs, and Sentences	✔					
Finding the Exact Word		✔				
Using Similes		✔				
Expanding Sentences		✔				
Rewriting Rambling Sentences		✔	✔			
Revising		✔				
Proofreading		✔				
Recognizing the Exact Meaning of Words			✔			
LETTER WRITING	C	D	E	F	G	H
Friendly Letters	✔	✔				
Invitations	✔					
Letters of Acceptance	✔					
Thank-You Letters	✔			✔		
E-Mail Messages	✔	✔		✔		

Envelopes	✔	✔				
Forms	✔	✔				
Business Letters				✔		
RESEARCH	C	D	E	F	G	H
Computer Catalog	✔					
Dictionary	✔	✔				
Encyclopedia	✔		✔			
Thesaurus		✔				
Internet		✔	✔	✔	✔	✔
Almanac			✔			
Atlas			✔		✔	
Guides to Periodicals				✔		
Biographical Information				✔		
The Dewey Decimal System				✔		
Books of Quotations					✔	
Books in Print					✔	
The Statistical Abstract of the United States						✔
Research Tools						✔

Sentence Analysis

Purpose

Sentence analysis is a classroom-tested strategy designed to aid students in the understanding of a sentence through the study of its grammatical components and their relationship to one another.

Sentence analysis begins with a careful and thoughtful reading of the sentence to determine that it does contain a complete thought. Students then determine the *use* of the sentence (for example, declarative). Next, they identify the subject and the predicate. They can then go on to analyze the details in the sentence.

It is often useful to conduct a sentence analysis as an oral exercise. Each student responds to one point in the analysis in some predetermined order—by row, by group, or by number. Keep the responses moving at a fairly fast pace to hold students' interest. Five minutes at the beginning of each grammar period will focus the students on the task. Prolonging the activity may make it a chore rather than a challenge.

Give each student a copy of the Sentence Analysis Chart (page TE16) or place a blown-up version where all students can see it. Select a sentence from this or another book and write it on the board for analysis.

Ideally, you should act as an observer during the activity, allowing students to perform the analysis without assistance. The students' performance will indicate their grasp of grammar and help you identify areas that need review.

Consistent practice in identifying grammatical concepts will ensure that students arrive at an understanding of how the English language is structured and how they can use its patterns to express their own thoughts.

Procedure

Display the Sentence Analysis Chart (page TE16) or distribute a copy to each student. Choose a sentence that contains the aspects of grammar recently taught or reviewed and write it on the board. The first few times you do the activity, you may also want to display or distribute the Sentence Analysis Questions (page TE15) to help students complete the task.

Now have students use the chart to work through the steps of analysis, identifying each part of the sentence.

1. Sentence

Have the sentence read aloud. You may want to have the class read as a whole or ask an individual to read. Students should recognize that a sentence has a subject and a predicate and forms a complete thought.

EXAMPLE SENTENCE: **Yesterday the happy children played drums noisily.**

2. Use

Students should be able to recognize that a sentence is declarative, interrogative, imperative, or exclamatory. In selecting sentences for analysis, vary your choice among the four types.

According to *use*, the example sentence is declarative because it makes a statement.

Note: You may want to have students practice steps 1 and 2 several times before moving on to step 3. Once the students are comfortable identifying sentences, add the following steps one at a time, practicing them in short sessions each day.

3. Predicate

The predicate is the part of a sentence that contains a verb. Because the verb is the focal point of the thought, it should be identified first. The verb expresses action or being.

The verb in the example sentence is *played.*

4. Subject

The verb tells what the subject does or is. The subject can be determined by asking *who* or *what* before the verb.

The subject of the example sentence is *children.*

5. Object/Complement

Sometimes the predicate verb is completed by a direct object or a subject complement. They answer the questions *whom, who,* or *what* after the verb.

The direct object of the example sentece is *drums.*

6. Modifiers

Adverbs modify verbs. Adverbs answer the questions *how, when,* or *where.*

In the example sentence, the adverb *yesterday* tells when the children played, and the adverb *noisily* tells how the children played.

Adjectives modify nouns or pronouns. Adjectives answer the questions *what, what kind, how many,* or *whose.* An article is an adjective that points out a noun.

In the example sentence, the article *the* points out the noun *children,* and the adjective *happy* tells what kind of children.

7. Parts of Speech

To close the activity, ask the students to name the part of speech of each word in the sentence, beginning with the first and moving through the sentence in order.

In the example sentence, *yesterday* is an adverb, *the* is an article, *happy* is an adjective, *children* is a noun, *played* is a verb, *noisily* is an adverb.

Sentence Analysis Questions

1. Sentence
Does the group of words form a complete thought with a subject and a predicate? (If it does, it's a sentence.)

2. Use
Is the sentence *declarative* (makes a statement), *interrogative* (asks a question), *imperative* (gives a command), or *exclamatory* (shows surprise or emotion)?

3. Predicate
The predicate of a sentence contains a *verb*. A verb shows action or being. What is the verb in the sentence? (The verb includes the main verb and any helping verbs: *swam/had swum, goes/is going.)*

4. Subject
The *subject* is a noun or a pronoun. The verb tells what the subject does or is. To find the subject, ask *who* or *what* before the verb.

5. Object/Complement
The direct object or subject complement complete the verb. To find them ask *whom, who,* or *what* after the verb.

6. Modifiers
Adverbs tell more about verbs. To find the adverbs, ask *how, when,* or *where* the action or being took place.

Adjectives describe nouns or pronouns. To find the adjectives, ask *what, what kind, how many,* or *whose* about each noun or pronoun. An article is an adjective that points out a noun.

7. Parts of Speech
- Which words name persons, places, or things? (Those words are *nouns.)*
- Which words take the place of nouns? (Those words are *pronouns.)*
- Which words express action or being? (Those words are *verbs.)*
- Which words tell more about verbs? (Those words are *adverbs.)*
- Which words describe nouns? (Those words are *adjectives.)*

Sentence Analysis Chart

Sentence

Use

Predicate

Subject

Object/Complement

Modifiers

Parts of Speech

EXERCISES IN ENGLISH

☆ GRAMMAR FOR LIFE ☆

LEVEL G

LOYOLAPRESS.

CHICAGO

Consultants

Therese Elizabeth Bauer
Martina Anne Erdlen
Anita Patrick Gallagher
Patricia Healey
Irene Kervick
Susan Platt

Linguistics Advisor

Timothy G. Collins
National-Louis University

Series Design: Karen Christoffersen
Cover Design: Vita Jay Schweighart
Cover Art: Jody Lepinot/prairiestudio.com
Cover Photoshop: John Petroshius/prairiestudio.com
Interior Art: Keith Ward
Character Education Portraits: Jim Mitchell
Back Cover Text: Ted Naron

Acknowledgments

page 160   Entry of "Dickens, Charles" reprinted with the permission of
                  R.R. Bowker, a division of Reed Elsevier Inc.
                  Copyright 1997, Reed Elsevier Inc.

0-8294-2020-7 ★

0-8294-1750-8 ★

Exercises in English® is a registered trademark of Loyola Press.

Manufactured in the United States of America.

03 04 05 06 07 08 QuebD ★ 10 9 8 7 6 5 4 3 2

03 04 05 06 07 08 QuebD ★ 10 9 8 7 6 5 4 3 2 1

Table of Contents

1. Identifying Sentences

A **sentence** is a group of words that expresses a complete thought. A sentence has a **subject** and a **predicate**. The subject is who or what the sentence is about. The predicate tells what the subject is or does. Every sentence begins with a capital letter.

SUBJECT	PREDICATE
Mosquitoes	**can transmit disease.**
Mosquito-control agencies	**try to reduce the mosquito population.**

A. Read each example. Write **S** on the line if the words form a sentence. Put a period at the end of each sentence.

__[S]__ 1. All mosquitoes have four stages of development [.]

_____ 2. Egg, larva, pupa, and adult

__[S]__ 3. Many mosquitoes lay eggs on the surface of stagnant water [.]

__[S]__ 4. This water is often found near the home [.]

_____ 5. In discarded tires, tin cans, birdbaths, or plant saucers

B. Read each sentence. Draw a line between the subject and the predicate.

1. Mosquito eggs | hatch quickly into larvae.

2. Larvae | grow rapidly in the hot summer months and become pupae.

3. Flying adult mosquitoes | emerge from the pupae in about a week.

4. Most mosquito species | produce many generations each year.

5. Adult mosquitoes | mate after emerging from the pupae.

6. The female mosquito | needs a blood meal for her eggs to develop.

7. The mosquito | lays her eggs and seeks another blood meal.

8. A female mosquito | can lay many batches of eggs without mating again.

9. The male mosquito | does not require blood meals.

10. Male mosquitoes | live only a short time after mating.

11. Malaria and yellow fever | are spread by mosquitoes.

12. Reducing amounts of stagnant water | can help control mosquitoes.

13. People | should dispose of old tin cans and tires.

14. Water in birdbaths and fountains | should be changed often.

15. Various kinds of insect repellents | protect against mosquito bites.

Review

2. Identifying Declarative and Interrogative Sentences

A **declarative sentence** makes a statement. A declarative sentence ends with a period.

The Great Wall of China is one of the wonders of the world.

An **interrogative sentence** asks a question. An interrogative sentence ends with a question mark.

When was the Great Wall built?

Decide whether each sentence is declarative or interrogative. Write your answer on the line. Add the correct end punctuation.

[interrogative] 1. When did construction of the Great Wall begin [?]

[declarative] 2. In the seventh century B.C. there were many warring states in China [.]

[declarative] 3. Each state built walls to keep out its enemies [.]

[declarative] 4. In 221 B.C. China was united under the emperor Shih huang-ti [.]

[declarative] 5. He restored the old walls and linked them with new construction [.]

[declarative] 6. The resulting wall was about 3,000 miles long [.]

[interrogative] 7. What was the wall made of [?]

[declarative] 8. Some parts of the Shih huang-ti wall are dry-laid stone [.]

[declarative] 9. Other parts are formed from layers of tightly packed earth [.]

[interrogative] 10. How long did this wall survive [?]

[declarative] 11. In 206 B.C. the Ch'in dynasty was overthrown [.]

[declarative] 12. The wall started to fall apart [.]

[interrogative] 13. Who rebuilt it [?]

[declarative] 14. In 206 B.C. the Han dynasty rose to power [.]

[declarative] 15. The emperor Han Wu-ti repaired the crumbling walls [.]

[declarative] 16. He extended the wall 300 miles more into the Gobi Desert [.]

[declarative] 17. The Han added beacon towers to the walls [.]

[interrogative] 18. What were the towers for [?]

[declarative] 19. Columns of smoke from the towers warned of enemy attacks [.]

[declarative] 20. The beacons relayed messages faster than a man on horseback could [.]

Name _____

3. Identifying Imperative and Exclamatory Sentences

> An **imperative sentence** gives a command or makes a request.
> An imperative sentence ends with a period.
>
> **Explain how the eye works.**
>
> An **exclamatory sentence** expresses a strong emotion.
> An exclamatory sentence ends with an exclamation mark.
>
> **That's impossible!**

A. Underline the sentences that are imperative.

1. Place a glass of water on a table.

2. Stand a pencil behind the glass of water.

3. Look through the glass.

4. You will see the image of two pencils in it.

5. Close your left eye.

6. The right-hand pencil will disappear.

7. What happens when you close your right eye?

8. The water acts as a cylindrical lens.

9. Each eye sees the image at a different angle.

10. Try the experiment with containers of other shapes.

B. Decide whether each sentence is imperative or exclamatory.
Write your answer on the line. Add the correct end punctuation.

____[imperative]____ 1. Fill a shallow dish with water [.]

____[imperative]____ 2. Rest a flat mirror at an angle in the dish [.]

____[exclamatory]____ 3. Be careful [!]

____[imperative]____ 4. Stand the dish so that sunlight hits the mirror [.]

____[imperative]____ 5. Hold a sheet of white paper in front of the mirror [.]

____[imperative]____ 6. Move the paper until you see a rainbow [.]

____[imperative]____ 7. Adjust the angle of the mirror if necessary [.]

____[exclamatory]____ 8. How amazing is that [!]

____[imperative]____ 9. Fix the mirror in position with some modeling clay [.]

____[imperative]____ 10. Show your prism to your friends [.]

4. Identifying the Four Kinds of Sentences

A sentence can be declarative, interrogative, imperative, or exclamatory.

Decide whether each sentence is declarative, interrogative, imperative, or exclamatory. Write your answer on the line. Add the correct end punctuation.

__[declarative]__ 1. Clara Barton was born on December 25, 1821 [.]

__[declarative]__ 2. As a child, Clara took care of sick or injured pets [.]

__[declarative]__ 3. When she was eleven, her brother fell off a barn roof [.]

__[exclamatory]__ 4. That's horrible [!]

__[declarative]__ 5. Clara nursed him for two seemingly long years [.]

__[interrogative]__ 6. What did she do as an adult [?]

__[declarative]__ 7. When she was seventeen, she became a teacher [.]

__[declarative]__ 8. During the Civil War Clara volunteered for the Union [.]

__[declarative]__ 9. She delivered medical supplies and food to the troops [.]

__[exclamatory]__ 10. What a fantastic person she was [!]

__[declarative]__ 11. In 1870 Clara was in Europe [.]

__[declarative]__ 12. She worked as a volunteer during the Franco-Prussian War [.]

__[declarative]__ 13. She helped refugees in Paris and other cities [.]

__[interrogative]__ 14. Why didn't she work for the International Red Cross [?]

__[declarative]__ 15. The International Red Cross did not allow women to join [.]

__[declarative]__ 16. In 1881 Clara helped form the American Red Cross [.]

__[declarative]__ 17. The International Red Cross provided only battlefield relief [.]

__[declarative]__ 18. The American Red Cross also serves in times of disasters [.]

__[declarative]__ 19. Clara personally helped victims of fires, floods, and hurricanes [.]

__[imperative]__ 20. Explain why you think Clara will always be remembered [.]

Clara Barton devoted her life to helping people during difficult times. Give an example of how you can help someone who is in need.

Name _____

5. Identifying Simple Subjects and Predicates

A sentence has a subject and a predicate. The **simple subject** is the noun or pronoun that names the person, place, or thing the sentence is about. The **simple predicate** is the verb that tells what the subject does or is.

SIMPLE SUBJECT

Engineers
Chinese engineers
Chinese engineers of the Ming dynasty

SIMPLE PREDICATE

build.
built the Great Wall.
built many miles of the Great Wall.

A. Write the simple subject and simple predicate of each sentence in the correct column.

	SIMPLE SUBJECT	SIMPLE PREDICATE
1. The Ming ruled China from 1368 to 1644.	[Ming]	[ruled]
2. Ming artists created beautiful porcelain.	[artists]	[created]
3. Chinese blue-and-white porcelain amazed Europeans.	[porcelain]	[amazed]
4. Ming trading ships sailed the seas.	[ships]	[sailed]
5. The ships carried tea, porcelain, silk, and spices.	[ships]	[carried]
6. The new drink became the rage in Europe.	[drink]	[became]
7. Ming engineers improved brick-making technology.	[engineers]	[improved]
8. Their bricks are as strong as modern masonry.	[bricks]	[are]
9. The Ming wall snakes across difficult terrain.	[wall]	[snakes]
10. The work of the Ming dwarfed earlier accomplishments.	[work]	[dwarfed]

B. Read each sentence. Draw one line under the simple subject. Draw two lines under the simple predicate.

1. During the Tang dynasty (618–906) the Chinese made the first true porcelain.

2. A potter shapes pieces of porcelain on a potter's wheel.

3. Porcelain workers decorate the pieces in a variety of ways.

4. Surface modification includes carving, perforating, or embossing a piece.

5. Many museums display Chinese painted porcelain.

5

6. Identifying Complete Subjects and Predicates

The **complete subject** of a sentence is the simple subject with all the words that describe it. The **complete predicate** of a sentence is the simple predicate with all the words that describe it.

COMPLETE SUBJECT
The 1900 Galveston hurricane

COMPLETE PREDICATE
destroyed almost the entire city.

SIMPLE SUBJECT
hurricane

SIMPLE PREDICATE
destroyed

Read each sentence. Draw a vertical line between the complete subject and the complete predicate. Draw one line under the simple subject. Draw two lines under the simple predicate.

1. Forecasters at the turn of the century | had no radar or satellites.

2. They | lacked information about the forces of nature.

3. The city of Galveston | is on an island off the coast of Texas.

4. A report about a tropical storm | reached Galveston on September 4, 1900.

5. The forecasters in the weather bureau | thought the storm would hit Florida.

6. Showery weather | began in Galveston on the morning of September 8.

7. A high surf | pounded the shore.

8. Galveston residents | watched the waves.

9. The breezes from the sea | cooled the unseasonably hot air.

10. The hurricane | struck about eight o'clock that night.

11. An enormous surge of water | swept about 6,000 people to their deaths.

12. The low-lying, three-mile-wide island | offered no protection from the storm.

13. Residents trying to escape | found the roads impassable.

14. The winds at the height of the storm | reached 135 miles per hour.

15. The force of the hurricane | leveled thousands of buildings.

16. Terrified islanders | strapped themselves together with ropes.

17. People huddling in churches | died when the roofs collapsed.

18. Only three children in Galveston's St. Mary's Orphanage | survived.

19. Almost one-sixth of the island's population | perished in the storm.

20. The Galveston hurricane | was the deadliest natural disaster in U.S. history.

Name _____

7. Forming Sentences

> A sentence has a subject and a predicate.

A. Make sentences by matching the complete subjects in Column A with the complete predicates in Column B. Write the correct letter on the line. Use each letter once. **[Answers may vary. Sample answers are given.]**

COLUMN A

_[e]_ 1. *The Wizard of Oz*

_[d]_ 2. Dorothy Gale and her dog

_[h]_ 3. The citizens of Munchkin City

_[g]_ 4. The power of the ruby slippers

_[j]_ 5. Each of the friends

_[f]_ 6. The Wicked Witch of the West

_[a]_ 7. A band of flying monkeys

_[i]_ 8. The Wizard

_[c]_ 9. Glinda the Good Witch

_[b]_ 10. Scarecrow, Tin Woodsman, and Lion

COLUMN B

a. captures Dorothy.

b. join Dorothy on her journey.

c. tells Dorothy how to get home.

d. are swept away to Oz by a tornado.

e. is a well-loved movie.

f. wants her sister's ruby slippers.

g. takes Dorothy back to Kansas.

h. tell Dorothy how to find the Wizard.

i. turns out to be a fraud.

j. asks the Wizard for a favor.

B. Choose the best simple predicate to complete each sentence. Use each word once. **[Answers may vary. Sample answers are given.]**

appeared   delighted   quit   starred   wrote

1. Lyman Frank Baum _____[wrote]_____ the book *The Wizard of Oz* in 1900.

2. The adventures of Dorothy _____[delighted]_____ children right from the start.

3. Soon afterward, Baum _____[quit]_____ his job as a journalist.

4. Thirteen more Oz books _____[appeared]_____ before he died in 1919.

5. Judy Garland _____[starred]_____ in the film version of the story in 1939.

8. Identifying Compound Subjects and Predicates

A **compound subject** consists of more than one simple subject.

<u>Heat</u>, <u>light</u>, and <u>electricity</u> are forms of energy.

A **compound predicate** consists of more than one simple predicate.

Energy <u>powers</u> our vehicles and <u>cooks</u> our food.

A. Each sentence has a compound subject or predicate. Draw a vertical line between the subject and the predicate. Underline the compound subject or predicate.

1. <u>Our brains and bodies</u> | use energy from food.

2. <u>Bread, rice, and pasta</u> | give us quick energy.

3. <u>Fats and oils</u> | keep our skin healthy.

4. Proteins | <u>build muscle, develop bones, and carry oxygen through our bodies.</u>

5. <u>Meat, dairy products, eggs, and soybeans</u> | are good sources of proteins.

6. <u>Food and sunlight</u> | provide the energy for all living things.

7. <u>Machines and other nonliving things</u> | use other kinds of energy.

8. <u>Flashlights and portable radios</u> | use chemical energy stored in batteries.

9. Machines | <u>move and lift things with the energy from burning gasoline.</u>

10. The energy in moving water | <u>turns mill wheels and powers generators.</u>

B. Read each sentence. Underline the compound subjects. Circle the compound predicates.

1. <u>Coal</u>, <u>oil</u>, and <u>natural gas</u> are fossil fuels.

2. <u>Dinosaurs and plants</u> died millions of years ago.

3. Their bodies (decomposed) and (lay) buried under the ground.

4. After millions of years, they gradually (changed) and (formed) fuels.

5. Miners (dig) coal or (scrape) it off the surface of the earth.

6. <u>Oil and gas</u> lie in deposits underground.

7. Companies (drill) and (pump) crude oil out of the ground.

8. <u>Pipelines or tanker ships</u> carry the crude oil to refineries.

9. The refineries (heat) and (split) the oil into different types of products.

10. <u>Clothes</u>, <u>fertilizers</u>, and <u>plastics</u> are made from oil.

Name _____

9. Identifying Direct Objects

> The **direct object** is the noun or pronoun that completes the action of the verb. Many sentences need direct objects to complete their meaning. To find the direct object of a sentence, ask *whom* or *what* after the verb.
>
> | SUBJECT | VERB | DIRECT OBJECT | |
> |---------|------|---------------|---|
> | Many people | decorate | their homes | during the holidays. |
> | Stores | sell | decorations | of all kinds. |

A. Circle the direct object in each sentence.

1. People first decorated Christmas (trees) in the 1500s.

2. Merchants in Germany had (fairs) at Christmas time.

3. Bakers shaped (ornaments) out of gingerbread.

4. Families hung these (souvenirs) of the fairs on their trees.

5. Manufacturers invented (tinsel) about 1610.

6. They used real (silver.)

7. Earlier in America people hadn't celebrated (Christmas.)

8. The Puritans did not like such (celebration.)

9. In 1659 the government of Boston outlawed the (holiday.)

10. In 1846 Prince Albert of Germany gave his wife, Queen Victoria of England, a (gift) of a Christmas tree.

11. Americans first enjoyed Christmas (trees) in the 1800s.

12. People imported (ornaments) from Germany.

13. Pioneers on the frontier made their own (decorations.)

14. They put (candles) in tin lanterns for lights.

15. The trees relieved the (harshness) of life on the prairie.

B. Complete each sentence by writing a direct object. **[Answers will vary.]**

1. My family celebrates _____.

2. On this holiday we usually eat _____.

3. Sometimes we buy _____.

4. I often make _____.

5. My whole family enjoys _____.

Review

10. Identifying Indirect Objects

Some sentences have two objects—the direct object and the indirect object. The **indirect object** is the noun or pronoun that tells *to whom* or *for whom* the action is done.

Mike sent <u>his aunt</u> a card. = Mike sent a card to <u>his aunt</u>.

He bought <u>her</u> a present too. = He bought a present for <u>her</u> too.

A. Read each sentence. Circle the indirect object. The direct object is underlined.

1. Mrs. Rawlins offered (Marco) a <u>job</u> at the library.

2. Marco reads the (children) <u>stories</u>.

3. He shows (adults) the latest <u>bestsellers</u>.

4. Sometimes he mails (people) overdue <u>notices</u>.

5. Yesterday Mrs. Rawlins gave (Marco) a <u>raise</u>.

6. Last week Carol lent her (sister) her red <u>sweater</u>.

7. Marla promised (Carol) a <u>favor</u> in return.

8. Carol's social studies teacher assigned the (class) a special <u>project</u>.

9. Carol had to write the (mayor) a <u>letter</u>.

10. Marla gave her (sister) <u>help</u> in composing it.

B. Read each sentence. Underline the direct object. Circle the indirect object.

1. The city council promised our (neighborhood) a new <u>park</u>.

2. The architect showed the (reporter) the <u>design</u>.

3. The design denied (children) any playground <u>equipment</u>.

4. All the neighbors wrote the (mayor) <u>letters</u>.

5. The mayor offered the (citizens) a weak <u>explanation</u>.

6. A television reporter asked the (mayor) a <u>question</u>.

7. The mayor gave the (reporter) a long rambling <u>answer</u>.

8. The reporter told the (city) the <u>truth</u>.

9. The mayor had promised the (architect) a <u>kickback</u>.

10. The citizens gave the (reporter) a standing <u>ovation</u>.

Name _____

11. Reviewing Sentences

A. Decide whether each sentence is declarative, interrogative, imperative, or exclamatory. Write your answer on the line. Add the correct end punctuation.

_____[declarative]_____ 1. Álvar Núñez Cabeza de Vaca was born in Spain in 1490 [.]

_____[declarative]_____ 2. He made an amazing journey across America [.]

_____[interrogative]_____ 3. When did his journey begin [?]

_____[declarative]_____ 4. He arrived in Florida on April 7, 1528 [.]

_____[declarative]_____ 5. The captain of the fleet claimed the land for Spain [.]

_____[declarative]_____ 6. His men captured the leader of the Apalachee tribe [.]

_____[exclamatory]_____ 7. A terrible deed was done [!]

_____[declarative]_____ 8. The Native Americans ambushed them and chased them to the coast [.]

_____[interrogative]_____ 9. How were they going to escape [?]

_____[declarative]_____ 10. The men built some crude rafts and sailed away [.]

_____[declarative]_____ 11. A hurricane blew them to the coast of Texas [.]

_____[exclamatory]_____ 12. What bad luck they had [!]

_____[declarative]_____ 13. For six years Cabeza de Vaca lived with Native Americans in Texas [.]

_____[declarative]_____ 14. In the spring of 1534, he and three companions escaped [.]

_____[interrogative]_____ 15. Where did they go [?]

_____[declarative]_____ 16. They were the first explorers in the American West [.]

_____[declarative]_____ 17. They arrived in Mexico City in 1536 [.]

_____[declarative]_____ 18. Cabeza de Vaca wrote about his adventures [.]

_____[declarative]_____ 19. He wanted people to treat the Native Americans in a humane way [.]

_____[imperative]_____ 20. Try to find out more about this great explorer [.]

B. Read each sentence. Underline the simple or compound subjects. Circle the simple or compound predicates.

1. Many species of wildlife (live) and (flourish) at the Grand Canyon.

2. Pine, oak, and juniper (are) the dominant trees on the south rim of the Canyon.

3. Cacti and other drought-resistant shrubs (grow) at the bottom of the Canyon.

Name _____

4. Mule deer (wander) through the meadows and (graze) on the grass.

5. Bobcats and coyotes (range) and (hunt) throughout the park.

6. Beavers, gophers, chipmunks, and other small mammals (inhabit) the forest.

7. Peregrine falcons and bald eagles (swoop) and (soar) over the hills.

8. Reptiles and amphibians (live) along the river.

9. Some species of fish (suffered) and (died) because of changes in the river.

10. Some squawfish and chub (are considered) endangered.

C. Read each sentence. Underline the direct object. Circle the indirect object.

1. The National Park Service provides the (Grand Canyon) protection.

2. The rangers teach (people) safe ways to enjoy the park.

3. Trail markers give (hikers) directions.

4. Concession stands offer (visitors) refreshments.

5. Some tourists show other (tourists) the sights.

Try It Yourself
Write four sentences about a park or other attraction you have visited.
Be sure each sentence is complete. Use correct punctuation.

_____

_____

_____

_____

Check Your Own Work
Choose a piece of writing from your portfolio or journal, a work in progress,
an assignment from another class, or a letter. Revise it, applying the skills
you have reviewed. The checklist will help you.

✔ Does each sentence express a complete thought?

✔ Does each sentence start with a capital letter?

✔ Does each sentence end with the correct punctuation mark?

12. Identifying Proper and Common Nouns

A **noun** is a name word. A **proper noun** names a particular person, place, or thing. A **common noun** names any one member of a group of persons, places, or things. Proper nouns are capitalized.

Daniel Defoe wrote a book that tells the story of a shipwrecked sailor.

A. Identify whether each underlined noun names a person, place, or thing. Write your answer on the first line. On the second line, write **P** if it is proper, **C** if it is common.

[thing]	[C]	1. There has long been interest in <u>stories</u> about survival.
[person]	[C]	2. Usually <u>people</u> in the stories need to use intelligence to survive.
[person]	[P]	3. One classic story by <u>Johann David Wyss</u> tells about a shipwrecked family.
[person]	[C]	4. The <u>family</u> has to learn how to survive on its own.
[thing]	[C]	5. The family faces dangers from <u>snakes</u> and lions.
[place]	[C]	6. The family manages to build a paradise on the <u>island</u>.
[thing]	[C]	7. Wyss's <u>book</u> is nearly two hundred years old.
[thing]	[P]	8. A movie called <u>Castaway</u> was popular more recently.
[thing]	[C]	9. It told the story of a man who survived a crash of a <u>plane</u>.
[person]	[C]	10. The movie focused on the loneliness of the <u>man</u>.

B. Underline each noun. Above each noun write **P** if it is proper, **C** if it is common.

1. A well-known <u>character</u> [C] from a <u>book</u> [C] is <u>Robinson Crusoe</u> [P].
2. <u>Crusoe</u> [P] was a <u>sailor</u> [C] who spent twenty-eight <u>years</u> [C] shipwrecked on an <u>island</u> [C].
3. His <u>ship</u> [C] sank in the <u>Caribbean Sea</u> [P], and the <u>Englishman</u> [P] was the only <u>survivor</u> [C].
4. <u>Crusoe</u> [P] had to get <u>food</u> [C], <u>shelter</u> [C], and <u>clothing</u> [C] on his own.
5. The <u>goats</u> [C] on the <u>island</u> [C] provided <u>milk</u> [C] and <u>cheese</u> [C].
6. Although not a <u>carpenter</u> [C], <u>Crusoe</u> [P] built <u>shelves</u> [C] and a <u>table</u> [C] and eventually a <u>house</u> [C].
7. <u>Crusoe</u> [P] was able to grow <u>corn</u> [C] and <u>grain</u> [C] from <u>seeds</u> [C] and so could make <u>bread</u> [C].
8. <u>Crusoe</u> [P] found a <u>valley</u> [C] with <u>fruits</u> [C] such as <u>grapes</u> [C], which the <u>sailor</u> [C] dried into <u>raisins</u> [C].
9. The shipwrecked <u>man</u> [C] found a <u>parrot</u> [C] and taught the <u>bird</u> [C] to say <u>words</u> [C] in <u>English</u> [P].
10. Eventually a <u>ship</u> [C] landed near the <u>shore</u> [C], and <u>Crusoe</u> [P] returned to <u>England</u> [P].

13. Identifying Collective Nouns

> A **collective noun** names a group of persons, places, or things considered as a unit.
> A collective noun usually takes a singular verb.
>
> **The class visited an exhibit of student paintings.**
>
> **One painting showed a flock of pure white doves on a blue background.**

A. Underline the collective noun(s) in each sentence.

1. I belong to a photography club.

2. Last week a group of us went to a photography exhibit.

3. The collection of pictures was interesting.

4. The exhibit was sponsored by a company that sells cameras.

5. The majority of the photographers whose pictures were in the exhibit were teenagers.

6. My favorite picture showed a nervous cast backstage before a play.

7. My favorite action picture showed a soccer team celebrating a victory.

8. One striking set of pictures showed a fleet of tall ships entering a harbor.

9. The most relaxing picture was of a herd of cows grazing on a peaceful green hill.

10. A committee of students and professional photographers will choose the best pictures.

B. Write a collective noun associated with each group. **[Suggested answers are given.]**

1. cattle _____[herd]_____
2. baseball players _____[team]_____
3. birds _____[flock]_____
4. singers _____[choir]_____
5. sailors _____[navy]_____
6. executives _____[management]_____
7. students _____[class]_____
8. boy scouts _____[troop]_____
9. soldiers _____[army]_____
10. fish _____[school]_____
11. workers _____[union/company]_____
12. musicians _____[orchestra]_____
13. wolves _____[pack]_____
14. president and congress _____[government]_____
15. ants _____[colony]_____
16. grapes _____[bunch]_____
17. husband and wife _____[couple]_____
18. parents and children _____[family]_____
19. actors in a play _____[cast]_____
20. people at a play _____[audience]_____

14. Identifying Concrete and Abstract Nouns

A **concrete noun** names something that can be seen or touched.

Teachers work in schools.

An **abstract noun** names a quality, a condition, or a state of mind. It names something that cannot be seen or touched.

Teachers need energy and dedication.

Circle the abstract nouns. Underline the concrete nouns.

1. Maria Montessori (1870–1952) was a pioneer in the (education) of children.

2. Through her (determination,) Maria was the first woman in Italy to become a doctor.

3. The young doctor began to work with children and study their (methods) of (learning.)

4. Montessori worked in a poor area of Rome.

5. Her (desire) to help children was strong.

6. Maria even had workers cut down chairs and desks for the (convenience) of small children.

7. Her basic (observation) was that children have a great (need) to work toward (goals.)

8. Educators need to set the right (environment) so young learners can experiment independently.

9. The (philosophy) of Montessori was to present children with (challenges.)

10. There are many schools around the world that follow the (principles) of Montessori today.

11. In the classrooms you will see beads, blocks, and maps—all on low shelves.

12. In Montessori schools, children work with materials that have specific (purposes.)

13. One such material is the pink tower, which is made of ten pink blocks.

14. For (success) with a tower, the child starts with the largest block first.

15. The tower helps children learn the (concept) of (size.)

Maria Montessori used her knowledge to help others.
Give an example of how you can use your talents to help others.

15. Identifying the Number of Nouns

A **singular noun** refers to one person, place, or thing. A **plural noun** refers to more than one person, place, or thing.

SINGULAR   PLURAL
One girl in the group of students on the train was waving out the window.

A. Write the plural form of each noun.

1. grape ____[grapes]____
2. canoe ____[canoes]____
3. gulf ____[gulfs]____
4. country ____[countries]____
5. mouse ____[mice]____
6. chimney ____[chimneys]____
7. piano ____[pianos]____
8. half ____[halves]____
9. potato ____[potatoes]____
10. wish ____[wishes]____

11. alumnus ____[alumni]____
12. daughter-in-law ____[daughters-in-law]____
13. sheep ____[sheep]____
14. fox ____[foxes]____
15. melody ____[melodies]____
16. zero ____[zeroes]____
17. belief ____[beliefs]____
18. radio ____[radios]____
19. branch ____[branches]____
20. calf ____[calves]____

B. Complete each sentence using the noun at the left in its plural form.

language   1. Some people can speak more than twenty ____[languages]____.

tomato   2. The Aztecs of Mexico introduced Europeans to ____[tomatoes]____.

memory   3. The ____[memories]____ in personal computers are constantly increasing.

zoo   4. Lincoln Park Zoo in Chicago, a free cultural institution, is one of the world's most famous ____[zoos]____.

college   5. Many high school students apply to several ____[colleges]____.

loaf   6. In French bakeries ____[loaves]____ of bread in many different shapes are sold.

echo   7. Some good places in which to hear ____[echoes]____ are caves and building lobbies.

babysitter 8. Many young teenagers get their first jobs as ____[babysitters]____.

valley   9. Low areas between mountains are called ____[valleys]____.

solo   10. Songs sung by one person are ____[solos]____; in opera they are called arias.

16. Using Nouns as Subjects and Subject Complements

A noun can be the subject of a sentence. The subject tells what the sentence is about.

Brazil is in South America.

A **subject complement** is a noun, pronoun, or adjective that completes the meaning of a linking verb in a sentence. It renames or describes the subject.

Brazil is a **country** in South America.

A. Underline the subjects. Circle any subject complements.

1. Brazil is a fast-growing (country.)
2. The capital of the country is (Brasilia.)
3. That city was built in the 1950s.
4. In Brazil, Portuguese is spoken.
5. Brazil is the economic (leader) of South America.
6. Coffee remains a major (export) of Brazil.
7. The production of automobiles has become an important (industry) for Brazil.
8. Brazil is the fifth largest (country) in the world in size and population.
9. Rio de Janeiro and São Paulo are other important (cities.)
10. The beaches of Rio de Janeiro are famous.
11. The area near the Amazon River is (home) to a large rain forest.
12. Carnival in Rio remains a popular (attraction) for Brazilians and tourists alike.
13. A stew with beans is a popular Brazilian (dish.)
14. *Bossa nova* is a (type) of Brazilian music popular around the world.
15. Will Brazil be a major (power) in the future?

B. Complete the sentences. Indicate whether you added a subject or subject complement on the line at the left. Write **S** for subject or **SC** for subject complement. [**Completed sentences will vary.**]

[SC]   1. The most important city in my area is _____.

[S]   2. _____ is a major attraction in my area.

[S]   3. In my area _____ is an important product.

[SC]   4. A popular sport in my area is _____.

[S]   5. In my area _____ is really good to eat.

17. Identifying Appositives

Nouns

> An **appositive** is a noun that follows another noun. It renames or describes the noun it follows.
>
> SUBJECT   APPOSITIVE
> **Biology, the study of plant and animal life, is a basic science.**

A. Underline the appositive in each sentence. Circle the noun it renames or describes.

1. The (cell), the smallest unit of life, is a basic field of scientific research.

2. Inside each cell is (DNA,) a material with key genetic information.

3. (James Watson), an American scientist, helped discover the structure of DNA in 1953.

4. (Francis Crick,) a British scientist, was also involved in the discovery.

5. The structure of DNA is a (double-helix,) a ladderlike form.

6. Humans' 46 (chromosomes,) the carriers of hereditary characteristics, contain DNA.

7. The only humans whose DNA is not unique are identical (twins,) children born from a single egg.

8. (Genes,) sections of DNA, govern life processes and determine things like hair color and height.

9. A (gene,) the structural unit of inheritance, is a segment of DNA with a specific purpose.

10. The (genome,) the sequence of genes within an organism, is being studied by scientists.

12. The human (genome,) the sum of all the genes in human chromosomes, is being mapped.

13. A (mouse,) a fellow mammal, has only 300 genes that differ from a human's genes.

14. A positive result of DNA research may be gene (therapy,) the repair of malfunctioning genes.

15. Among the important sciences of the future is (genetics,) the scientific study of heredity.

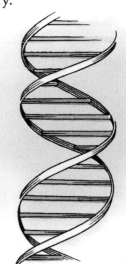

B. Add an appositive to rename or describe each *italicized* noun. [Answers will vary.]

1. *Biology,* _____, is my favorite class.

2. Our *teacher,* _____, is also a researcher.

3. Her research topic is *genetics,* _____.

4. My *brother,* _____, works at a laboratory.

5. His biology *textbook,* _____, is used at our school.

Name _____

18. Reviewing Nouns Used as Subjects, Subject Complements, and Appositives

A. Above each *italicized* noun, write **S** if it is used as a subject, **SC** if it is used as a subject complement, or **APP** if it is used as an appositive.

1. Kamehameha I, [APP] *king* of all the Hawaiian islands, united them into one kingdom.

2. The last king of Hawaii, [APP] *Kamehameha V,* made June 11 a holiday honoring Kamehameha I.

3. Kamehameha Day is a [SC] *time* for all kind of festivities.

4. The day is the state [SC] *holiday* of Hawaii.

5. In the city of Honolulu, [S] *singers* chant songs in front of the king's statue.

6. Leis, a [APP] *type* of wreath made with flowers, decorate the king's memorial.

7. After this ceremony a big [S] *parade* takes place.

8. One [S] *float* carries a man dressed as the king.

9. Eight princesses, [APP] *representatives* of the eight major islands, ride on horseback.

10. A [S] *luau,* a festive Hawaiian [APP] *party,* concludes the day.

B. Underline the subjects. Circle the subject complements. Draw two lines under the appositives.

1. Mardi Gras is the (day) before Ash Wednesday.

2. Lent, a season of fasting and penance, begins on Ash Wednesday.

3. Mardi Gras has been a (day) of fun and parades for many centuries.

4. People may wear elaborate costumes as clowns, lions, or famous personalities.

5. In New Orleans, Mardi Gras has been an important (celebration) since the 1700s.

6. Many floats take part in each Mardi Gras parade, a spectacular sight.

7. Some spectators arrive before dawn for a good viewing spot.

8. Colorful beads are the (souvenirs) of Mardi Gras.

9. The riders on the floats throw the beads at spectators.

10. Doubloons, toy coins, are also (remembrances) of the day.

Nouns

19. Forming Possessive Nouns

> The **possessive form** of a noun expresses possession, ownership, or connection.
>
> SINGULAR POSSESSIVE
> **The singer's voice was powerful and full.**
>
> PLURAL POSSESSIVE
> **In a choir the singers' voices have different qualities.**

A. Write the singular possessive and the plural possessive of each noun.

	SINGULAR POSSESSIVE	PLURAL POSSESSIVE
1. neighbor	[neighbor's]	[neighbors']
2. enemy	[enemy's]	[enemies']
3. farmer	[farmer's]	[farmers']
4. uncle	[uncle's]	[uncles']
5. wife	[wife's]	[wives']
6. parent	[parent's]	[parents']
7. child	[child's]	[children's]
8. princess	[princess's]	[princesses']
9. camel	[camel's]	[camels']
10. sister-in-law	[sister-in-law's]	[sisters-in-law's]

B. Underline the nouns in possessive form. Above each write
S if it is singular, **P** if it is plural.

1. In ancient times the night air rang with the telling of <u>heroes'</u> [P] stories.
2. Storytelling was <u>humans'</u> [P] basic form of entertainment in the distant past.
3. <u>Homer's</u> [S] famous poems, the *Iliad* and the *Odyssey*, are classics from ancient Greece.
4. Some scholars say that the poems are not one <u>poet's</u> [S] work.
5. The poems arose out of the ancient <u>Greeks'</u> [P] tradition of telling stories.
6. The *Iliad* tells about those who fought in the Trojan War and about the <u>warriors'</u> [P] bravery.
7. The *Odyssey* tells one <u>man's</u> [S] story—a man named Odysseus who fought in the Trojan War.
8. It took Odysseus 10 years to return home, and the <u>hero's</u> [S] adventures were numerous.
9. The ancient Greeks believed in gods, and the <u>gods'</u> [P] roles in the poems are important.
10. The stories from the ancient <u>storytellers'</u> [P] creative imaginations still fascinate us today.

Name _____

20. Using Possessive Nouns

The possessive form of a noun expresses possession, ownership, or connection.

A. Complete each sentence with the possessive form of the noun at the left. In some sentences you will use the singular possessive and in other sentences, the plural possessive.

Greek   1. The ancient _____[Greeks']_____ love of sports was expressed in the Olympics Games.

Frenchman   2. One _____[Frenchman's]_____ efforts resulted in the revival of the Olympic games in 1896.

Coubertin   3. _____[Coubertin's]_____ idea was to have an international gathering of athletes.

man   4. In the 1896 Olympics there were only _____[men's]_____ events.

woman   5. Since 1900 there have also been _____[women's]_____ events.

city   6. Cities bid to host the Olympics, and each _____[city's]_____ bid is analyzed by the Olympic committee.

committee   7. The _____[committee's]_____ decision is announced long before the start of the games.

winner   8. A _____[winner's]_____ prize at the modern Olympics is a gold medal.

winner   9. The _____[winners']_____ prizes in the original Olympics were crowns of laurel.

athlete   10. _____[Athletes']_____ names become instantly known because TV sends their images to millions around the world.

minute   11. For many athletes years of training come down to a _____[minute's]_____ performance.

loser   12. Audiences see both a winner's joy and a _____[loser's]_____ disappointment.

crowd   13. The _____[crowd's]_____ favorite is often the gymnastic events.

gymnast   14. A _____[gymnast's]_____ grace, strength, and skill are amazing.

swimmer   15. _____[Swimmers']_____ speeds in races are faster and faster every Olympics.

CONTINUED

judge 16. Some sports, like figure skating, are decided by several
_____[judges']_____ opinions.

computer 17. Other sports, like the races, are decided by a ___[computer's]___ precision.

animal 18. The Olympics are open even to ___[animals']___ involvement
and participation.

horse 19. In equestrian events a ___[horse's]___ role is to carry a rider
over jumps and across fields.

individual 20. But at the heart of the Olympics remain an ___[individual's]___
efforts and skill.

B. Write sentences using the possessive form of the noun provided. [Answers will vary.]

athlete, singular 1. _____

_____

coach, plural 2. _____

_____

girl, singular 3. _____

_____

boy, singular 4. _____

_____

winner, plural 5. _____

_____

loser, plural 6. _____

_____

professional, singular 7. _____

_____

teacher, singular 8. _____

_____

swimmer, plural 9. _____

_____

runner, plural 10. _____

_____

Nouns

Name _____

21. Identifying Separate and Joint Possession

When two or more people own something together, it is called joint possession. To show joint possession, use 's after the last noun only.

JOINT OWNERSHIP: **Martin and Paul's band plays Latin music.** (one band)

When two or more people each own a separate thing, it is called separate possession. To show separate possession, use 's after each noun.

SEPARATE OWNERSHIP: **Jason's and Peter's bands play rock music.** (two bands)

A. On the line write **J** if the sentence indicates joint ownership or **S** if it indicates separate ownership.

___[S]___ 1. Mozart's and Haydn's symphonies are more than two hundred years old but are still played.

___[J]___ 2. Leonard Bernstein and Stephen Sondheim's musical of 1957, *West Side Story*, is based on the story of Romeo and Juliet.

___[J]___ 3. Elton John and Tim Rice's musical *Aida*, set in ancient Egypt, was popular recently on Broadway.

___[S]___ 4. Elvis Presley's and Chuck Berry's music was influential in the development of rock and roll in the 1950s.

___[S]___ 5. Ricky Martin's and Gloria Estefan's albums are representative of Latin pop music.

B. Write sentences with possessives to show separate or joint ownership.

1. Oscar and Ivan have a band. It plays jazz.

   [Oscar and Ivan's band plays jazz.]

2. Lillian has a band. Rita has a band. Their bands play country music.

   [Lillian's and Rita's bands play country music.]

3. Michael and Fiona have the same piano teacher. Her name is Ms. Suarez.

   [Michael and Fiona's piano teacher is Ms. Suarez.]

4. Ona and Petra sang together. Their song was judged the best in the recital.

   [Ona and Petra's song was the judged the best in the recital.]

5. Wilson and Richard each have a new keyboard. The keyboards have great sound.

   [Wilson's and Richard's keyboards have great sound.]

22. Identifying Nouns Used as Direct Objects

A noun can be used as the direct object of a verb. A direct object answers the question *whom* or *what* after the verb.

My mother practices <u>karate</u>.

A. Underline the direct object in each sentence.

1. Over the past decades more and more people have shown an <u>interest</u> in karate.

2. Many movies and TV shows feature this <u>type</u> of martial art.

3. Growing numbers of people are learning <u>karate</u> as a means of defense.

4. Colleges, karate clubs, and other schools teach its <u>techniques</u>.

5. The Japanese word *karate* means "<u>empty hand</u>."

6. With karate a person strikes <u>parts</u> of somebody else's body.

7. Some martial arts, such as *tae kwon do*, emphasize <u>kicking</u>.

8. Others, such as *kung fu*, use a circular <u>motion</u> of the hands.

9. A karate blow can hurt or kill a <u>person</u>.

10. With practice a person's hand may reach a <u>velocity</u> of 21 to 30 miles an hour.

11. Originally Buddhist monks used <u>karate</u> for protection against wild animals.

12. Today for many people in the United States, karate offers <u>fun</u> and <u>exercise</u>.

13. People hold karate <u>competitions</u>.

14. Karate competitors can get special <u>belts</u>.

15. The color of their belts show their <u>expertise</u> in the sport.

B. Complete each sentence with a noun used as a direct object. **[Answers will vary.]**

1. As far as sports go, I can play _____.

2. For exercise I often play _____.

3. As a viewer of sports on TV, I sometimes watch _____.

4. Sports like tennis require _____.

5. To play a sport well, you need _____.

23. Identifying Nouns in Prepositional Phrases

> **Prepositions** can show place, time, direction, or relationship. Some common prepositions are *in, into, on, to, by, for, from, at, with,* and *without*. A noun that follows a preposition in a prepositional phrase is called the object of the preposition.
>
> PREPOSITION   OBJECT   PREPOSITION   OBJECT
> **The center of some cities is filled with skyscrapers.**

A. Circle each preposition. Underline its object.

1. Skyscrapers are the pyramids and cathedrals (of) the modern age.

2. They show the age's amazing achievements (in) technology.

3. The Petronas Towers (in) Malaysia extend 1,483 feet (into) the sky.

4. The design (of) the towers is based (on) geometric characteristics (of) Muslim architecture.

5. (Without) the invention (of) the elevator, however, no skyscrapers would be practical.

6. Initially elevators were not considered safe (for) humans.

7. Then a special safety brake (for) elevators was invented (by) Elisha G. Otis.

8. Chicago is called the birthplace (of) the skyscraper.

9. The first building (with) a frame (of) steel was built there (in) the late nineteenth century.

11. Early skyscrapers were covered (with) stone.

12. One example (of) this kind (of) skyscraper is the Empire State Building.

13. This building (in) New York was the tallest building (in) the world (for) many decades.

14. Now the frame (of) most skyscrapers is covered (with) glass.

15. Streets (in) big cities (with) tall buildings are canyons made (by) humans.

B. Complete each sentence with an appropriate preposition. More than one choice may be correct. Underline the object of the preposition.

1. Cesar Pelli was born and raised _____[in]_____ Argentina,

   but he lives _____[in]_____ the United States.

2. The Petronas Towers were designed _____[by]_____ Pelli.

3. Pelli wanted the buildings to offer good quality _____[to/for]_____

   the people who used them.

4. The windows are shaded _____[with/by]_____ stainless steel

   bands to give protection _____[from]_____ the sun.

5. The Petronas Towers have been praised _____[for]_____ their design.

24. Identifying Appositives

Nouns

> A subject, subject complement, direct object, indirect object, and object of a preposition can have an appositive.
>
> DIRECT OBJECT   APPOSITIVE
> **Many people have <u>myopia</u>, the <u>inability</u> to see things far away.**

A. Underline the appositive in each sentence. Circle the noun it explains.
Write **DO** over direct objects that have appositives.

1. The human eyeball houses the (retina,) a layer of nerve tissues with light receptors. [DO]

2. The eyeball has a (sclera,) a tough shell that covers the eyeball. [DO]

3. The eyeball contains vitreous (humour,) a jellylike liquid, to help it keep its shape. [DO]

4. The part that lets light pass through the eye is the (cornea,) a segment of the sclera.

5. Behind the cornea the eye has an (iris,) a set of muscles that open and close. [DO]

6. Light enters through the (pupil,) an opening at the center of the iris.

8. The retina contains (rods and cones,) the receptor cells. [DO]

9. Receptors send images to the optic (nerve,) the link between the eye and the brain.

10. Perceiving shapes and brightness is done by (rods,) light-sensitive cells.

11. (Cones,) light-sensitive cells of another type, perceive color and fine detail.

12. (Thomas Young,) an English physician, theorized the existence of color receptors in 1801.

13. Existence of the color (receptors,) the cones, finally was confirmed in the 1960s.

14. Lack of a set of cones explains color (blindness,) the inability to see red, green, or blue. [DO]

15. For example, people with (protanopia,) blindness to red, cannot distinguish red and green.

B. Use the phrase at the right as an appositive for each underlined object.

1. We can see <u>light</u>.   a kind of radiant energy
   [We can see light, a kind of radiant energy.]

2. Light moves in <u>waves</u>.   an up-and-down motion
   [Light moves in waves, an up-and-down motion.]

3. Light has its own <u>wavelength</u>.   the distance between the tops of two waves
   [Light has its own wavelength, the distance between the tops of two waves.]

4. People use <u>microwaves</u> to cook food.   another kind of radiant energy
   [People use microwaves, another kind of radiant energy, to cook food.]

5. Waves of different lengths form the <u>light spectrum</u>.   an array of six colors
   [Waves of different lengths form the light spectrum, an array of six colors.]

25. Identifying Nouns Used as Indirect Objects

A noun can be used as the indirect object of a verb. The indirect object tells *to whom* or *for whom* the action was done.

INDIRECT OBJECT   DIRECT OBJECT

Sally told her <u>friend</u>   the <u>story</u> of her first job.

A. Underline the indirect object in each sentence. Circle the verb it goes with.

1. Mrs. Rivera (offered) <u>Sally</u> a job as a babysitter.

2. Mr. and Mrs. Rivera (showed) <u>Sally</u> their house.

3. They (gave) the <u>teenager</u> instructions.

4. Mrs. Rivera said, "(Give) the <u>baby</u> some juice when she wakes up."

5. She (handed) <u>Sally</u> a number to call in case of emergency.

6. Sally (read) <u>Molly</u> a book about a dragon.

7. Sally (tossed) <u>Tommy</u> the bean bag.

8. Molly and Tommy (drew) <u>Sally</u> pictures.

9. Sally (made) the <u>children</u> sandwiches for supper.

10. Sally (sang) the <u>baby</u> songs so that she would go back to sleep.

11. The children (told) <u>Sally</u> stories about their favorite cartoon characters.

12. The children (showed) the <u>babysitter</u> their pet, a long green snake.

13. When she got home, Mrs. Rivera (gave) the <u>baby</u> a big kiss.

14. Mr. Rivera (handed) <u>Sally</u> money for her work.

15. Back home Sally (wrote) her <u>friend</u> a long e-mail about her first babysitting job.

B. Underline the indirect object in each sentence. Circle the direct object.

1. My grandfather told his <u>grandchildren</u> the (story) of his first job.

2. His father's friend offered my <u>grandfather</u> a (job) in an ice cream parlor.

3. At first my grandfather served <u>customers</u> (sundaes.)

4. He usually gave <u>customers</u> very large (scoops) of ice cream.

5. My grandfather's boss soon gave my <u>grandfather</u> the (job) of washing dishes instead.

26. Reviewing Uses of Nouns

Above each *italicized* noun, write **DO** if it is used as a direct object, **IO** if it is used as an indirect object, **OP** if it is used as an object of a preposition, or **APP** if it is used as an appositive.

1. Philadelphia was the birthplace of *Marian Anderson,* [OP] a famous *singer.* [APP]

2. From an early *age,* [OP] Marian had only one *dream* [DO]—to become a great singer.

3. She often sang *spirituals,* [DO] African-American religious *songs,* [APP] with her *sisters.* [OP]

4. Her family bought *Marian* [IO] a secondhand *piano.* [DO]

5. With a *piano* [OP] she could perform her *songs* [DO] with musical *accompaniment.* [OP]

6. Friends gave *Marian* [IO] *money* [DO] for *lessons.* [OP]

7. Eventually her outstanding voice won *Marian* [IO] a *number* [DO] of *scholarships.* [OP]

8. She studied in *Europe.* [OP]

9. There her singing earned the young *woman* [IO] wide *praise.* [DO]

10. She gained *fame* [DO] as the world's greatest contralto, a woman's *voice* [APP] of the lowest pitch.

11. She had a successful *career* [DO] as a *recitalist.* [OP]

12. In 1939 a group refused to give *Marian* [IO] *permission* [DO] to sing in their hall.

13. Instead, Marian sang at the *Lincoln Memorial* [OP] before a *crowd* [OP] of about 75,000.

14. In 1955 Marian was the first African-American woman to sing with the *Metropolitan Opera* [OP] in *New York City.* [OP]

15. The audience gave *Marian* [IO] a standing *ovation* [DO] even before she sang.

16. In 1963 the government awarded *Marian* [IO] the *Presidential Medal of Freedom.* [DO]

17. After that, Marian spent two *years* [DO] on a successful worldwide farewell *tour.* [OP]

18. She attributed her *success* [DO] to many *people.* [OP]

19. She had the *help* [DO] of friends, but she also had an inner *wealth,* [DO] her own spirit of *determination.* [APP]

20. Marian died in 1993, but people still listen to her wonderful *voice* [DO] on *recordings.* [OP]

Marian Anderson had to fight against prejudice because of her race.
Give an example of how you can fight against prejudice in your everyday life.

27. Reviewing Nouns

A. Identify the *italicized* nouns. In Column 1 write **C** for common or **P** for proper. In Column 2 write **C** if the noun is a collective noun. In Column 3 write **A** for abstract or **C** for concrete.

	COLUMN 1	COLUMN 2	COLUMN 3
1. The tourists visited *Turkey*.	[P]		[C]
2. The *group* visited a famous mosque.	[C]	[C]	[C]
3. It had once been a Christian *church*.	[C]		[C]
4. Its name is *Hagia Sophia*, or Holy Wisdom.	[P]		[A]
5. The tourists appreciated the *beauty* of the place.	[C]		[A]
6. People worship at the *mosque* daily.	[C]		[C]

B. Above each *italicized* noun write how it is used. Write **S** if it is used as a subject, **SC** if it is used as a subject complement, and **APP** if it is used as an appositive.

1. Does *Linda* [S] know who developed Norse mythology?
2. In Norse mythology *gods* [S] and *giants* [S] are superhuman *creatures* [SC].
3. *Asgar* [S], the *home* [APP] of the gods, is connected to the land of the humans by a bridge.
4. Hel is the *goddess* [SC] of the dead, and Hel was the *name* [SC] for the land of the dead.
5. *Valhalla* [S] was the *home* [SC] of dead warriors, who fought during the day and feasted at night.
6. *Odin* [S] is the supreme *ruler* [SC] in Norse mythology.
7. *Thor* [S], Odin's oldest *son* [APP], was god of thunder and lightning.
8. In Norse myths a *tree* [S] called Yggdrasil held up the world.
9. *Loki* [S], the evil *son* [APP] of a giant, causes the end of the world.

C. Underline the nouns in possessive form. Above each write **S** if it is singular or **P** if it is plural.

1. The development of the steam engine changed <u>humans'</u> [P] lives.
2. Previously, people depended on their own power, <u>animals'</u> [P] power, or <u>nature's</u> [S] power.
3. Many <u>inventors'</u> [P] ideas went into the development of the steam engine.
4. Some books say that the engine was <u>James Watt's</u> [S] invention.
5. His creation was an improvement on earlier <u>experimentors'</u> [P] work, because it used less fuel.

CONTINUED

Nouns

Name _____

D. Write whether the *italicized* nouns show separate or joint ownership.

_____[joint]_____ 1. The science-fair judges chose *Marco and Lillian's* project for first place.

_____[separate]_____ 2. *Roberto's and Guong's* entries tied for second place.

_____[separate]_____ 3. Everyone watched *Vic's and Sy's* faces as third place was announced.

_____[joint]_____ 4. They were disappointed; *Rose and Bob's* project came in third.

_____[separate]_____ 5. *Richard's and Robert's* projects were good, but they were both on photosynthesis.

E. Above each *italicized* noun, write **DO** if it is used as a direct object, **IO** if it is used as an indirect object, **OP** if it is used as an object of a preposition, or **APP** if it is used as an appositive.

1. France gave the [IO] *United States* the [DO] *Statue of Liberty,* a [APP] *symbol* of freedom.

2. It stands 46 meters high in the [OP] *harbor* of [OP] *New York.*

3. During each [OP] *year* countless tourists see the famous [DO] *sight.*

4. On the statue's [OP] *pedestal,* visitors can read "The New Colossus," a [APP] *poem* by [OP] *Emma Lazarus.*

5. The Statue of Liberty gives [IO] *people* the [DO] *promise* of [OP] *freedom* and [OP] *hope.*

Try It Yourself
Write a paragraph about a famous monument in the United States. Be sure that you use capital letters and apostrophes correctly.

_____

_____

_____

_____

_____

Check Your Own Work
Choose a piece of writing from your portfolio or journal, a work in progress, an assignment from another class, or a letter. Revise it, applying the skills you have reviewed. The checklist will help you.

✔ Have you capitalized all proper nouns?

✔ Have you used the correct forms of plurals?

✔ Have you used apostrophes in possessives correctly?

Name _____

28. Identifying Personal Pronouns

A **pronoun** is a word that takes the place of a noun or nouns.

> **Sharon wanted to see the new film, so <u>she</u> checked the Internet for the movie times.**

A personal pronoun shows the speaker (first person); the person spoken to (second person); or the person, place, or thing spoken about (third person).

FIRST PERSON: **Jack and I wanted to see the film too, but <u>we</u> didn't have the schedule.**

SECOND PERSON: **Do <u>you</u> have the movie times, Ling?**

THIRD PERSON: **The movie was great. I really liked <u>it</u>.**

A. Write **1** above each pronoun in the first person, **2** above each pronoun in the second person, and **3** above each pronoun in the third person.

1. Where were [2] you last night, Marcus?

2. Sandy and [1] I wanted to go to the movies.

3. [3] She heard some friends talk about a scary movie playing at the Cineplex.

4. [3] It was a film that none of [1] us had seen.

5. [1] We met Sam and Ramona at the theater.

6. [1] We met [3] them at the box office.

7. [3] They asked where [2] you were.

8. Sam treated all of [1] us to popcorn.

9. [1] I could hardly eat [3] it because the movie was so scary.

10. [2] You missed a great film!

B. Complete each sentence with the correct pronoun.

2nd, singular 1. Have ____[you]____ ever seen *Phantom of the Opera*?

1st, singular 2. ____[I]____ was really impressed by the musical.

3rd, singular 3. ____[It]____ was about a strange masked man who lived in the Paris Opera House.

3rd, singular 4. ____[He]____ falls in love with a beautiful singer.

3rd, plural 5. Lindy and John took me to the play, since ____[they]____ had an extra ticket.

Name _____

29. Using Personal Pronouns as Subjects

> A personal pronoun can be used as the subject of a sentence.
> The subject pronouns are *I, we, you, he, she, it,* and *they.*
>
> **I can play the guitar.**

A. Circle the correct pronoun for each sentence.

1. David and (him (he)) are philatelists, collectors of stamps.

2. Richard and ((they) them) sometimes go to shows for stamp collectors.

3. Alicia and ((I) me) know how to put up Web pages.

4. May ((we) us) help you design your Web page?

5. Pedro and ((she) her) can play the guitar and drums.

6. Are ((they) them) going to start a band?

7. Petra and (them (they)) take ballet lessons.

8. ((We) Us) have been invited to their dance recital.

9. Emilio and (him (he)) like to play soccer.

10. My friend and ((I) me) sometimes play soccer with them.

B. Replace the *italicized* word or words with the correct pronoun. Write it on the line.

_____[They]_____ 1. *The nature walkers* formed groups and scouted the area.

_____[She]_____ 2. *Beth* and a few others walked through the woods to the south.

_____[He]_____ 3. *Louis* went by himself along a dirt path that led to a waterfall.

_____[They]_____ 4. *Lillian and Carmen* followed a path near the road.

_____[we]_____ 5. Trish asked, "May *Nancy and I* help you collect fern samples?"

_____[She]_____ 6. *Mrs. Tordoff* answered, "OK, if you don't mind the ravine."

_____[they]_____ 7. After several hours *the groups* met to discuss what they had seen.

_____[He]_____ 8. *Bill* told them about the field of moss he had seen.

_____[She]_____ 9. *Sandra* passed around bark that had unusual lichens on it.

_____[They]_____ 10. *Several students* showed drawings that they had made of plants.

30. Using Personal Pronouns as Subject Complements

A subject pronoun can replace a noun used as a subject complement.
A subject complement follows a linking verb and refers back to
the same person or thing as the subject.

It was <u>they</u> who found the missing jewels in the library.

A. Circle the correct pronoun for each sentence.

1. It was (us **we**) who wanted to watch the mystery on TV.

2. Is it (them **they**) who have to find the jewel thief?

3. The person who was alone in the library was (**he** him).

4. Jennifer said it was (**she** her) who opened the library door.

5. Richardson said it was (**he** him) who turned off the lights.

6. Was that (**they** them) who came late to the party?

7. Is that (**he** him) who found the lost set of keys?

8. Can the person who stole the jewels be (her **she**)?

9. That was (him **he**) who asked everyone to gather in the library.

10. The person who guessed the guilty person was (me **I**).

B. Rewrite the sentences, using a pronoun as a subject complement and confirming the information given. Follow the example.

I think Sarah and Ed like mystery stories.

Yes, it is they who like mystery stories.

1. I think Encyclopedia Brown is a fictional ten-year-old who helps solve crimes.
[Yes, it is he who is a fictional ten-year-old who helps solve crimes.]

2. I think it is Virginia Hamilton who wrote *The House of Dies Drear* about a missing treasure.
[Yes, it is she who wrote *The House of Dies Drear* about a missing treasure.]

3. I think that it was Edgar Allan Poe who wrote the first mystery story.
[Yes, it was he who wrote the first mystery story.]

4. I think that it was Sherlock Holmes and Dr. Watson who were created by
Arthur Conan Doyle.
[Yes, it was they who were created by Arthur Conan Doyle.]

5. I think that it is Agatha Christie who is called the queen of mystery.
[Yes, it is she who is called the queen of mystery.]

31. Reviewing Subject Pronouns

A. Complete each sentence with an appropriate pronoun. Sometimes more than one answer is possible. On the line identify how the pronoun is used. Write **S** for subject or **SC** for subject complement. [Suggested answers are given.]

__[SC]__ 1. It was ____[they]____ who were planning a camping trip.

__[S]__ 2. Leslie and ____[I]____ started to put up our tent.

__[S]__ 3. Lorraine, Carmen, and ____[she]____ were swimming in the lake.

__[S]__ 4. In the rowboat were Eugene, Luis, and ____[he]____.

__[S]__ 5. Len and ____[she]____ wanted to play volleyball.

__[SC]__ 6. Was it ____[they]____ who forgot the volleyball net?

__[S]__ 7. Richard and ____[he]____ told scary stories.

__[SC]__ 8. Was it ____[they]____ who were roasting marshmallows over the campfire?

__[S]__ 9. Tom and Allen got up late. ____[They]____ skipped breakfast.

__[S]__ 10. Sally and ____[I]____ got into the car to leave, and it started to rain.

B. Replace the underlined word or words in each sentence with the correct pronoun. Write it on the line. Write **S** or **SC** above the underlined word or words to identify how the pronoun is used.

____[We]____ 1. Sheena and I rented the video of *Beauty and the Beast*.

____[They]____ 2. Many books and films retell the classic story.

____[she]____ 3. In most versions of the story, Beauty is one of several daughters.

____[They]____ 4. Beauty and her sisters live with their father.

____[he]____ 5. Unfortunately Beauty's father is captured by the ugly Beast.

____[she]____ 6. To save her father, Beauty goes to live with the very frightening Beast.

____[she]____ 7. The most generous character in the story is Beauty.

____[they]____ 8. Eventually Beauty and Beast fall in love.

____[he]____ 9. The Beast was actually a handsome prince.

____[she]____ 10. It is Beauty who saves the prince with her love.

32. Using Personal Pronouns as Direct Objects

> A personal pronoun can be used as the direct object of a verb.
> The object pronouns are *me, us, you, him, her, it,* and *them.*
>
> **My friends invited <u>us</u> to an international food fair.**

A. Circle the correct pronoun for each sentence.

1. My friends invited my sister and (I (me)) to the international food fair.

2. They called ((us) we) with the invitation, and we arranged to meet at noon.

3. We met Omar and (he (him)) near the entrance.

4. The workers directed my friends and (I (me)) to the ticket booth.

5. We saw Marietta and (she (her)) near the Mexican food booth.

6. The worker helped Peter and (they (them)) with directions to the Chinese booth.

7. Some people told Kathleen and (we (us)) about the tasty Thai spring rolls.

8. Some old friends of their family recognized Martin and (she (her)).

9. Unfortunately I lost my sister and ((them) they) in the crowd.

10. Then I got an idea: I called (she (her)) on her cell phone.

B. For each sentence write the pronoun that correctly replaces the *italicized* word or words.

___[them]___ 1. Last week a distant cousin called *my mom and dad.*

___[us]___ 2. He was coming to town, and he wanted to see *my mom, dad, sister, and me.*

___[him]___ 3. We recognized *Paul* as he stepped off the plane.

___[her]___ 4. He surprised *my mom* with a gift—an album of family pictures.

___[him]___ 5. My mom thanked *Paul* for the gift.

___[her]___ 6. Paul told *my mom* about some of her family members.

___[them]___ 7. My mom hasn't seen *Paul's mother and father* for many years.

___[us]___ 8. Paul was seeing *my sister and me* for the first time.

___[him]___ 9. We liked *Paul* immediately.

___[them]___ 10. When he left, Paul thanked *my mom and dad* for their hospitality.

Pronouns

33. Using Personal Pronouns as Indirect Objects

> An object pronoun can be used as the indirect object of a verb.
> **George mailed <u>her</u> an invitation to the Halloween party.**

A. Circle the correct pronoun for each sentence.

1. George and David sent (I (me)) an invitation to their Halloween party.
2. Ann showed Juanita and ((me) I) her ghost costume.
3. Her sister had lent (she (her)) the costume.
4. David's mother made his brother and (he (him)) skeleton costumes.
5. The hosts served (we (us)) apple juice and pretzels.
6. Lydia brought ((them) they) some pumpkin-shaped cookies.
7. I owed George and (he (him)) an apology for being late.
8. I told (they (them)) the problem: I couldn't get my Dracula teeth to stay in.
9. My sister gave (I (me)) some special glue for the teeth.
10. Dressing as salt-and-pepper shakers won Philippa and ((her) she) a prize for best costume.

B. For each sentence write the object pronoun that correctly replaces the underlined word or words.

_[them]_____ 1. In the *Iliad* the ancient Greeks send <u>the Trojans</u> a huge horse.

_[them]_____ 2. The horse affords <u>the Greek soldiers</u> a hiding place while they enter Troy.

_[him]_____ 3. In a Roman myth the goddess Venus gives <u>Paris</u> some golden apples.

_[her]_____ 4. Hippomenes wins a race against Atalanta when he throws <u>the young woman</u> the apples and distracts her.

_[him]_____ 5. In the Bible Jacob gives <u>his son Joseph</u> a coat of many colors.

_[him]_____ 6. The Magi bring <u>the baby Jesus</u> gold, frankincense, and myrrh.

_[them]_____ 7. Tom Sawyer tells <u>his friends</u> a not-quite-true story about why he is painting a fence.

_[him]_____ 8. The other children offer <u>Tom</u> things so that they too can paint the fence.

_[him]_____ 9. In O. Henry's story "The Gift of the Magi," the wife gives <u>her husband</u> a chain for his watch.

_[her]_____ 10. In the same story the husband buys <u>his wife</u> a set of combs for her hair.

Pronouns

34. Using Personal Pronouns as Objects of Prepositions

> An object pronoun can be used as the object of a preposition.
> **The report was presented to <u>them</u> by Shirley and <u>me</u>.**

A. Circle the correct pronoun for each sentence.

1. The work on the history project was divided among Jed, Jim, Valerie, Judy, and (I (me)).

2. Research on the Internet about the Incas was done by Jed and (she (her)).

3. The graphics were prepared by Judy and ((him) he).

4. All of (we (us)) decided on the organization of the project.

5. The section on the amazing Inca road system was prepared by Valerie and (she (her)).

6. The Maya and the Inca are old civilizations, and we made comparisons between ((them) they).

7. The task of proofreading the report was divided between Valerie and (I (me)).

8. We asked Jed and ((her) she) to make copies of our report.

9. Some excellent questions were asked by Richard and (he (him)).

10. We received some good feedback from Mr. Robertson and (they (them)).

B. For each sentence write the object pronoun that correctly replaces the *italicized* word or words.

___[her]___ 1. A report on *Cleopatra* was presented by Tom and Sue.

___[them]___ 2. She was a ruler of *the Egyptians* about two thousand years ago.

___[them]___ 3. She was considered fascinating and alluring by *the people of her time.*

___[them]___ 4. For a while Cleopatra ruled Egypt with each of *her brothers.*

___[him]___ 5. Later Cleopatra was able to regain power with help from *Julius Caesar.*

___[him]___ 6. Eventually she was married to *Mark Antony, a Roman leader.*

___[her]___ 7. The aim of Antony and *Cleopatra* was to gain more power.

___[them]___ 8. They were defeated in several battles by *the Romans.*

___[him]___ 9. The story of Cleopatra and *Antony* ends unhappily.

___[her]___ 10. Many stories and plays have been written about *Cleopatra.*

35. Reviewing Object Pronouns

A. Write on the line the correct pronoun to replace the *italicized* word or words in each sentence. Above the *italicized* word or words identify how the pronoun is used. Write **DO** if it is used as a direct object, **IO** if it is used as an indirect object, or **OP** if it is used as the object of preposition.

___[them]___ 1. In social studies we are studying about *world leaders*. **[OP]**

___[him]___ 2. Last week we focused on *Mohandas Gandhi*. **[OP]**

___[them]___ 3. Gandhi, called the Father of India, freed *his people* **[DO]** from British control.

___[him]___ 4. Indians gave *Gandhi* **[IO]** another name, Mahatma, meaning "Great Soul."

___[them]___ 5. Gandhi taught *his followers* **[IO]** the principles of nonviolent protest.

___[them]___ 6. The Indian leader once led *his followers* **[DO]** on a march to the sea.

___[them]___ 7. There they made salt from seawater, as a protest against *the British Salt Acts*. **[OP]**

___[him]___ 8. Fasting for five or six days was one protest sometimes undertaken by *Gandhi*. **[OP]**

___[us]___ 9. Mrs. Lee assigned *Teri and me* **[IO]** further research on Gandhi.

___[her]___ 10. Our class will study next about *Golda Meir*, **[OP]** a former prime minister of Israel.

B. Complete each sentence with a correct pronoun. Write its use on the line at the left. Use the key in the directions for Part A.

__[DO]__ 1. While discussing classic films, Rita told ___[us]___ about *It's a Wonderful Life*.

__[IO]__ 2. I hadn't seen the film, so Rita lent Elaine and ___[me]___ a video of the film.

__[DO]__ 3. The main character, George Bailey, has lost some money at his building and loan. He is afraid the police will arrest ___[him]___.

__[IO]__ 4. An enemy of George is causing ___[him]___ problems.

__[OP]__ 5. An angel finds George and talks to ___[him]___ about his troubles.

__[OP]__ 6. George realizes that his town is a better place because of ___[him]___.

__[OP]__ 7. George returns to his family, and he is happy to be with ___[them]___.

__[IO]__ 8. His family and friends then help him and give ___[him]___ money for the bank.

__[IO]__ 9. The movie taught ___[me]___ the importance of family and of helping others.

__[DO]__ 10. We returned the film to Rita and thanked ___[her]___ for the video.

Pronouns

Name _____

36. Using Pronouns after <u>Than</u> and <u>As</u> Correctly

> The conjunctions *than* and *as* are used to compare a noun and a pronoun or two pronouns.
>
> If the noun with which the pronoun is compared is a subject or a subject complement, the pronoun following the conjunction must also be a subject pronoun. If the noun is an object, the pronoun following the conjunction must be an object pronoun.
>
> **Sarah likes picnics as much as I.** (Sarah likes picnics as much as I like picnics.)
>
> Sometimes words are left out of sentences that make comparisons. Figuring out the missing words will help you decide if the pronoun is used as a subject or object.
>
> **The snake scared me more than him.** (The snake scared me more than it scared him.)

A. In each sentence circle the pronoun that agrees with the *italicized* word.

1. The children looked forward to the picnic, and the *adults* were as excited as (they) them).

2. Because they took a shortcut, *the Edwards family* arrived earlier than (we) us).

3. It took *Pedro* longer to set up the grill than (he (him)).

4. *Michael* makes better potato salad than (she) her).

5. *I* ate as many hot dogs as (she) her).

6. *Wayne* ate more cookies than (I) me).

7. The heat bothered *Jude* more than (they (them)).

8. The mosquitoes annoyed *Samantha* more than (he (him)).

9. *Carol* played volleyball better than ((he) him).

10. The game entertained *Carol* more than (he (him)).

B. Use the information below to write sentences with *than* or *as* followed by pronouns.

	Ernesto	Ellie	Bev
Newspapers delivered	74	85	85
Time worked	50 minutes	50 minutes	1 hour

Compared with Bev: [Sentences may vary. Suggestions are given.]

Ellie delivered as many newspapers as she.
It took Ellie less time to deliver 85 newspapers than her.

1. [Ernesto delivered fewer newspapers than she.]
_____

Compared with Ellie:

2. [Bev delivered as many newspapers as she.]
_____

3. [It took Ernesto as much time to deliver his newspapers as her.]
_____

Compared with Ernesto:

4. [Bev delivered more newspapers than he.]
_____

5. [It took Ellie as much time to deliver her newspapers as him.]
_____

37. Using Possessive Pronouns and Possessive Adjectives

> Possessive pronouns and possessive adjectives show possession or ownership.
> A **possessive adjective** modifies a noun. The possessive adjectives are *my, our, your, his, her, its,* and *their.*
>
> > **Their** *sneakers* **are red and black.**
>
> A **possessive pronoun** takes the place of a noun and its possessive adjective.
> The possessive pronouns are *mine, ours, yours, his, hers, its,* and *theirs.*
>
> > **The yellow sneakers under the table are mine.**

A. Underline each possessive pronoun. Circle each possessive adjective.

1. The things in the garage sale are ours.
2. My old Batman comic book sold for five dollars.
3. Deciding on prices is her job; mine is to give change.
4. Their offer for his old bike was too low.
5. But that ugly painting is now theirs!
6. My coat is beside hers on the rack; those coats are not for sale.
7. You may use my pen if you have lost yours.
8. Someone bought our old broken lamp for two dollars.
9. His old golf clubs got the highest price.
10. Come to our sale again next year.

B. Replace the *italicized* words in each sentence with a possessive. Then write **A** if it is a possessive adjective or **P** if it is a possessive pronoun.

[ours]	[P]	1. All the stuff in the attic was *my family's and mine.*
[mine]	[P]	2. Don't put those old stuffed animals on sale. They're *my stuffed animals.*
[her]	[A]	3. The table with the broken leg was in *Sally's* room. We can't sell it.
[his]	[P]	4. That old phonograph was *my grandfather's.*
[his]	[A]	5. The guitar missing a string was once *Dad's* favorite guitar.
[hers]	[P]	6. The old cameras were *Mom's.*
[theirs]	[P]	7. The old model planes were *my Dad's and his brother's.*
[mine]	[P]	8. The tiny baby shoes were once *my shoes.*
[her]	[A]	9. That was *my sister's* old tricycle.
[their]	[A]	10. The large wardrobe once was in *my grandparents'* house.

38. Using Reflexive and Intensive Pronouns

A **reflexive pronoun** ends in *-self* or *-selves*. A reflexive pronoun is often the object of a verb or of a preposition. It refers to the same person, place, or thing as the subject of the sentence.

> **Walt Disney had confidence in <u>himself</u> and gained success.**

When a reflexive pronoun is used as an appositive immediately after a noun or pronoun to show emphasis, it is called an **intensive pronoun**.

> **Walt Disney <u>himself</u> did much of the work on his films.**

A. Underline the reflexive or intensive pronoun in each sentence. Circle the words it refers to.

1. (Walt Disney) made a name for <u>himself</u> as a producer of cartoon features.

2. At first, (Disney) <u>himself</u> drew his cartoons.

3. Since (animals) lent <u>themselves</u> to animation, Disney's first character was a mouse.

4. (Disney) <u>himself</u> provided Mickey Mouse's voice.

5. At first, (Walt) had a small business, and he <u>himself</u> did most of the work.

6. (Mickey Mouse) would eventually earn <u>himself</u> a worldwide following.

7. Disney was not an overnight success; (he) very slowly worked <u>himself</u> to the top.

8. (*Snow White and the Seven Dwarfs*) gained <u>itself</u> a place in movie history.

9. The cartoon's (characters) won permanent places for <u>themselves</u> in the hearts of audiences.

10. Even the (songs) from the films <u>themselves</u> are still sung today.

B. Complete each sentence with a reflexive or intensive pronoun. Circle the word(s) it refers to.

1. (Rachel Carson) ____[herself]____ said that she loved nature from an early age.

2. (Carson) earned ____[herself]____ a degree in zoology in 1932.

3. Her (writings) about the ocean earned ___[themselves]___ a large audience.

4. (Carson) quit her job, and she devoted _____[herself]_____ to scientific writing.

5. Carson studied the use of synthetic pesticides, and she decided that the (pesticide) _____[itself]_____ was a potential danger to the environment.

6. According to Carson, (we) ____[ourselves]____ are part of the ecosystem.

7. Pesticides might ultimately harm (humans) ___[themselves]___ .

8. Pesticide (manufacturers) aligned _____[themselves]_____ against Carson's book about pesticides.

9. (Carson and her supporters) found ___[themselves]___ under attack.

10. (Carson) ___[herself]___ testified before Congress on behalf of the environment shortly before her death in 1964.

Name _____

39. Making Reflexive Pronouns and Antecedents Agree

> Reflexive and intensive pronouns agree with their antecedents
> in person, number, and gender.
>
> ANTECEDENT   REFLEXIVE PRONOUN
>
> **_She_** taught <u>herself</u> chess from a book.
> (The antecedent and reflexive pronoun are 3rd person, singular, female.)

A. Underline the reflexive or intensive pronoun in each sentence.
Circle its antecedent. Write the person, number, and gender (if appropriate)
of the pronoun on the line.

[2nd, singular, m/f] 1. (You) yourself can learn to do many things from books.

[3rd, singular] 2. A (book) itself is a teaching tool.

[2nd, plural, m/f] 3. (You) can teach yourselves anything from beekeeping to Web design.

[3rd, plural, m/f] 4. (Many people) repair things around the house themselves.

[3rd, singular, m] 5. (My father) used a book to fix the kitchen sink himself.

[3rd, singular, f] 6. My (mother) herself designed a rock garden with the help of a book.

[3rd, singular, f] 7. My (sister) taught herself needlepoint from a book.

[3rd, plural, m] 8. My (brothers) taught themselves origami with a kit.

[1st, singular, m/f] 9. (I) myself used a simple cookbook to make guacamole.

[1st, plural, m/f] 10. (We) now have a shelf full of self-teaching books in the
basement for ourselves.

B. Complete each sentence with a reflexive or intensive pronoun.
Be sure it agrees with its antecedent.

1. The students _____[themselves]_____ made all the food and
decorations for the ethnic party.

2. We _____[ourselves]_____ made the guacamole dip.

3. Help _____[yourselves]_____ to the guacamole, Ben and Barb.

4. Did you make the fried rice _____[yourself]_____, Ruth?

5. Cynthia _____[herself]_____ made the tabbouleh salad.

6. Did she cut _____[herself]_____ when she was making the salad?

7. They helped _____[themselves]_____ to an extra serving of pierogi,
Polish dumplings.

8. Vladimir _____[himself]_____ ate most of the caviar.

9. I _____[myself]_____ had never before tasted tempura.

10. We made _____[ourselves]_____ a promise to have another potluck dinner.

Name _____

40. Using Interrogative Pronouns

An **interrogative pronoun** is used when asking a question.

Who, whom, and *whose* are used when asking about persons. *Who* is used when the pronoun is the subject of the question. *Whom* is used when the pronoun is the object of the verb or of a preposition. *Whose* is used when asking about a possession.

Which is used when asking about one of a class or group of persons, places, or things.

What is used when asking about things and in seeking information.

A. Circle the interrogative pronoun in each sentence. On the line write whether it refers to a person, a place, a thing, or is seeking information.

_____[person]_____ 1. By (whom) was *The Wizard of Oz* written?

_____[thing]_____ 2. (What) is a wizard?

_____[information]_____ 3. (What) happens in the book?

_____[person]_____ 4. (Which) of the characters lacks courage?

_____[information]_____ 5. (What) did the scarecrow want?

_____[person]_____ 6. (Who) were Dorothy's companions on the trip?

_____[place]_____ 7. (Which) is Dorothy's home—Kansas or Illinois?

_____[thing]_____ 8. (What) is a tornado?

_____[person]_____ 9. (Who) starred in the movie version of *The Wizard of Oz*?

_____[person]_____ 10. (Whose) book is this?

B. Complete each sentence with an interrogative pronoun.

1. _____[Who]_____ wrote the Harry Potter books?

2. With _____[whom]_____ did Harry Potter live at first?

3. _____[What]_____ did Harry learn about himself when he was eleven?

4. _____[Who/What]_____ were Harry's parents?

5. _____[What]_____ is the name of Harry Potter's new school?

6. _____[Who]_____ is Hermione?

7. _____[Which]_____ of his classmates is Harry's rival?

8. _____[Which]_____ of the adventures in the books is the most exciting?

9. _____[What]_____ makes the Harry Potter books special?

10. _____[Which]_____ of the Harry Potter books have you read?

41. Using Interrogative Pronouns <u>Who</u> and <u>Whom</u> Correctly

Who is used when the pronoun is the subject of a question.
> **<u>Who</u> said, "A penny saved is a penny earned"?**

Whom is used when the pronoun is the direct or indirect object of a verb or the object of a preposition.
> **By <u>whom</u> was Frankenstein created?**

A. Underline the interrogative pronoun in each sentence. On the line write how it is used. Write **S** if it is a subject, **DO** if it is a direct object, **IO** if it is an indirect object, or **OP** if it is the object of a preposition.

[OP]   1. By <u>whom</u> was paper money first developed?

[IO]   2. The Magna Carta gave <u>whom</u> liberties?

[OP]   3. After <u>whom</u> were the Americas named?

[S]   4. <u>Who</u> signed the Declaration of Independence first?

[OP]   5. After <u>whom</u> was the guillotine named?

[S]   6. <u>Who</u> is the Liberator of South America?

[DO]   7. <u>Whom</u> did Stanley meet in Africa?

[S]   8. <u>Who</u> founded the Red Cross?

[DO]   9. <u>Whom</u> did Whistler paint?

[S]   10. <u>Who</u> was the first person to walk on the moon?

B. Complete each sentence with *who* or *whom*.

1. ____[Who]____ was in the parlor eating bread and honey?

2. ____[Whom]____ couldn't all the king's horses and men put together again?

3. With ____[whom]____ was the lamb sure to go?

4. ____[Who]____ went up the hill to fetch a pail of water?

5. Before ____[whom]____ was the pie with four and twenty blackbirds set?

6. ____[Who]____ went to the cupboard to fetch the poor dog a bone?

7. For ____[whom]____ did Old King Cole call?

8. ____[Whom]____ did Georgie Porgie kiss?

9. ____[Who]____ was eating curds and whey?

10. ____[Whom]____ did the spider frighten away?

Name _____

42. Identifying Relative Pronouns

A **relative pronoun** connects a dependent clause to the person, place, or thing it modifies. A dependent clause describes or gives information about the person, place, or thing. The relative pronouns are *who, whom, whose, which,* and *that. Who, whom,* and *whose* usually refer to persons. *Which* refers to places or things. *That* refers to persons, places, or things. Use *who* when the pronoun is the subject of the dependent clause. Use *whom* when the pronoun is the object of a verb or of a preposition.

DEPENDENT CLAUSE

Marco Polo, *who lived in the thirteenth century,* made a dangerous journey to China.

Underline the relative pronoun in each sentence.
Circle the person, place, or thing it modifies.

1. The (Silk Road,) which was a 4,000-mile trading route, connected China with Europe.

2. According to legend, (General Zhang Qian,) who lived in the second century B.C., first traveled the route.

3. (Zhang Qian,) whom a Chinese emperor sent on a mission, spent thirteen years on his journey to find allies to the west.

4. Silk was one of the (goods) that traveled to Europe along the route.

5. (Silk,) which the Chinese could make, was much prized in Europe.

6. (Goods) that went east along the route were wool, gold, and such foods as pomegranates.

7. A famous traveler along the Silk Route was (Marco Polo,) whose travel reports introduced the wonders of China to Europeans.

8. Part of the Great Wall of China was built to protect the route from (bandits) who attacked caravans.

9. One danger was the (Takla Makan Desert,) whose name meant "go in and you won't come out."

10. The (areas) that the route crossed included Afghanistan.

11. It went on to the (Levant,) which is the name for the countries on the eastern Mediterranean.

12. (Ships,) on which the goods were then put, made the journey across the sea.

13. (Caravans,) which included people, camels, and horses, traveled the route at a slow pace.

14. (People) who traveled the entire length of the route were rare.

15. The (Silk Route,) which a German scholar in the 1800s named, was replaced by safer sea routes by the 1400s.

43. Using Relative Pronouns as Subjects

> A relative pronoun can be the subject of a dependent clause.
> **Deserts, <u>which</u> cover about one fifth of the earth's land, lack water.**

A. In each sentence underline the dependent clause and circle the relative pronoun.

1. According to scientists, deserts are places (that) receive less than ten inches of rain a year.

2. The Gobi Desert, (which) is an example of a cold desert, has temperatures of −40 degrees Fahrenheit.

3. Many animals (that) survive in the desert get their water from their food.

4. Camels, (which) can go without water for two weeks, store fat for food in their humps.

5. Some people (who) live in the desert have a nomadic life and move in search of food and water.

6. Desert plants such as cactuses have spines, (which) protect them from hungry animals.

7. Most deserts are in areas (that) lie 30 degrees latitude north or south of the equator.

8. Movement of moist air from the hot area of the equator creates the deserts (that) ring our planet.

9. The Sonoran Desert, (which) extends from Mexico into the southwestern United States, lies in a rain shadow.

10. In a rain shadow, rain falls on the mountainside (that) faces the ocean, not on the opposite side.

B. Combine each pair of sentences with a relative pronoun used as a subject of a dependent clause. Write the dependent clause after the underlined noun. [Sample answers are given.]

1. The <u>Sahara</u> covers an area almost the size of the United States. The Sahara is the world's largest desert.
   [The Sahara, which covers an area almost the size of the United States, is the world's largest desert.]

2. The word "Sahara" comes from an Arabic <u>word</u>. The Arabic word means "desert."
   [The word "Sahara" comes from an Arabic word that means "desert."]

3. <u>Ergs</u> cover only part of the mostly rocky desert. Ergs are vast seas of sand.
   [Ergs, which are vast seas of sand, cover only part of the mostly rocky desert.]

4. Most of the Saharan people are <u>nomads</u>. These nomads tend herds of sheep, goats, and cattle.
   [Most of the Saharan people are nomads who tend herds of sheep, goats, and cattle.]

5. Crops such as dates and wheat are raised on <u>oases</u>. Oases are fertile areas with water.
   [Crops such as dates and wheat are raised on oases, which are fertile areas with water.]

Pronouns

44. Identifying Relative Pronouns as Direct Objects

> A relative pronoun can be the object of a verb. When the relative pronoun is the object of a verb, the clause is written with the direct object coming before the verb.
>
> **At dawn tourists come to see the Taj Mahal, <u>which</u> sunlight *turns* to gold.**

A. Underline the relative pronoun in each sentence. Write the verb of which the pronoun is the direct object.

_____[built]_____ 1. The Taj Mahal, <u>which</u> a Mughal emperor built, stands in India.

_____[loved]_____ 2. According to legend, the emperor erected the tomb to honor his wife, <u>whom</u> he loved.

_____[visit]_____ 3. The tomb, <u>which</u> millions of tourists visit yearly, was erected from 1630 to 1653.

_____[call]_____ 4. Visitors are amazed by the beauty of the tomb, <u>which</u> people call the world's eighth wonder.

_____[respected]_____ 5. The tomb was built by an architect <u>whom</u> some people respected as a great master.

_____[erected]_____ 6. White marble covers the tomb, <u>which</u> about twenty thousand workers erected.

_____[produced]_____ 7. The tomb is decorated with floral designs <u>that</u> artisans produced from precious stones.

_____[divides]_____ 8. The front gardens, <u>which</u> a huge reflecting pool divides, enhance the beauty of the site.

_____[have produced]_____ 9. The damage <u>that</u> time, pollution, and tourists have produced on the Taj Mahal worries experts.

_____[designated]_____ 10. The Taj Mahal, <u>which</u> the United Nations designated as a World Heritage site in 1983, should stand for centuries with preservation.

B. Combine each pair of sentences with a relative pronoun used as a direct object. Write the relative pronoun after the underlined noun. [Sample answers are given.]

1. St. Peter's <u>Basilica</u> is a special place for Roman Catholics. Popes built the basilica.
   [St. Peter's Basilica, which popes built, is a special place for Roman Catholics.]

2. The <u>square</u> is in the shape of welcoming arms. The artist Bernini designed the square.
   [The square, which the artist Bernini designed, is in the shape of welcoming arms.]

3. The <u>square</u> is the site of many outdoor ceremonies. Thousands of pilgrims fill the square.
   [The square, which thousands of pilgrims fill, is the site of many outdoor ceremonies.]

4. The <u>dome</u> is one of the largest in the world. The artist Michelangelo designed the dome.
   [The dome, which the artist Michelangelo designed, is one of the largest in the world.]

5. Inside the church is the *Pietà*. Michelangelo sculpted the *Pietà*.
   [Inside the church is the *Pietà*, which Michelangelo sculpted.]

Pronouns

45. Using Relative Pronouns as Objects of Prepositions

> A relative pronoun can be the object of a preposition.
> **Many objects are named after the places *in* which they originated.**

A. Underline each relative pronoun. Circle the preposition of which the pronoun is the object.

1. Louis Dobermann, (after) whom Dobermans are named, was the first to breed these dogs.

2. The shrub fuchsia, (on) which purplish flowers grow, is named for a German botanist.

3. The Earl of Cardigan, (after) whom a collarless sweater is named, fought in the Crimean War.

4. *Silk* is from a Greek word for "Oriental people," (from) whom the thread was first obtained.

5. The Italian town of Cantalupo, (in) which cantaloupe was first grown, gave the melon its name.

6. Kashmir goats gave their name to the cloth cashmere, (from) which sweaters are often made.

7. A gas-run aircraft (in) which passengers could ride was named after Ferdinand von Zepplin.

8. The decibel, (by) which noise level is measured, was named to honor Alexander Graham Bell.

9. Ceres, (from) whom we get the word *cereal*, was the Roman goddess of agriculture.

10. The Earl of Sandwich, (after) whom the sandwich was named, was the first to eat one.

B. Complete each sentence with a relative pronoun used as the object of a preposition.

1. Samuel Morse, by ____[whom]____ a system of communicating letters in dots and dashes called the Morse code was invented, was a well-known American artist.

2. Conestoga wagons were named after the town in Pennsylvania in ____[which]____ they were built.

3. The resort of Tuxedo Park in New York, at ____[which]____ tuxedos were first worn, gave its name to a formal suit.

4. The nickel coin is named for the grayish-white metal of ____[which]____ it is made.

5. The word *magnet* comes from Magnesia, Greece, in ____[which]____ the special iron ore was found.

46. Using Relative Pronouns as Possessive Adjectives

> The relative pronoun *whose* is used to refer to the possessor or possessors of something.
> **The artist, whose paintings I liked best, was from Spain.**

A. Underline each relative pronoun used as a possessive adjective.
Circle the noun it modifies.

1. The (artist) whose works were most influential in the twentieth century was Pablo Picasso.

2. Picasso's painting (Guernica,) whose subject is the horrors of war, is a powerful work.

3. (Claude Monet,) whose favorite subject became waterlilies, was important in impressionism.

4. (Impressionism,) whose characteristics include short brush strokes of bright colors, was an important art movement in the 1800s.

5. (Frida Kahlo,) whose self-portraits are well known, was a Mexican artist.

6. (Kahlo,) whose health was affected by an accident, often illustrated women's hard lives.

7. An American artist was (Jackson Pollock,) whose technique was to splatter paint on canvas.

8. Pollock belonged to the abstract expressionist (movement,) whose characteristic was an emphasis on form and color without painting real-life objects.

9. (Andy Warhol,) whose art movement was called pop art, became prominent in the 1960s.

10. His (paintings,) whose subjects included familiar products, often used bright colors.

B. Circle the possessive form of the relative pronoun.
On the line write its person and number.

___[3rd, singular]___ 1. Georgia O'Keeffe, (whose) paintings hang in many museums, was born in 1887.

___[3rd, plural]___ 2. Her works, (whose) inspiration came from nature, often showed flowers.

___[3rd, plural]___ 3. Her flowers, (whose) petals are often huge, make a powerful impact.

___[3rd, plural]___ 4. Her art teachers, (whose) support helped O'Keeffe, recognized her talent.

___[3rd, singular]___ 5. O'Keeffe, (whose) decision to be an artist was made at an early age, was clearly special.

___[3rd, singular]___ 6. In her twenties, she left an art school (whose) methods disappointed her.

___[3rd, singular]___ 7. Later she found an art teacher (whose) methods inspired her.

___[3rd, singular]___ 8. Her husband, (whose) influence in the art world was significant, helped her career.

___[3rd, singular]___ 9. In 1928 a painting (whose) subject was a lily sold for $25,000.

___[3rd, singular]___ 10. O'Keeffe lived her later years in New Mexico, (whose) landscape inspired her work.

47. Reviewing Relative Pronouns

Underline the relative pronoun in each sentence. On the line write **S** if it used as a subject, **O** if it is an object, or **M** if it modifies. For pronouns used as subjects, write the related verb. For pronouns used as objects, write the related verb or preposition. For modifiers, write the noun the pronoun modifies.

__[S, lived]__ 1. Peter Cooper, who lived from 1791 to 1883, was an inventor and philanthropist.

__[M, ingenuity]__ 2. Cooper, whose ingenuity was noteworthy, established many businesses.

__[M, schooling]__ 3. Cooper, whose formal schooling lasted one year, became an apprentice to a coach maker at a young age.

__[O, served]__ 4. The coach maker, whom he served well, helped Cooper in his career.

__[S, had]__ 5. Cooper, who had a head for business, first made machines for cutting cloth.

__[O, for]__ 6. The accomplishment for which he first gained fame was designing a railroad locomotive.

__[S, was called]__ 7. The locomotive, which was called the *Tom Thumb*, could pull 40 persons at 10 miles an hour.

__[S, enjoyed]__ 8. Cooper, who enjoyed inventing, supported the work of other inventors.

__[O, devised]__ 9. Inventions that he devised included a washing machine.

__[O, after]__ 10. Cooper, after whom the Cooper Union in New York was named, founded it in 1859.

__[M, mission]__ 11. The Cooper Union, whose mission was to educate working people, helped many.

__[O, supported]__ 12. The institution, which Cooper's donations supported, offered free courses in science, engineering, and art.

__[S, can meet]__ 13. It is still open today to any student who can meet requirements.

__[O, take]__ 14. Cooper supported reforms that we take for granted, including public schools.

__[S, said]__ 15. Cooper, who said, "The object of life is to do good," died at 92.

Peter Cooper founded a community institution to help the poor. Give an example of how you can help less fortunate people in your community.

48. Using Relative Pronouns Who and Whom Correctly

> The relative pronoun *who* is used when the pronoun is the subject of the dependent clause.
>
> **All good things come to those who wait.** —English Proverb
>
> The relative pronoun *whom* is used when the pronoun is an object in the dependent clause.
>
> **The limits of tyrants are prescribed by the endurance of those whom they oppose.**—Frederick Douglass, *African-American Leader*

Circle the correct relative pronoun for each sentence. On the line write **S** if it is used as a subject, **DO** if it is a direct object, or **OP** if it is an object of a preposition. Write the related verb or preposition.

[S, is sending] 1. I am a little pencil in the hand of a writing God (who whom) is sending a love letter to the world.
—Mother Teresa, *Humanitarian*

[S, don't know] 2. Those (who whom) don't know how to weep with their whole heart don't know how to laugh either.
—Golda Meir, *Politician*

[OP, with] 3. We cannot really love anybody with (who whom) we never laugh.
—Agnes Repplier, *Writer*

[DO, love] 4. Among those whom I like, I can find no common denominator, but among those (who whom) I love, I can; all of them make me laugh.
—W. H. Auden, *Poet*

[DO, choose] 5. Life is partly what we make it, and partly what it is made by the friends (who whom) we choose.
—Chinese proverb

[S, are] 6. Misfortune shows those (who whom) are not really friends.
—Aristotle, *Ancient Greek Philosopher*

[S, doesn't know] 7. An ignorant person is one (who whom) doesn't know what you have just found out.
—Will Rogers, *American Humorist*

[S, has made] 8. An expert is a person (who whom) has made all the mistakes that can be made in a very narrow field.
—Niels Bohr, *Scientist*

[OP, to] 9. Do not withhold good from those to (who whom) it is due when it is in your power to do it.
—Bible: Hebrew, Proverbs 3:27

[S, prepare] 10. The future belongs to those (who whom) prepare for it today.
—Malcolm X, *African-American Leader*

49. Reviewing Relative Pronouns in Clauses

A relative pronoun connects a dependent clause to the person, place, or thing it modifies. A dependent clause describes or gives information about the person, place, or thing. The relative pronouns are *who, whom, whose, which,* and *that.*

A. Underline the relative pronoun in each sentence. Circle the antecedent.

1. (Eratosthenes,) who accurately measured Earth's circumference, was an ancient astronomer.
2. His (calculation,) which was 7,850 miles, was only 50 miles off Earth's actual diameter.
3. According to Ptolemy, it was the (sun) that revolved around Earth.
4. Ptolemy's (theory,) which people accepted for centuries, put Earth at the universe's center.
5. (Copernicus,) who lived in the sixteenth century, theorized that Earth orbits the sun.
6. (Copernicus,) whose theory many people first rejected, created a controversy.
7. According to Kepler, the (orbits) that planets follow are oval shaped and not circles.
8. (Galileo Galilei,) by whom the telescope was first used, made important discoveries.
9. He verified Copernicus's (theory,) which said the sun was at the center of our solar system.
10. He first saw Jupiter's satellites and the (craters) that cover the moon.
11. Isaac Newton's contribution was the law of (gravity,) which explained the nature of orbits.
12. The theory of gravity explains the (attraction) that exists between particles of matter.
13. (Edmond Halley,) for whom a famous comet is named, first calculated a comet's orbit.
14. William Herschel studied the stars and (nebulae,) which are clusters of gases and dust in space.
15. According to (Edwin Hubble,) who gave his name to Hubble's law, the universe is expanding.

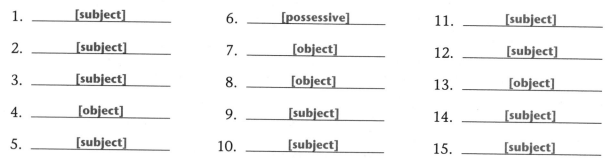

B. On the line write whether each relative pronoun in Part A is a subject pronoun, a possessive pronoun, or an object pronoun.

1. _____[subject]_____	6. _____[possessive]_____	11. _____[subject]_____
2. _____[subject]_____	7. _____[object]_____	12. _____[subject]_____
3. _____[subject]_____	8. _____[object]_____	13. _____[object]_____
4. _____[object]_____	9. _____[subject]_____	14. _____[subject]_____
5. _____[subject]_____	10. _____[subject]_____	15. _____[subject]_____

Name _____

50. Using Demonstrative Pronouns

A **demonstrative pronoun** points out a definite person, place, or thing. Use *this* and *these* to point out what is near; use *that* and *those* to point out what is distant.

This is the best store in the area.

Those over there are rotten apples.

A. Underline each demonstrative pronoun. On the line write **N** if it indicates objects that are near or **F** for objects that are farther away.

__[N]__ 1. This is the biggest supermarket in the area.

__[F]__ 2. Let's get one of those to hold our groceries.

__[N]__ 3. This is a large produce department.

__[N]__ 4. Do you think that these are the best-looking apples?

__[F]__ 5. Let's get some of those—they're on sale.

__[N, F]__ 6. These are more expensive than those.

__[F]__ 7. That is a good brand of cereal.

__[F]__ 8. Don't get near that—the whole stack of cans might fall!

__[N]__ 9. These are the freshest loaves of bread.

__[F]__ 10. That is the shortest check-out line.

B. Complete each sentence with the correct demonstrative pronoun. Use the information at the left.

far   1. Is ____[that]____ the bag with the eggs? Be careful!

near   2. Are ____[these]____ all the bags we have?

far   3. ____[That]____ goes in the refrigerator.

near   4. Where does ____[this]____ belong?

far   5. ____[Those]____ go in the fruit bowl.

near   6. I can't carry ____[this]____—it's too heavy.

far   7. These bananas look riper than ____[those]____.

near   8. ____[These]____ are great-looking grapes.

far   9. ____[That]____ is the largest can—put it on the bottom.

near   10. ____[This]____ is the last thing to put away. Hooray!

51. Identifying Indefinite Pronouns

> An **indefinite pronoun** refers to any or all of a group of persons, places, or things.
> The indefinite pronouns are *anybody, anyone, anything, everybody, everyone, everything, one, nobody, no one, nothing, somebody, someone, something, both, few, many, several, all, some.*
> The indefinite pronouns *each, either,* and *neither* refer separately to each member of a group of persons, places, or things.
>
> **Many enjoy the sport of ballooning.**
> **Each of the hot-air balloons was in a bright color.**

A. Underline the indefinite pronouns.

1. My two brothers wanted to do <u>something</u> different during summer vacation.

2. <u>Both</u> of them are interested in sports and like a challenge.

3. A <u>few</u> of their friends had talked to them about hot-air ballooning.

4. My brothers went up in a balloon with <u>someone</u> who was an experienced pilot.

5. After <u>several</u> of the trips, they wanted to learn to pilot themselves.

6. <u>Either</u> of the community colleges offered classes.

7. <u>Each</u> of the students would get ten hours of flight experience with an instructor.

8. Passing a written examination was a requirement for <u>everyone</u> in the class.

9. <u>No one</u> who missed class would be able to get a license.

10. <u>Neither</u> of my brothers missed a class, and now they have their licenses.

B. Circle the indefinite pronouns. On the line write **S** if it is used as a subject, **DO** if it is a direct object, **IO** if it is an indirect object, or **OP** if it is the object of a preposition.

[DO] 1. My brothers looked for ballooning sites on the Web, and they found (many.)

[S] 2. (Neither) of them had known about the Balloon Fiesta in New Mexico before.

[OP] 3. The information they discovered really made an impression on (each) of them.

[S] 4. (Everyone) told me that more than 1,000 balloons participate in the fiesta.

[S] 5. (Many) of the balloons are in odd shapes—such as a piggy bank or a motorcycle.

[DO] 6. My brothers found (someone) who had been to the fiesta.

[IO] 7. The person told (both) of them stories about the fiesta and the mass balloon ascensions.

[S] 8. (Either) of my brothers could participate in future fiestas.

[OP] 9. The fiesta is open to (anyone) who is qualified.

[OP] 10. I'll be rooting for (both) of them to win prizes in the contests.

Name _____

52. Using Correct Agreement for Indefinite Pronouns

> Some indefinite pronouns are always singular; others are always plural.
>
> SINGULAR: each, either, neither, every, everyone, everybody, everything, one, anyone, anybody, anything, no one, nobody, nothing
>
> PLURAL: all, both, few, many, several, some
>
> **Each *wants* to help.   Many *are* needed.**

Circle the verb that agrees with the pronoun.

1. All of the cleanup volunteers (was (were)) supposed to bring their sign-up cards with them.

2. Everyone ((was mailed) were mailed) a sign-up card.

3. Each of them ((was) were) assigned to a work group for the day.

4. All of them (was (were)) given a ticket with their group number.

5. If anybody ((wants) want) gloves for the work, they are available.

6. A few of the volunteers ((have brought) has brought) their gloves.

7. Nobody (have brought (has brought)) a shovel.

8. Several of the groups ((work) works) on the south end of the beach.

9. One of the groups (clean (cleans)) the parking areas.

10. Each of the volunteers ((fills) fill) his or her bag with garbage.

11. No one but the volunteers ((was allowed) were allowed) on the beach during the cleanup.

12. Many of the beach users (has left (have left)) cans and bottles from picnics on the beach.

13. All of the bottles and cans (was put (were put)) in separate bags.

14. Ed found a shoe. Someone ((has left) have left) the beach with only one shoe.

15. If someone ((fills) fill) a bag, one of the two managers provides another bag.

16. After a couple of hours, neither of the beach managers ((has) have) any bags left.

17. Some of the bags (breaks (break)) when full.

18. Many of the groups (was finished (were finished)) with their areas before noon.

19. All (works (work)) hard.

20. Everyone ((was pleased) were pleased) with the results—a clean beach.

Name _____

53. Using Nothing and Anything Correctly

The negative of *something* is *nothing*. Because *nothing* is a negative, it is not used when a sentence contains another negative word such as *not* or *never*; use *anything* instead.

There was <u>nothing</u> good in the refrigerator.
There was *never* <u>anything</u> good in the refrigerator.

A. Complete each sentence with *nothing* or *anything*.

1. When my family arrived at our new house, there was _____[nothing]_____ in it.

2. My parents called the moving company, but it couldn't tell us _____[anything]_____ about our van.

3. There was _____[nothing]_____ to do but wait for the van to arrive.

4. We found a refrigerator in the kitchen, but it didn't contain _____[anything]_____ at all.

5. We hadn't had _____[anything]_____ to eat since breakfast, and we were hungry.

6. There was _____[nothing]_____ we could do but call for a pizza.

7. We had _____[nothing]_____ with which to eat it—so we used our hands.

8. Since we couldn't find _____[anything]_____ to sit on, we sat on the floor.

9. Since we couldn't do _____[anything]_____, we were bored.

10. When the van finally arrived, the drivers said _____[nothing]_____ about why they were so late.

B. Rewrite the sentences in Part A. For sentences with *nothing*, use *anything*. For sentences with *anything*, use *nothing*. Be sure to make all the necessary changes to have correct sentences.

1. [When my family arrived at our new house, there wasn't anything in it.]

2. [My parents called the moving company, but it could tell us nothing about our van.]

3. [There wasn't anything to do but wait for the van to arrive.]

4. [We found a refrigerator in the kitchen, but it contained nothing at all.]

5. [We had had nothing to eat since breakfast, and we were hungry.]

6. [There wasn't anything we could do but call for a pizza.]

7. [We hadn't anything with which to eat it—so we used our hands.]

8. [Since we could find nothing to sit on, we sat on the floor.]

9. [Since we could do nothing, we were bored.]

10. [When the van finally arrived, the drivers didn't say anything about why they were so late.]

Pronouns

Name _____

54. Reviewing Pronouns

A. Circle the correct form of the pronoun for each sentence. On the line write
S if it is used as a subject, **SC** if it is a subject complement, **DO** if it is a direct object,
IO if it is an indirect object, or **OP** if it is the object of a preposition.

___[IO]___ 1. Ancient myths have given (we (us)) many famous characters.

___[OP]___ 2. Names such as Hercules are familiar to (we (us)) all.

___[SC]___ 3. Also well-known is the story of Daedalus. It was ((he) him) who invented wings.

___[DO]___ 4. A king had imprisoned (he (him)) and his son Icarus.

___[S]___ 5. ((They) Them) wanted to escape.

___[S]___ 6. His son and ((he) him) were able to fly with the wings, but the story ends unhappily for Icarus.

___[DO]___ 7. Daedalus had warned ((him) he) about the danger of the sun.

___[OP]___ 8. But the warning was forgotten by (he (him)) in the excitement of flying.

___[S]___ 9. The sun melted the wax on his wings, and ((they) them) came off.

___[S]___ 10. Both the wings and ((he) him) fell deep into the ocean.

B. Complete each sentence with a possessive pronoun, intensive pronoun, or a reflexive pronoun.

1. Zeus was the chief god, and the most important place on Mount Olympus was
   _____[his]_____.

2. He could turn _____[himself]_____ into an animal or a human.

3. The gods and goddesses often quarreled among _____[themselves]_____.

4. They _____[themselves]_____ often behaved foolishly.

5. Despite this, the gods and goddesses were powerful, and the power over
   humans was _____[theirs]_____.

C. Circle the relative pronoun in each sentence. On the line write
S if it is used as a subject, **DO** if it is a direct object, **OP** if it is an
object of a preposition, or **PA** if it is a possessive adjective.

___[PA]___ 1. Hercules, (whose) father was Zeus, was very powerful.

___[OP]___ 2. Hercules had to perform twelve difficult tasks, to (which) the name Labors of Hercules has been given.

___[DO]___ 3. Hercules wore the skin of a lion, (which) he had killed with his bare hands.

57

___[S]___   4. For a while he took over the job of Atlas, (who)
carried the sky on his back.

___[S]___   5. He even traveled to the fearful underworld to fetch Cerberus,
(which) was Pluto's three-headed dog.

D. Identify each *italicized* pronoun. On the line write **IN** if it is interrogative,
DEM if it is demonstrative, or **ID** if it is indefinite.

___[IN]___   1. *What* do you know about ancient mythology?

___[DEM]___   2. *This* is a topic that interests many people.

___[ID]___   3. I got two books from the library, but *neither* had the story of Ariadne.

___[ID]___   4. *Both* were nice books with beautiful illustrations.

___[ID]___   5. I have read versions of *many* of the stories before.

E. Complete each sentence with *who* or *whom*.

1. Hermes, ____[whom]____ the Romans called Mercury, was the messenger of the gods.

2. Athena, after ____[whom]____ Athens is named, was the goddess of wisdom.

3. Poseidon, by ____[whom]____ the sea was ruled, was Zeus' brother.

4. Hephaestus, ____[who]____ was the god of fire, was called Vulcan by the Romans.

5. Apollo, ____[who]____ was the god of music, was one of the most important Greek gods.

F. Circle the correct pronoun in parentheses.

1. The class doesn't know (nothing (anything)) about the story of Arachne.

2. Everyone ((looks) look) for the names in the dictionary.

3. A few (does (do)) an Internet search.

4. Mark helps Carrie: he found some information faster than ((she) her).

5. Lee and Inez were as interested in the topic as ((they) them).

Try It Yourself

On a separate sheet of paper, write a paragraph about a famous person you've learned about recently. Be sure that you use correct forms of pronouns and pronoun agreement.

Check Your Own Work

Choose a piece of writing from your portfolio or journal, a work in progress, an assignment from another class, or a letter. Revise it, applying the skills you have reviewed. The checklist will help you.

✔ Are the personal pronouns correct?

✔ Are *who* and *whom* used correctly in questions and dependent clauses?

✔ Are possessive pronouns in the correct form—without apostrophes?

✔ Are *nothing* and *anything* used correctly?

Name _____

Adjectives

55. Identifying Descriptive Adjectives

An **adjective** describes or limits a noun or a pronoun.

> **Gloria Estefan is a famous singer.**

A **proper adjective** is formed from a proper noun. It is capitalized. All other adjectives are common adjectives.

> **Gloria Estefan is a Cuban-American singer.**

Underline the descriptive adjectives in each sentence. Write **P** above the proper adjectives and **C** above the common adjectives.

1. Gloria Estefan is a [C] popular singer.
2. She sings [P] Latin music.
3. As a child, Gloria had a [C] hard life.
4. Her family was from the [C] tropical island of Cuba.
5. They had come to the United States because of [C] political problems.
6. Gloria's father became [C] sick, and she was an [C] important caregiver for him.
7. She used to listen to [C] current music and sing the [C] jazzy songs to herself.
8. Gloria's mother encouraged her to sing with a [C] local group.
9. Although Gloria was [C] shy at first, she became a [C] confident performer.
10. Gloria's [C] smooth voice made her a success with audiences.
11. [P] Latin-American audiences really appreciated her group's music.
12. Early on, the group sang [P] Spanish songs.
13. Then her group had a [C] huge success with an [P] English song called "Dr. Beat."
14. Gloria now had a [C] famous and [C] wealthy life.
15. Then, in 1990, she was in a [C] serious accident in a bus.
16. She suffered a [C] broken back and had to have [C] major surgery.
17. Gloria wanted her [C] musical career back.
18. She was [C] courageous and [C] hard-working, and her efforts paid off.
19. She rebuilt a [C] successful career after the accident.
20. She always performs in an [C] interesting, [C] lively, and [C] creative way.

Gloria Estefan is an example of a person who is determined to reach her goals. Give an example of how you can show determination to reach a goal.

56. Placing Adjectives Correctly

A descriptive adjective may come before or after a noun or after a linking verb. An adjective that follows a linking verb is a subject complement.

BEFORE A NOUN: **Popcorn and tomatoes were Native American crops.**

AFTER A NOUN: **Tomatoes, rich and juicy, can be eaten raw.**

AS A SUBJECT COMPLEMENT: **Popcorn is very tasty.**

A. Underline the adjectives in each sentence. Identify the position of each. Write **BN** if it is before the noun, **AN** if it is after the noun, or **SC** if it is a subject complement.

[SC] 1. Popcorn isn't new.

[BN] 2. At excavations in New Mexico, archaeologists have found ancient popcorn.

[AN] 3. The popcorn, still fluffy and white, had been in tombs for hundreds of years.

[SC] 4. Native Americans were creative in their uses of popcorn.

[BN] 5. They made popcorn into decorative headdresses and necklaces.

[BN] 6. They even made an unusual soup from popcorn.

[SC] 7. In the United States, popcorn is popular today.

[BN] 8. People love to eat buttery popcorn at the movies.

[AN] 9. In a year an American snacks on 70 quarts of popcorn, inexpensive and easy-to-fix.

[BN] 10. Popcorn is a seed with a tiny embryo in it.

[BN] 11. Around the embryo is a starchy material.

[SC] 12. The material becomes large when it is heated.

[BN] 13. It creates the fluffy area of the popcorn.

[SC] 14. Popcorn isn't always healthful for you.

[AN] 15. Popcorn, buttered and salted, should not be overeaten.

B. Write the appropriate adjective(s) to complete each sentence. On the line identify the position of each. Use **BN**, **AN**, or **SC** as in Part A.

poisonous   decorative   popular   red, round   rich and thick

[SC] 1. The tomato has become very _____[popular]_____ around the world.

[BN] 2. The _____[red, round]_____ tomato is actually a fruit and not a vegetable.

[SC] 3. In the 1600s, Europeans thought that the tomato was _____[poisonous]_____.

[BN] 4. They used the tomato for _____[decorative]_____ purposes.

[AN] 5. Eventually the Italians put the tomato into pasta sauces, _____[rich and thick]_____.

Adjectives

57. Identifying Articles and Numeral Adjectives

The **articles** *a, an,* and *the* point out a noun. The indefinite articles *a* and *an* refer to any one of a class of things. The definite article *the* refers to one or more specific things.

>**We went to visit a museum in Washington, D.C.**
>**The museum displays historic aircraft.**

A **numeral adjective** tells how many.

>**I went to the museum with my two brothers. It was our first visit.**

Adjectives such as *few* and *many* tell about how many.

>**There were many airplanes to see.**

In each sentence underline the article(s) and circle the numeral adjectives.

1. There are (many) things to see at the National Air and Space Museum in Washington, D.C.

2. The museum houses pioneer aircraft in history.

3. There are at least (four) types of aircraft: planes, balloons, rockets, and space ships.

4. (One) aircraft is the plane in which the Wright brothers made the (first) flight in 1903.

5. A major attraction is the spacecraft from the (first) lunar-landing mission.

6. This spacecraft was used by the (first) astronauts to walk on the moon.

7. Visitors to the museum can actually touch a moon rock.

8. This moon rock is (several billion) years old.

9. The museum houses the (first) balloon to travel around the world.

10. In 1999 Bertrand Piccard and Brian Jones used the balloon to go around the world.

11. It took them nearly (twenty) days.

12. It also has the (first) aircraft to make a transatlantic flight.

13. The (first) flight was made by Charles Lindbergh in 1929.

14. The flight helped show that the airplane could be a safe means of transportation.

15. The (first) rocket propelled by liquid fuel is also here.

16. The rocket made a flight of less than (three) seconds in 1926.

17. It can take a (few) visits to see everything in the museum.

18. Visitors can see only part of the collection at a time.

19. There are more than (three hundred) aircraft in the museum's collection.

20. The museum is also an important center for research in aviation history.

Adjectives

58. Identifying More Types of Adjectives

Demonstrative adjectives point out definite persons, places, or things. The demonstrative adjectives are *this, that, these,* and *those.*

>   **these songs**   **that microphone**

Possessive adjectives show possession or ownership. The possessive adjectives are *my, your, his, her, its, our,* and *their.*

>   **his CD**   **their duets**

Indefinite adjectives refer to any or all of a group of persons, places, or things. The indefinite adjectives include *both, few, every, several, all, some, many, each, either,* and *neither.*

>   **every listener**

Interrogative adjectives ask a question. The interrogative adjectives are *what, which,* and *whose.*

>   **Which song was best?**

A. Identify the type of each *italicized* adjective. On the line write **DEM** for demonstrative, **P** for possessive, **IND** for indefinite, or **INT** for interrogative.

[INT]   1. *Which* students have signed up to participate in the karaoke night?

[DEM]   2. *This* event is going to take place in the cafeteria.

[IND]   3. *Every* participant has to choose a song.

[IND]   4. Participants can choose *any* song from a list.

[P]   5. The students have to write *their* choices on the list in the cafeteria.

[P]   6. Many students are choosing songs by *their* favorite groups.

[P]   7. Yolanda chose to sing *her* favorite song by the Beatles.

[IND]   8. *Some* students want to sing with partners.

[P]   9. I am having trouble deciding on *my* favorite song.

[INT]   10. *What* song do you think I should sing?

B. Complete each sentence with the type of adjective named.

interrogative   1. **[Which/What]** students do you think sang the best? **[Answers may vary.]**

indefinite   2. **[Each/Every]** student got a lot of applause.

possessive   3. Wilma and Rita did a great job on ____**[their]**____ duet.

indefinite   4. **[Some/Many]** students didn't want to participate.

demonstrative 5. ____**[This]**____ kind of event can be fun for everyone.

59. Understanding When to Repeat the Article

> When two or more nouns joined by *and* refer to different people, places, or things, use an article before each noun.
>
> **The circus performer and the musician performed a program of circus music.**
>
> When two or more nouns joined by *and* refer to the same person, place, or thing, use an article before the first noun only.
>
> **The manager and director of the circus was in the audience.**

A. On the line write the article if it should be repeated. If it should not be repeated, write *no*.

1. The ringmaster and _____[no]_____ announcer was a tall man in a tuxedo.

2. The juggler and _____[the]_____ tightrope walker were the first performers in the ring.

3. The tightrope walker's costume included a shiny pink leotard and _____[a]_____ white scarf.

4. The white and _____[the]_____ brown horses trotted in the ring—a white one, a brown one, then a white one, and so on.

5. The rider and _____[the]_____ horse worked as a team with precision moves.

6. The clown in the black pants and _____[the]_____ white shirt looked sad.

7. The owner and _____[no]_____ director of the circus was an elegant woman.

8. The drummer and _____[no]_____ xylophone player was at the back of the orchestra.

9. The lion tamer and _____[the]_____ trapeze artist performed at the same time.

10. A lion and _____[a]_____ tiger were in the ring at the same time.

B. Write sentences to show the following situations. Be careful to repeat or not repeat articles to make your meaning clear.

1. Charmaine is a singer. Charmaine is a circus performer.
   [Charmaine is a singer and circus performer.]

2. I enjoyed the lion tamer. I also enjoyed the elephant trainer.
   [I enjoyed the lion tamer and the elephant trainer.]

3. A special shoe worn by a clown was blue and red. It lit up.
   [A special blue-and-red shoe worn by a clown lit up.]

4. The tall man is a violinist. The tall man is a saxophonist.
   [The tall man is a violinist and saxophonist.]

5. The director of the circus was in the ring. The owner of the circus was also in the ring.
   [The director and the owner of the circus were in the ring.]

Adjectives

60. Forming Comparative and Superlative Degrees

The **positive degree** of an adjective shows a quality of a noun.
The **comparative degree** shows a quality of two nouns in greater or lesser degree.
The **superlative degree** shows a quality of a noun in the greatest or least degree.

POSITIVE DEGREE	COMPARATIVE DEGREE	SUPERLATIVE DEGREE
large	larger	largest
creative	more creative	most creative

A. Write the comparative and superlative degrees of each of the adjectives.

POSITIVE	COMPARATIVE	SUPERLATIVE
1. short	[shorter]	[shortest]
2. efficient	[more efficient]	[most efficient]
3. charming	[more charming]	[most charming]
4. wide	[wider]	[widest]
5. long	[longer]	[longest]
6. popular	[more popular]	[most popular]
7. simple	[simpler]	[simplest]
8. colorful	[more colorful]	[most colorful]
9. cloudy	[cloudier]	[cloudiest]
10. graceful	[more graceful]	[most graceful]

B. Identify the degree of comparison of each *italicized* adjective. On the line write **P** if it is positive, **C** if it is comparative, or **S** if it is superlative.

[S] 1. Some of the *most unusual* animals in the world are on the Galapagos Islands.

[P] 2. The islands, in the Pacific Ocean off South America, are *volcanic* ones.

[C] 3. There are thirteen large islands in the Galapagos group and six *smaller* ones.

[P] 4. The islands were *remote,* and animals and plants there developed in unique ways.

[C] 5. The animals on the island were *tamer* than animals elsewhere because the island animals had no natural predators.

[S] 6. The flightless cormorant is one of the *oddest* creatures on the island.

[P] 7. It doesn't fly, but it is a *swift* swimmer.

[S] 8. It is one of the *rarest* birds—there are only about 1,000 left.

[S] 9. The giant tortoises live the *longest* lives of all animals—more than 150 years.

[C] 10. The islands' giant tortoises live mostly in the *higher* elevations.

Adjectives

Name ______________________________

61. Using the Comparative and the Superlative Degree

The comparative degree is used when two things are compared. It is often used with *than.*

Earth is much smaller than Jupiter.

The superlative degree is used when more than two things are compared.

Jupiter is the largest planet in the solar system.

A. In each sentence circle the correct form for the adjective used in a comparison.

1. Of the nine planets, Mercury is the planet that is (closer (closest)) to the sun.
2. Temperatures on Mercury are the (more extreme (most extreme)) in the solar system.
3. Venus is the (brighter (brightest)) planet of all.
4. Venus looks ((brighter) brightest) than any other object in the sky except the sun and the moon.
5. Venus was considered the ((most beautiful) more beautiful) of all the planets.
6. The (more enormous (most enormous)) volcano in the solar system is Olympus Mons, which is about 16 miles tall and is on Mars.
7. Mars is much ((smaller) smallest) in size than Earth.
8. Earth is ((flatter) flattest) at the poles and ((wider) widest) in the middle than a true sphere would be.
9. The (more unusual (most unusual)) feature of Jupiter is its Red Spot, which is an intense storm of gases.
10. Jupiter is much ((larger) largest) than Earth—about 1,300 Earths would fit into it.

B. For each sentence write the correct degree of comparison of the adjective given.

cold	1. Pluto is the **[coldest]** planet, with temperatures of –387°F.
long	2. Of all the planets, Pluto takes the **[longest]** time to orbit the sun.
remarkable	3. The **[most remarkable]** feature of Saturn is the rings that circle its equator.
short	4. A year on Mercury is much **[shorter]** than a year on Earth.
faint	5. The rings of Jupiter are **[fainter]** than those of Saturn.
close	6. Venus comes **[closer]** to Earth than any other planet.
hot	7. Venus's clouds create a greenhouse effect to make it the **[hottest]** planet of all.
massive	8. Jupiter is **[more massive]** than the other planets.
important	9. Jupiter's name comes from the **[most important]** Roman god.
interesting	10. What is the **[most interesting]** fact you've learned about the planets?

Adjectives

62. Using **Fewer** and **Less** Correctly

Use *fewer* and *less* to compare quantities. Use *fewer* to compare things you can count.

There were fewer fans in the stands.

Use *less* to compare things you cannot count.

There was less noise from the crowd.

A. Circle the correct word in parentheses.

1. (**Fewer** Less) spectators attended this year's basketball tournament than last year's.

2. There were (**fewer** less) students from our school there than there were last year.

3. There was (**less** fewer) applause when the teams took the court.

4. Our team scored (**fewer** less) points in the first half than the other team.

5. There was (**less** fewer) tension in the second half because our team was far behind.

6. The other team made (**fewer** less) mistakes and deserved its lead.

7. Our team seemed to play with (fewer **less**) energy in the second half.

8. There were (**fewer** less) cheers from the fans and the cheerleaders.

9. There was (fewer **less**) hope that the team would win.

10. There were (**fewer** less) smiles on the ride home than there were last year when our team won.

B. Complete each sentence with *fewer* or *less*.

1. Basketball teams have ____[fewer]____ players than baseball teams.

2. There is ____[less]____ time in a basketball quarter than in a hockey period.

3. There are ____[fewer]____ minutes in a polo period than in a basketball quarter—there are only seven and one half minutes in a period in polo.

4. There is ____[less]____ interest in professional soccer in the United States than in many other countries.

5. Professional baseball players earned ____[fewer]____ dollars twenty years ago.

6. A football field has ____[less]____ area than a soccer field.

7. Soccer requires ____[fewer]____ pieces of equipment than football.

8. The NBA championship has ____[fewer]____ TV viewers than the World Cup.

9. ____[Fewer]____ points are scored in soccer than in many other sports.

10. Some people say that golf requires ____[less]____ athletic ability than other sports.

Adjectives

63. Using Demonstrative Adjectives

> The demonstrative adjectives *this, that, these,* and *those* agree in number with the nouns they modify.
>
> *This* and *these* refer to objects that are near. *That* and *those* refer to objects that are farther away.
>
> **This kind of backpack holds a lot of things.**
>
> **Those tents are good for camping in the woods.**

A. Circle the correct demonstrative pronoun in parentheses.

1. (this (these)) chairs
2. (this (these)) types of tents
3. ((that) those) camp stove
4. ((that) those) bag of apples
5. (this (these)) boxes of matches
6. (this (these)) compasses
7. ((that) those) sweater
8. ((that) those) pair of boots
9. ((that) those) bag of marshmallows
10. ((this) these) kind of sleeping bag

B. Complete each sentence with a demonstrative adjective.
Use the information at the left.

near   1. ____[This]____ new type of tent isn't very bulky.

far   2. Don't forget ____[those]____ tent stakes.

near   3. ____[These]____ sleeping pads will be comfortable to sleep on.

far   4. We might take ____[that]____ futon mattress instead.

far   5. ____[Those]____ shirts will make good pillows for our heads.

near   6. ____[This]____ recipe for campfire corn-on-the-cob sounds good.

far   7. Pack ____[that]____ can of kidney beans for my easy chili.

far   8. We need to take ____[that]____ can opener also.

near   9. I'll take ____[these]____ bananas for my grilled banana recipe.

near   10. ____[This]____ type of camp stove burns propane gas.

near   11. ____[These]____ boxes of plastic utensils will come in handy.

far   12. You should take ____[those]____ warm socks.

near   13. Don't forget ____[these]____ rain ponchos.

near   14. Put ____[these]____ bottles of water into the cooler.

far   15. Can you carry all ____[that]____ gear?

Adjectives

67

64. Identifying Words Used as Nouns and Adjectives

A noun is a name word. An adjective describes a noun or pronoun.

USED AS NOUN: **One <u>animal</u> that was in danger was a penguin in Australia.**

USED AS ADJECTIVE: **<u>Animal</u> protection is important to environmentalists— and to everyone.**

A. On the line write **N** if the *italicized* word is used as a noun or **A** if it is used as an adjective.

___[A]___ 1. An *oil* spill in Australia recently threatened the lives of penguins.

___[N]___ 2. Deadly *oil* covered the penguins.

___[N]___ 3. The penguins might ingest the poisonous oil that covered their *feathers*.

___[A]___ 4. The penguins' *feather* coat, which keeps them warm, could lose its natural oils.

___[N]___ 5. This meant that the penguins would have no protection from the *cold*.

___[A]___ 6. The waters that the penguins live in are very *cold* and icy.

___[A]___ 7. *Rescue* workers needed to capture and clean the penguins.

___[N]___ 8. The unusual rescue plan was to dress each penguin in a tiny *sweater*.

___[A]___ 9. To help, many people downloaded *sweater* patterns from the Internet.

___[N]___ 10. They went to stores to buy skeins of *wool* and knitting needles.

___[A]___ 11. They knitted tiny *wool* sweaters especially designed for the penguins.

___[N]___ 12. Each *penguin* captured was dressed in one of the sweaters.

___[A]___ 13. The penguin was then put into a tank with *salt* water.

___[N]___ 14. The sweater was eventually eaten up by the *salt,* but in the meantime the penguin's natural oils had returned.

___[A]___ 15. The *penguin* rescue was successful, and many penguins were returned to the ocean.

B. Complete each sentence with one of the given words. On the line write **N** if the word is used as a noun or **A** if it is used as an adjective. **[Suggested answers are given.]**

ocean   rescue   volunteer

___[A]___ 1. The plan to save the penguins was carried out by _____[volunteer]_____ workers.

___[N]___ 2. Every _____[volunteer]_____ was dedicated to saving the penguins.

___[N]___ 3. The workers at first didn't know if the _____[rescue]_____ would be successful.

___[A]___ 4. The _____[rescue]_____ plan saved many penguins.

___[A]___ 5. Many penguins are now back in the _____[ocean]_____ waters off Australia.

Name _____

65. Reviewing Adjectives

A. In Column 1 write **D** if the *italicized* adjective is descriptive, **A** if it is
an article, or **N** if it is a numeral adjective.
In Column 2 write **BN** if the adjective is before the noun,
AN if it is after the noun, or **SC** if it is a subject complement.

COLUMN 1	COLUMN 2	
[A]	[BN]	1. People give meanings to *the* colors.
[D]	[BN]	2. Here are some common meanings in *Western* culture.
[D]	[SC]	3. Black is *stylish* and timeless.
[A]	[BN]	4. Nowadays *the* color black is very popular for clothes.
[D]	[BN]	5. Black is often worn by *evil* people in fiction—think of Dracula.
[D]	[SC]	6. Red is *intense*.
[A]	[BN]	7. Every head turns when someone in *a* red oufit walks by.
[D]	[BN]	8. Red cars are *popular* targets for thieves.
[D]	[AN]	9. Blue, *peaceful* and calming, is a popular color.
[N]	[BN]	10. *Many* scientists think that people are more productive in blue rooms.
[D]	[BN]	11. Green is a *relaxing* color.
[A]	[BN]	12. We have green "blackboards" because green is the easiest color on *the* eye.
[D]	[AN]	13. This color, calming and *refreshing*, is used in many hospitals.
[D]	[SC]	14. Yellow is attention-getting and *optimistic*.
[D]	[BN]	15. Yellow is used for *legal* pads because it helps a person's concentration.

B. Identify each *italicized* adjective.
Write **DEM** if it is demonstrative, **P** if it is possessive,
IND if it is indefinite, or **INT** if it is interrogative.

[INT] 1. *What* color is your favorite?

[IND] 2. *Many* people like the color blue.

[IND, P] 3. *Every* jacket in *my* closet is black.

[DEM] 4. *That* jacket in red looks very good on you.

[IND] 5. There are *few* purple jackets in the store.

CONTINUED

C. Underline the correct adjective for each sentence. Identify the degree of comparison by writing **P** if it is positive, **C** if it is comparative, or **S** if it is superlative.

1. The (shorter <u>shortest</u>) [S] day of the year in the Northern Hemisphere is usually on or about December 21.

2. On that day the North Hemisphere is actually tilted (closer <u>closest</u>) [S] to the sun.

3. In areas near the North Pole, the day is almost completely (<u>dark</u> [P] darker).

4. Days gradually become (<u>longer</u> [C] longest) after that date.

5. On the other hand, in the Southern Hemisphere, that very day is the (longer <u>longest</u>) [S] day of the year.

D. Circle the correct word or *no change* for each sentence.

1. There are (fewer) less) hours of daylight in the winter months.

2. (Fewer (Less)) sunlight makes me want to stay indoors.

3. Do owls catch ((fewer) less) mice in winter?

4. The biologist and (the (no change)) lecturer who works at the museum might know the answer.

5. The planets and ((the) no change) constellations can be seen best on clear nights.

E. Circle the correct demonstrative adjective in each sentence.

1. ((This) These) planet has an axial tilt of almost twenty-four degrees.

2. ((That) Those) tilt causes solar rays to strike one hemisphere more intensely at different seasons of the year.

3. Where (this (these)) rays are most direct, the season is warmer.

4. Two days each year have days and nights of equal length: (that (those)) days are equinoxes.

5. ((This) These) word means "equal night."

Try It Yourself

On a separate sheet of paper, write a description of two places you visited. Tell how they are alike or different. Be sure to use capital letters and comparisons correctly.

Check Your Own Work

Choose a piece of writing from your portfolio or journal, a work in progress, an assignment from another class, or a letter. Revise it, applying the skills you have reviewed. The checklist will help you.

✔ Have you capitalized all proper adjectives?

✔ Have you used the correct forms of adjectives for the comparisons?

✔ Do demonstrative adjectives agree with the nouns they modify?

66. Identifying Verb Phrases

> A **verb** is a word used to express an action or a state of being.
>> **Many different animals and plants <u>live</u> in rain forests.**
>
> A **verb phrase** is a group of words used to do the work of a single verb.
>> **Tropical rain forests <u>are found</u> near the equator.**
>> **<u>Can</u> you <u>describe</u> a rain forest?**

Underline the verb or verb phrase in each sentence.

1. What <u>do</u> you <u>know</u> about tropical rain forests?

2. These rain forests <u>can</u> also <u>be called</u> jungles.

3. Their climate <u>is characterized</u> by high temperatures and abundant rain.

4. The rainfall <u>might reach</u> as much as 400 inches a year!

5. Tropical rain forests <u>are located</u> in Asia, Africa, South America, and Central America.

6. A rain forest <u>is divided</u> into four levels.

7. The canopy <u>has</u> trees as tall as 200 feet.

8. The third level, with small trees and vines, <u>is called</u> the understory.

9. The fourth level <u>is</u> the forest floor.

10. The rain forest's diversity of plant life <u>surpasses</u> any other habitat in the world.

11. Many of the plants for medicines <u>can</u> only <u>be found</u> in tropical rain forests.

12. An extraordinary variety of animal life <u>lives</u> there.

13. Scientists <u>discover</u> new species of insects and reptiles each year.

14. Unfortunately many species <u>are becoming</u> extinct.

15. Tropical rain forests <u>have existed</u> for about 300 million years.

16. <u>Will</u> they <u>survive</u> much longer?

17. Human activities severely <u>disrupt</u> the rain forests.

18. Millions of acres of rain forests <u>are destroyed</u> each year.

19. Farming, logging, and mining <u>may eliminate</u> them completely.

20. <u>Should</u> this destruction <u>be allowed</u> to continue?

67. Identifying Regular and Irregular Verbs

A verb has four principal parts: the **present**, the **present participle**, the **past**, and the **past participle**. The present participle is formed by adding *-ing* to the present form of the verb. The simple past and past participle of **regular verbs** are formed by adding *-d* or *-ed* to the present form. The simple past and past participle of **irregular verbs** are not formed by adding *-d* or *-ed* to the present form.

PRESENT	PRESENT PARTICIPLE	PAST	PAST PARTICIPLE
live	living	lived	lived
see	seeing	saw	seen

Many lords lived in castles.   **I have seen pictures of castles.**

A. For each sentence draw one line under the subject and two lines under the verb or verb phrase. On the line write whether the verb is regular or irregular.

_____[regular]_____ 1. During the Middle Ages most people lived in small villages.

_____[regular]_____ 2. The Middle Ages lasted from about A.D. 500 to A.D. 1400.

_____[regular]_____ 3. Society was divided into three groups: nobles, peasants, and clergy.

_____[irregular]_____ 4. The nobles fought for the protection of the land and the people on it.

_____[regular]_____ 5. The land was owned by the nobles.

_____[irregular]_____ 6. The nobles got their land from the king or queen.

_____[regular]_____ 7. The peasants farmed the land.

_____[irregular]_____ 8. The peasants gave part of their crops to the lord.

_____[irregular]_____ 9. The clergy taught people about the Christian religion.

_____[irregular]_____ 10. The clergy held a great deal of power in medieval society.

B. Write the present participle, past, and past participle of each verb.

	PRESENT PARTICIPLE	PAST	PAST PARTICIPLE
1. fly	[flying]	[flew]	[flown]
2. decide	[deciding]	[decided]	[decided]
3. think	[thinking]	[thought]	[thought]
4. wear	[wearing]	[wore]	[worn]
5. eat	[eating]	[ate]	[eaten]
6. forget	[forgetting]	[forgot]	[forgotten]
7. fix	[fixing]	[fixed]	[fixed]
8. keep	[keeping]	[kept]	[kept]
9. sell	[selling]	[sold]	[sold]
10. hurt	[hurting]	[hurt]	[hurt]

Verbs

68. Using Irregular Verbs Correctly

A. Circle the correct form of the verb in parentheses.

1. The Hopi of Arizona have long (grew *grown*) crops of corn and lived in pueblos.

2. The Hopi have long (hold *held*) ceremonies to call for rain, like the Snake Dance.

3. Also, the Hopi have (tell *told*) a story about the origin of the sun and the moon.

4. The Hopi believed that they had (*risen* rose) up to this world from an underworld.

5. The world they (*came* come) into was dark, and life was difficult for them.

6. One day they (seen *saw*) a light in the distance.

7. A messenger was (send *sent*) by the chiefs of the Hopi to find the cause of the light.

8. In a field the messenger (find *found*) a great fire and a handsome man called Skeleton.

9. The Hopi were (gave *given*) corn for roasting by Skeleton.

10. With Skeleton's help, the Hopi (build *built*) fires and learned to grow crops.

B. Complete each sentence with the past or past participle form of the verb at the left.

make 1. The darkness of the world still ___[made]___ life difficult for the Hopi.

have 2. The Hopi had ___[had]___ a moon in the underworld, and so they decided to make one in this world.

cut 3. They ___[cut]___ a huge circle from buffalo hide and painted it white.

put 4. The circle was ___[put]___ on a huge wooden loop.

throw 5. They ___[threw]___ the circle into the sky.

sing 6. As they swung the circle, they ___[sang]___ a magical song.

become 7. Suddenly there was a light in the sky that ___[became]___ brighter and brighter—the moon.

do 8. But there still wasn't enough light, and so something else was ___[done]___.

take, weave 9. The Hopi ___[took]___ a special piece of cloth that they had ___[woven]___ in the underworld.

swing 10. They ___[swung]___ the copper-colored cloth into the sky, and it became the sun.

Verbs

73

69. Using Troublesome Verbs Correctly

The verb *lie (lying, lay, lain)* means "to rest or recline." It doesn't take a direct object.

The bulbs have <u>lain</u> in the ground all winter.

The verb *lay (laying, laid, laid)* means "to put or place in position." It takes a direct object.

I've <u>laid</u> the gardening tools somewhere.

The verb *sit (sitting, sat, sat)* means "to have or keep a seat."

I <u>sat</u> on the wobbly lawn chair.

The verb *set (setting, set, set)* means "to place or fix."

I <u>set</u> the rake against the wall.

The verb *rise (rising, rose, risen)* means "to ascend or move up." It doesn't take a direct object.

The first bulb sprouts <u>rose</u> from the ground in March.

The verb *raise (raising, raised, raised)* means "to lift." It takes a direct object.

We <u>raise</u> flowers in our front garden.

The verb *let (letting, let, let)* means "to permit or allow."

Mom <u>let</u> me plant the seeds.

The verb *leave (leaving, left, left)* means "to abandon or depart from."

I <u>left</u> my seed catalogs in the garden.

A. Circle the correct verb in parentheses.

1. My family (rises (raises)) vegetables for our use.

2. When the temperature ((rises) raises) in the spring, we get ready.

3. How long has that rake ((lain) laid) in the yard?

4. Don't ((sit) set) on that dirty chair—it's been outside all winter.

5. Don't ((lie) lay) down on the grass—it's wet and cold.

6. The key for the shed ((lay) laid) unnoticed in the grass all winter.

7. (Let (Leave)) the seed packages in the wagon.

8. ((Let) Leave) me do the raking.

9. I (lay (laid)) my gloves somewhere. Where did I put them?

10. I'll (sit (set)) the seeds carefully in each hole.

11. Let's ((raise) rise) pumpkins this year.

12. Where can I ((set) sit) the tomato cages?

13. Just ((lay) lie) them in the corner.

14. We can (let (leave)) those chives where they are.

15. You should just ((lie) lay) down and rest.

CONTINUED

Verbs

Name _____

B. Complete each sentence with the correct form of a troublesome verb from this exercise. More than one answer may be possible.

1. The price of seeds has _____[risen]_____ since last year.

2. This year we're going to _____[raise]_____ tomatoes and peppers.

3. Where did you _____[lay/set]_____ the garden tools?

4. The garden hose has _____[lain]_____ at the back of the shed all winter.

5. _____[Let]_____ Mom hoe the ground—she makes straight rows.

6. Who _____[left]_____ that rake there? Someone might trip on it.

7. The cat _____[sat]_____ right in the middle of the row where we were working.

8. It was _____[lying]_____ in our way.

9. I _____[set/laid]_____ the zucchini seeds somewhere.

10. _____[Let]_____ me _____[sit]_____ down on that chair. I'm tired!

11. _____[Set]_____ the birdbath toward the back of the garden.

12. Oh, there's the cat _____[lying]_____ in the catnip.

13. We can _____[let]_____ her stay there.

14. What plant could we _____[raise]_____ for the dog?

15. He likes the place where we have _____[laid]_____ the chair cushions.

C. Circle the correct verb in parentheses.

1. Where did the boys (lie (lay)) the tickets for the concert.

2. How long have the tickets (lay (lain)) there?

3. The audience is (setting (sitting)) in the front of the huge hall.

4. (Leave (Let)) me accompany you to the concert tonight.

5. We are ((leaving) letting) promptly at six o'clock.

6. Frank, (sit) set) where you have the best view.

7. Please be seated; the curtain is (raising (rising)).

8. In scene one an actor is (laying (lying)) on top of a piano.

9. Rosi (lay (laid)) her program on the seat of her chair.

10. Everyone (raised (rose)) to cheer the actor's performance.

70. Identifying Words Used as Nouns and Verbs

> Some words can be used as either nouns or verbs. A noun is a name word.
> A verb generally expresses action or being.
>
> NOUN: **A bird may make its <u>nest</u> in the same place year after year.**
>
> VERB: **Some birds <u>nest</u> in the same place year after year.**

On the line write whether each *italicized* word is a noun or a verb.

_____[noun]_____ 1. The nature of bird migration remains
a fascinating *question* for scientists.

_____[noun]_____ 2. A blackpoll warbler—no bigger than a sparrow—
flies approximately 2,500 miles without a *rest*.

_____[noun]_____ 3. It will winter in South America after a nonstop *journey* of some 90 hours.

_____[verb]_____ 4. Many birds *journey* much farther—11,000 miles from the Arctic to the Antarctic.

_____[verb]_____ 5. Of course, such birds *rest* along the way.

_____[verb]_____ 6. Many North American birds *winter* in South America.

_____[noun]_____ 7. South American birds don't fly farther north than the tropics for the *winter*.

_____[verb]_____ 8. Many migrating birds *return* to nest in the same place every year.

_____[noun]_____ 9. In North America the *return* of the birds means spring.

_____[verb]_____ 10. The reason for the migration of birds is simple: a bird *needs* food.

_____[noun]_____ 11. For some species there aren't enough insects in winter for their *needs*.

_____[verb]_____ 12. What factors *trigger* migration? How do birds know winter is coming?

_____[noun]_____ 13. A change in hormone production because of less daylight may be one *trigger*.

_____[verb]_____ 14. Scientists can't positively *answer* why birds return to the same nests
year after year.

_____[noun]_____ 15. Actually scientists have come up with more than one *answer*.

_____[noun]_____ 16. Landmarks such as rivers and mountain ranges may act as *guides*.

_____[verb]_____ 17. Some birds may *use* the stars for navigation.

_____[verb]_____ 18. Some scientists say the earth's magnetic field *guides* the birds.

_____[verb]_____ 19. Others *question* these explanations as incomplete.

_____[noun]_____ 20. The *use* of stars and magnetic fields would require complex sensory organs,
which scientists haven't yet located in birds.

71. Identifying Transitive and Intransitive Verbs

A **transitive verb** expresses an action that passes from a doer to a receiver.
The receiver of the action is the direct object.

DIRECT OBJECT

The ancient Mayas built *temples*.

An **intransitive verb** does not have a receiver of an action. It does not have a direct object.

The Mayas lived in Mexico and Central America.

Underline the verb in each sentence. If it has a direct object, circle the object. On the line write **T** if the each verb is transitive or **I** if it is intransitive.

[I] 1. In the rain forest of Central America stands a stone pyramid.

[T] 2. The pyramid honored the Maya (gods) of sun, moon, and rain.

[T] 3. The ancient Mayas built the (pyramid) about 1,000 years ago.

[I] 4. The pyramid rises to a height of almost 80 feet.

[T] 5. The pyramid has nine large stone (terraces).

[I] 6. The terraces lead to the temple at the top.

[I] 7. Only the Maya priests went into the temple.

[T] 8. The Maya priests sacrificed (animals) to the gods.

[T] 9. In Maya beliefs the gods needed (blood) for survival.

[T] 10. So the Mayas killed (animals,) such as dogs and jaguars.

[I] 11. All the classes in Maya society worshiped at the pyramid.

[I] 12. In 1952 a Cuban archaeologist, Alberto Ruiz Lhuiller, explored deep into the pyramid.

[T] 13. He made an amazing (discovery.)

[T] 14. He found a secret (crypt.)

[I] 15. Inside the crypt lay the body of a king.

[T] 16. A shroud of cotton with sprinkles of red dye covered the (body.)

[I] 17. In Maya belief the king fell into the underworld at his death.

[T] 18. In the tomb the king's followers put (food) for the king's stay in the underworld.

[I] 19. A jade mask lay over the king's face.

[T] 20. The Mayas valued (jade) highly.

Verbs

72. Distinguishing Verbs That Can Be Transitive and Intransitive

Some verbs can be transitive or intransitive, depending on their use in a sentence.

TRANSITIVE: **The campers drove their new van.**

INTRANSITIVE: **The campers drove to the lake.** (no direct object)

A.   Underline the verb or verb phrase in each sentence. On the line write **T** if the verb is transitive or **I** if it is intransitive.

__[I]__   1. I could see across the lake with my new binoculars for bird watching.

__[T]__   2. I saw a yellow-bellied sapsucker in a tree on my first day.

__[T]__   3. We cooked corn right in the campfire.

__[I]__   4. The corn cooked rapidly in the heat.

__[T]__   5. Mari poured the hot cider for us.

__[I]__   6. The marshmallows burned quickly over the campfire.

__[T]__   7. We burned firewood for heating and cooking.

__[I]__   8. The rain poured down for the last two days of our trip.

__[I]__   9. So we could not play outside.

__[T]__   10. Instead we played computer games inside our cabin.

B.   Write two sentences for each verb at the left. Use the verb as transitive and intransitive, in any form you choose. [Sample sentences are given.]

sing   1. [The class sang together.]

    2. [We sang the National Anthem at the baseball game.]

hide   3. [Ann hid the cookies from the class.]

    4. [George hides from the snake.]

continue   5. [The group continued the tour of the art museum.]

    6. [The game continued after the rain delay.]

burst   7. [Mary burst the water balloon.]

    8. [The bicycle tires burst.]

play   9. [Jim and Bill played Monopoly.]

    10. [Agnes and I played with the dog.]

Verbs

Name _____

73. Identifying Linking Verbs

A **linking verb** links the subject of a sentence with a subject complement (a noun, a pronoun, or an adjective). Verbs of being are the most common linking verbs.

Helen Keller and Anne Sullivan <u>were</u> courageous, dedicated *people*.
(The subject complement is a noun.)

Helen Keller and Anne Sullivan <u>are</u> *famous* in American history.
(The subject complement is an adjective.)

Circle each linking verb. Underline its complement. On the line write **N** if the subject complement is a noun, **P** if it is a pronoun, or **A** if it is an adjective.

__[A]__ 1. As a small child Helen Keller (was) very <u>sick</u>.

__[N]__ 2. Two effects of the illness (were) <u>loss</u> of sight and hearing.

__[N]__ 3. Helen's only means of contact with the world (was) <u>touch</u>.

__[A]__ 4. She (was) <u>eager</u> for communication with others.

__[N]__ 5. Anne Sullivan (was) Helen's <u>teacher</u>.

__[N]__ 6. The day of Anne's arrival (was) an important <u>day</u> in Helen's life.

__[P]__ 7. It (was) <u>she</u> who first communicated with Helen through the sense of touch.

__[N]__ 8. The method of communication (was) the <u>use</u> of finger movements for letters.

__[A]__ 9. Before this time Helen (had been) <u>lonely</u> in a world of her own.

__[A]__ 10. School attendance (was) now <u>possible</u> for Helen.

__[N]__ 11. By 1904 she (was) a college <u>graduate</u>.

__[N]__ 12. Helen Keller (was) later a <u>lecturer</u>.

__[N, N]__ 13. Her topics (were) often the <u>story</u> of her life and <u>stories</u> of inspiration.

__[A]__ 14. Her lecture money (was) <u>helpful</u> in improving conditions for those without sight.

__[A]__ 15. The story of Helen's life (is) <u>fascinating</u> to readers of her autobiography.

Helen Keller showed great courage to overcome her problems and help others. Give an example of how you might show courage to overcome a problem.

74. Identifying Other Linking Verbs

> The verbs *appear, become, continue, feel, grow, look, remain, seem, smell, sound, stay,* and *taste* can be used as linking verbs. These verbs can be considered linking verbs if some form of the verb *be* can be substituted for them.
>
> **The Narnia chronicles <u>became</u> a well-loved *series* of books.**
>
> **The world of Narnia <u>seems</u> *green* and *fresh* at first.**

A. Circle each linking verb. Underline its complement. On the line write **N** if the subject complement is a noun or **A** if it is an adjective.

__[N]__ 1. At the start of *The Chronicles of Narnia,* Digory and Polly (become) <u>friends</u>.

__[N]__ 2. With Digory's uncle's rings, they (become) <u>participants</u> in a magical world.

__[A]__ 3. In the story an evil witch (appears) very <u>beautiful</u>.

__[A]__ 4. The lion's special song of creation (sounds) <u>sweet</u>.

__[A]__ 5. The lion's world of Narnia with its talking animals (seems) <u>wonderful</u>.

__[A]__ 6. Eventually the children (grow) <u>hungry</u>.

__[N]__ 7. In the magic land a piece of toffee candy (becomes) a toffee <u>tree</u>.

__[A]__ 8. Its fruit (tastes) <u>delicious</u> and <u>juicy</u>.

__[A]__ 9. Back at home the children (feel) <u>happy</u> about the good results of their adventures.

__[A]__ 10. Digory's mother (becomes) <u>well</u> through the magic of Narnia.

B. Underline the verb in each sentence. On the line write **T** if it is transitive, **I** if it is intransitive, or **L** if it is linking.

__[L]__ 1. C. S. Lewis <u>was</u> the author of the Narnia chronicles.

__[T]__ 2. Lewis <u>created</u> a world of talking animals and valiant battles.

__[T]__ 3. The forces of evil <u>fight</u> the forces of good in the books.

__[I]__ 4. Ordinary children, as well as mythical beings, <u>appear</u> in the books.

__[L]__ 5. The books <u>have become</u> popular around the world.

__[T]__ 6. The series <u>contains</u> seven books in all.

__[I]__ 7. According to Lewis, the idea for the books <u>grew</u> from three images: a fawn, a witch on a sled, and a magnificent lion.

__[T]__ 8. Lewis <u>wrote</u> *The Lion, the Witch, and the Wardrobe* first, in 1950.

__[T]__ 9. Lewis <u>taught</u> literature at Oxford University.

__[L]__ 10. The professor <u>became</u> an author of children's books.

Verbs

75. Identifying the Active and Passive Voice

In the **active voice**, the subject is the doer of the action.

DOER

Renaissance *artists* <u>painted</u> religious and mythological subjects.

In the **passive voice**, the subject is the receiver of the action.

RECEIVER

Religious and mythological *subjects* <u>were painted</u> by Renaissance artists.

Linking verbs are not action verbs; therefore, they do not have voice.

A. Underline the verb in each sentence. On the line write **A** if it is active, **P** if it is passive, or **L** if it is linking.

[P] 1. The period from about 1400 to about 1600 <u>is named</u> the Renaissance.

[A] 2. Its name <u>means</u> "rebirth."

[P] 3. The medieval focus on religion and the other world <u>was rejected</u> in the Renaissance.

[P] 4. The works of ancient Greek and Roman authors <u>were studied</u> by Renaissance thinkers.

[A] 5. Advances in science and technology <u>occurred</u>.

[P] 6. Botany, zoology, and even magic <u>were developed</u> as a result of the study of ancient texts.

[L] 7. Art <u>became</u> more realistic.

[P] 8. Objects <u>were drawn</u> to scale and in perspective.

[L] 9. The city of Florence in the central part of Italy <u>was</u> the center of the Renaissance.

[P] 10. Many works of art <u>were produced</u> in Florence by artists like Leonardo da Vinci.

B. Rewrite the sentences using the voice indicated.

1. Florence was ruled by rich, powerful families.

   active   **[Rich, powerful families ruled Florence.]** _____

2. Rich and powerful families ordered many works of art.

   passive   **[Many works of art were ordered by rich and powerful families.]** _____

3. The citizens of Florence appreciated art.

   passive   **[Art was appreciated by the citizens of Florence.]** _____

4. Many churches and palaces were decorated by Florentine artists.

   active   **[Florentine artists decorated many churches and palaces.]** _____

5. Thousands of tourists visit Florence each year.

   passive   **[Florence is visited by thousands of tourists each year.]** _____

Verbs

76. Identifying Simple Tenses

> The simple present tense tells about an action that happens again and again.
>
> **Many people like ice hockey.**
>
> The simple past tense tells about an action that happened in past time.
>
> **Canadians invented the sport of ice hockey.**
>
> The future tense tells about an action that will happen in future time.
>
> **The hockey season will start next October.**

A. Underline the verb in each sentence. Write its tense on the line: present, past, or future.

[past] 1. The game of ice hockey began in Canada in the 1800s.

[past] 2. The game became popular in other countries, such as Russia and the United States.

[present] 3. The fast-paced sport of hockey is played by two teams on an ice-covered rink.

[present] 4. Six skating players and a goalie compose a hockey team.

[present] 5. A player scores by hitting the puck into the other team's net with a stick.

[future] 6. The team with the most goals will win the game.

[present] 7. Hockey has swifter action than many other sports.

[future] 8. Any potential hockey players will require excellent skating ability and balance.

[present] 9. Hockey spectators need quick reflexes for the fast-moving puck.

[past] 10. Hockey was established as an Olympic sport in 1920.

B. Complete each sentence with the indicated tense and voice of the verb.

win (future, active) 1. Who ____[will win]____ the Stanley Cup next year?

name (present, passive) 2. The cup ____[is named]____ for Lord Stanley, a governor of Canada.

give (past, active) 3. He ____[gave]____ the cup as an annual prize for the best hockey team.

award (past, passive) 4. The cup ____[was awarded]____ for the first time in 1893.

compete (present, active) 5. National Hockey League teams ____[compete]____ for the cup every year.

Verbs

77. Identifying Progressive Tenses

Progressive tenses express continuing action. The progressive tenses are formed with the present participle and a form of *be*.

The present progressive tense tells about something that is happening right now.

> **Katherine is paying for summer camp.**

The past progressive tells about something that was happening in the past.

> **Jay was paying for summer school.**

The future progressive tense tells about something that will be happening in the future.

> **Elizabeth will be paying for all her music lessons next year.**

A. Underline the verb in each sentence. Write its tense on the line: **PR** for present progressive, **PT** for past progressive, or **FP** future progressive.

[FP] 1. Juan will be kayaking in Baja next summer.

[PR] 2. His brother is working at a camp now.

[FP] 3. His friend, Jorge, will be counseling two more years after this summer.

[PR] 4. No one is staying home this summer.

[PT] 5. I was thinking about going to school.

[PR] 6. Dad and Uncle Pete are planning a fishing trip.

[FP] 7. My music teacher will be performing in a musical.

[PT] 8. Mom was investigating the schedule for swimming classes.

[PR] 9. Am I the only one who is not planning something fun?

[PT] 10. I was looking forward to a long rest.

B. Write a sentence for each verb listed. Use the verbs in the present progressive, past progressive, or future progressive tenses.

    sail   act   grow   study   listen

1. [Answers will vary.] _____

2. _____

3. _____

4. _____

5. _____

Name _____

78. Identifying Perfect Tenses

> The **perfect tenses** are formed with a past participle and a form of *have*.
> The present perfect tense tells about an action that took place at an indefinite time in the past.
>
> **People have used computers in offices since the 1970s.**
>
> The past perfect tense tells about a past action that was completed before another past action started.
>
> **People had used typewriters before the invention of computers.**
>
> The future perfect tells about an action that will be completed before a specific time in the future.
>
> **People will have developed faster computers before the end of this decade.**

A. On the line write the tense of the *italicized* verb.

[present perfect] 1. The developments in technology *have occurred* quickly.

[present perfect] 2. The lives of people *have been changed* by these developments.

[past perfect] 3. Before the 20th century even started, some people *had foreseen* the world of the future.

[past perfect] 4. Before 1900 the French writer Jules Verne *had made* some accurate predictions.

[past perfect] 5. He *had predicted* skyscrapers of glass and steel and gas-powered cars.

[present perfect] 6. What *have* scientists *predicted* for the twenty-first century?

[future perfect] 7. Some predict that by 2025 self-driving cars *will have been developed*.

[future perfect] 8. By then tiny sensors *will have been placed* in highways to guide traffic.

[present perfect] 9. Already some car owners *have installed* a system for tracking the speed and position of the car ahead.

[future perfect] 10. *Will* people *have forgotten* the rules of the road by 2030?

B. On the line write the tense and voice of the *italicized* verb.

[present perfect, active] 1. The term "digital electronics" *has existed* for only about the last sixty years.

[past perfect, active] 2. Before then, no one *had heard* of the term.

[future perfect, active] 3. Some experts predict that by the year 2025 electric plugs *will have disappeared*.

[future perfect, passive] 4. Appliances *will have been changed* to run on batteries or radio frequencies.

[present perfect, active] 5. Many inventions *have appeared* in homes over the last fifty to seventy years.

Verbs

84

79. Identifying the Imperative Mood

> The imperative mood is used to give commands. To form a command in the second person, use the simple present tense of the verb.
>
> **Study the risks of extreme sports.**
>
> To form a command in the first person plural, use *let's*.
>
> **Let's both take the first aid class.**

A. Underline the verb in each sentence. Put a check on the line if the sentence is in the imperative mood.

_____ 1. Rock climbing has dangers.

_____ 2. What are the basic rules for safe climbs?

[✔] 3. Always go in a group with an experienced climber.

[✔] 4. Approach the rocks with confidence but not foolhardiness.

_____ 5. Expert rock climbers have a good sense of balance and good technique.

_____ 6. Rock climbers usually use rope for safety on steep climbs.

[✔] 7. At all times, maintain three points of contact with the rock—two hands and a leg or two legs and a hand.

_____ 8. A belayer, usually on the ground, feeds rope to the climbers.

_____ 9. This person acts as an anchor for the climbers.

[✔] 10. As basic equipment, get climbing shoes, an artificial fiber rope, and a harness.

B. Rewrite the sentences in the imperative mood.

1. It is very important to get instruction from an experienced rock-climbing teacher.
   [Get instruction from an experienced rock-climbing teacher.] _____

2. It is a good idea to start with bouldering—climbing less steep rocks without a rope.
   [Start with bouldering—climbing less steep rocks without a rope.] _____

3. Each climber has to move with rhythm and balance.
   [Move with rhythm and balance.] _____

4. It is important to stay as close to the rock as possible.
   [Stay as close to the rock as possible.] _____

5. You need to use balance and body position—not strength—to climb.
   [Use balance and body position—not strength—to climb.] _____

80. Identifying the Indicative Mood

> The indicative mood is used to make statements and ask questions.
> **What monument is being built to honor Crazy Horse?**
> **It is a carving in the Black Hills of South Dakota.**

A. Write the mood of each sentence: imperative or indicative.

_____[indicative]_____ 1. A monument to the Sioux chief Crazy Horse has been under construction since 1948.

_____[indicative]_____ 2. Sculptor Korczak Ziolkowski began work on the monument at the request of Sioux chief Henry Standing Bear.

_____[indicative]_____ 3. Would you believe the statue is carved right in the mountainside?

_____[imperative]_____ 4. Let's see it when we visit the Black Hills.

_____[indicative]_____ 5. Crazy Horse's face was completed in June 1998 and is 88 feet high.

_____[indicative]_____ 6. The statue, when finished, will be 563 feet high and 641 feet long.

_____[indicative]_____ 7. Crazy Horse is considered a great leader by the Sioux.

_____[indicative]_____ 8. How many people will visit the monument?

_____[imperative]_____ 9. Read the story of the Sioux before you go.

_____[indicative]_____ 10. The statue is an impressive sight.

B. Rewrite the sentences in the indicative mood. **[Sample answers are given.]**

1. Read the chapter on the Plains Indians tonight.
   [Our homework is to read the chapter on the Plains Indians tonight.]

2. Learn how they depended on the buffalo for food, clothing, and implements.
   [We will learn how they depended on the buffalo for food, clothing, and implements.]

3. Write the definitions of the vocabulary words.
   [We are also supposed to write the definitions of the vocabulary words.]

4. Let's do the map project together.
   [You and I can do the map project together.]

5. Don't forget to read the Internet article Mrs. Lauer assigned.
   [We need to read the Internet article Mrs. Lauer assigned.]

Verbs

81. Identifying Modal Auxiliary Verbs

The **modal auxiliary verbs** *may, might, can, could, must, should,* and *would* are used to express permission, possibility, ability, necessity, and obligation.

POSSIBILITY: **The students <u>might need</u> more items for the white elephant sale.**

PERMISSION: **Anyone <u>may participate</u>.**

ABILITY: **Jackson <u>can fix</u> old radios.**

NECESSITY: **The students <u>must put</u> all the clothes on racks.**

OBLIGATION: **We <u>should have paid</u> on time.**

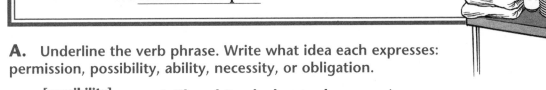

A. Underline the verb phrase. Write what idea each expresses: permission, possibility, ability, necessity, or obligation.

__[possibility]__   1. The white elephant sale <u>may raise</u> more money for charity this year than it did last year.

__[possibility]__   2. The students <u>may have collected</u> more old things this year than last.

__[ability]__   3. Charlie <u>can assemble</u> tables faster than anyone else.

__[permission]__   4. <u>May</u> I <u>help</u> you with that heavy box?

__[necessity]__   5. You <u>must be careful</u> with that box of old china.

__[ability]__   6. Laura <u>could have helped</u> you unpack that box.

__[possibility]__   7. Many people <u>may want</u> to look at the used clothes.

__[possibility]__   8. We <u>might need</u> another clothes rack.

__[obligation]__   9. Maybe we <u>should have charged</u> more money for those old records.

__[possibility]__   10. I <u>might like</u> that red-and-white sweater myself.

__[necessity]__   11. We <u>must clean</u> out the school basement completely.

__[ability]__   12. We <u>can donate</u> any leftover items to another charity.

__[possibility]__   13. We <u>may have</u> another sale in a few months.

__[permission]__   14. According to the principal, we <u>may have</u> another sale this year.

__[obligation]__   15. We <u>should start</u> to collect right now.

B. Complete the sentences with a verb phrase containing a modal auxiliary verb. Use the verb and the meaning indicated at the left. **[Answers will vary.]**

plan—necessity   1. The students ___[must/should plan]___ for the next sale.

make—ability   2. Elizabeth ___[can make]___ signs on her computer.

make—possibility   3. She ___[may/might make]___ a flier for the sale.

collect—necessity   4. The students ___[must collect]___ a variety of items.

store—permission   5. According to the teacher, the students ___[may store]___ items in the school basement.

Verbs

87

82. Making Subjects and Verbs Agree

A subject and a verb always agree. With most verbs the only time a change is needed is in the present tense with a third person singular subject. The ending -s or -es is added to the base form.

Our country celebrates special holidays.

Mexicans celebrate the Day of the Dead.

A. Underline the subject in each sentence. Circle the correct verb form in parentheses.

1. The Day of the Dead (occurs / occur) on November 1 and 2.

2. Mexicans (observes / observe) this traditional holiday.

3. By remembering their dead, Mexicans (honor / honors) the cycle of life and death.

4. The holiday (mark / marks) a special time.

5. According to popular belief, dead souls (returns / return) to their homes at this time.

6. Families (sets / set) up special altars in their houses for their dead members.

7. The altar's purpose (is / are) to welcome the souls of dead family members.

8. The altar (honors / honor) the dead.

9. A special bread (lies / lie) on the altar for the dead.

10. Candy skulls (is / are) also sometimes placed there.

11. Families (goes / go) to cemeteries to care for graves of relatives.

12. A picnic (is / are) sometimes eaten in the cemetery.

13. Traditional music (is / are) played by a mariachi band during the picnic.

14. The mood (is / are) joyful.

15. People (celebrates / celebrate) the memory of dead relatives and friends.

B. Complete each sentence with the present tense form of the verb at the left.

have   1. The marigold _____[has]_____ a special role in the Day of the Dead.

drop   2. People _____[drop]_____ the petals from the flower along the route to the cemetery.

help   3. In popular belief the flower's scent _____[helps]_____ the dead find their way home.

hold   4. Families _____[hold]_____ special ceremonies in cemeteries.

place   5. One person _____[places]_____ a marigold in a special wreath for the dead.

83. Using <u>Doesn't</u> and <u>Don't</u> and <u>You Are</u> and <u>You Were</u> Correctly

If the subject of the sentence is third person singular, use *doesn't*.

<u>Doesn't</u> a *foxglove* have poisonous leaves?

If the subject of the sentence is in the first or second person singular or third person plural, use *don't*.

<u>Don't</u> *farmers* grow roses for perfumes?

Use *are* and *were* with *you*, whether it is singular or plural.

<u>Are</u> *you* going to grow foxgloves in your garden?

A. Complete each sentence with *doesn't* or *don't*.

1. Roses ____[don't]____ grow from bulbs.

2. ____[Doesn't]____ a Venus's-flytrap plant eat insects?

3. Venus's-flytraps ____[don't]____ trap insects in their flowers—they trap them in their leaves.

4. A cactus ____[doesn't]____ need a lot of water.

5. You ____[don't]____ know the name of your state flower!

6. ____[Don't]____ all states have a state flower?

7. Janet ____[doesn't]____ know the name of the official state flower of Rhode Island.

8. ____[Don't]____ apples and pears belong to the family of rose plants?

9. ____[Doesn't]____ natural vanilla come from an orchid plant?

10. ____[Don't]____ sunflowers turn their heads to follow the sun?

B. Circle the correct verb form in parentheses.

1. You (is (are)) really an excellent gardener!

2. (Was (Were)) you the winner of the prize for best orchid at the floral show last year?

3. ((Was) Were) it wet in the garden this morning?

4. You (is (are)) developing your own kind of orchid, I hear.

5. You (was (were)) on a gardening show on television last month, I think.

6. ((Were) Was) you able to get a bulb for a purple tulip?

7. ((Is) Are) the floral show in June this year?

8. (Is (Are)) you going to show me your prize flowers?

9. You (is (are)) going to be a winner again this year for sure!

10. What (is (are)) you going to plant next spring?

Verbs

Name _____

84. Using <u>There Is</u> and <u>There Are</u> Correctly

There is (was, has been) should be used when the subject is singular. *There are (were, have been)* should be used when the subject is plural. When *there* introduces a sentence, the sentence generally is inverted, so the subject follows the verb.

PLURAL SUBJECT: **There <u>are</u> seven *continents* in the world.**

SINGULAR SUBJECT: **There <u>is</u> one *nation* that covers an entire continent.**

A. Circle the correct verb form in parentheses.

1. There (is **are**) more than 18 million people in Australia.

2. There (**have** has) been many new immigrants to Australia in the last 50 years.

3. There (is **are**) about 360,000 indigenous people in Australia.

4. How many stars (is **are**) there on the flag of Australia?

5. In Australia, there (**is** are) a prime minister who is the head of government.

6. There (is **are**) six states and two territories in Australia.

7. There (is **are**) many farms and ranches in Australia.

8. (Is **Are**) there many natural resources in Australia?

9. There (**is** are) iron ore in Australia.

10. (**Was** Were) there a gold rush in Australia's past?

11. There (is **are**) large areas of empty dry land called the outback.

12. There (**is** are) a magnificent harbor in Sydney.

13. There (was **were**) many visitors to Sydney for the Olympic games in the year 2000.

14. There (**is** are) a strange huge rock in the middle of an area of flat land, in Uluru National Park.

15. There (**is** are) an unusual Australian food called Vegemite, made from yeast extract, celery, and onions.

B. Complete each sentence with *is* or *are*.

1. There _____**[is]**_____ a huge reef off the coast of Australia called the Great Barrier Reef.

2. There _____**[are]**_____ approximately 1,500 kinds of fish in the reef's waters.

3. There _____**[are]**_____ several animals found only in Australia—such as kangaroos and koalas.

4. There _____**[is]**_____ an unusual bird in Australia—the black swan.

5. _____**[Are]**_____ there any questions about Australia?

85. Using Verbs Correctly with Intervening Phrases and Parenthetical Expressions

Sometimes a phrase comes between a subject and a verb. The verb must agree with the subject, not the phrase.

A **serving** of beans **is** one half cup.

Milk, together with yogurt and cheese, **forms** a basic food group.

A. Underline the subject of the sentence. Circle the correct verb form in parentheses.

1. <u>Fruit</u>, as well as vegetables, (is) are) a basic food group.

2. <u>Meat</u>, along with fish, beans, eggs, and nuts, (belongs) belong) to another group.

3. <u>Fats</u>, together with sweets and oils, (are) is) to be eaten sparingly.

4. Vegetable <u>oil</u>, as well as butter and eggs, (contains) contain) fat.

5. Two to four <u>servings</u> of fruit (is (are)) recommended daily.

6. Three to five <u>servings</u> of vegetables (is (are)) recommended per day.

7. A <u>serving</u> of vegetables (is) are) one cup of leafy vegetables.

8. A <u>serving</u> of fruit (is) are) one piece of fruit.

9. <u>Carrots</u>, as well as spinach and cantaloupe, (supplies (supply)) vitamin A, which is good for eyesight.

10. Citrus <u>fruit</u>, along with potatoes, (has) have) vitamin C.

11. Grain <u>foods</u>, such as bread and rice, (supply) supplies) carbohydrates, an excellent source of energy.

12. <u>Bread</u>, as well as broccoli and eggs, (is) are) rich in vitamin B, which turns fat into energy.

13. <u>Milk</u>, together with cheese and sardines, ((contains)) contain) calcium, which builds bones.

14. One <u>piece</u> of fudge (has) have) as many calories as three slices of bread.

15. Thirty-five <u>pieces</u> of celery (has (have)) as many calories as one piece of fudge!

B. Complete each sentence with *is* or *are*.

1. A bowl of cabbage soup _____[is]_____ recommended once a day in one fad diet.

2. The opinion of nutritionists _____[is]_____ that fad diets don't work.

3. A problem with fad diets _____[is]_____ that they don't change eating habits.

4. A good diet low in fat and high in fruits and vegetables _____[is]_____ what almost everyone needs.

5. Moderate consumption of food, together with exercise, _____[is]_____ recommended.

Verbs

91

86. Making Compound Subjects and Verbs Agree

Compound subjects connected by *and* usually require a plural verb.

London and Edinburgh are the capitals of England and Scotland, respectively.

If the subjects connected by *and* refer to the same person, place, or thing or express a single idea, the verb is singular.

In Britain, the prime minister and leader of the majority is the same person.

A. Circle the correct verb form in parentheses.

1. England, Scotland, and Wales (makes **make**) up the United Kingdom— along with part of Ireland.

2. The nominal head of state and head of the church (**is** are) the monarch.

3. The prime minister and the cabinet (has **have**) the real executive power of government.

4. The prime minister and the Parliament (shares **share**) the powers of government.

5. Rain and fog (characterizes **characterize**) London weather.

6. The stores and theaters (attracts **attract**) many tourists to London.

7. The Tower of London and Buckingham Palace (is **are**) important tourist sites.

8. A famous British writer and dictionary maker (**has** have) written, "When a man is tired of London, he is tired of life."

9. The monarch and the royal family (has **have**) a huge castle at Windsor, near London.

10. Fish and chips (**is** are) a popular English dish.

11. Bread and butter (is **are**) sometimes served at tea time.

12. Gardening and fishing (has **have**) long been popular pastimes in the countryside.

13. Soccer and cricket (is **are**) popular sports in England.

14. King Arthur and Robin Hood (was **were**) legendary figures in British history.

15. J. K. Rowling and Prince William (is **are**) famous current British citizens.

B. Complete the sentences with compound subjects and verbs that agree. **[Answers will vary.]**

1. _____ and _____ _____ important cities in my state.

2. _____ and _____ _____ important historical sites in my country.

3. _____ and _____ _____ important people in American history.

4. _____ and _____ _____ favorite pastimes in my area.

5. _____ and _____ _____ sometimes eaten for dessert.

Verbs

87. Making Subjects Preceded by Each, Every, Many a, or No and Verbs Agree

When *each*, *every*, *many a*, or *no* precede two or more singular subjects connected by *and* or *or*, use a singular verb.

Each writer and editor needs to use a dictionary or online tool to check spelling.

A. Circle the correct verb form in parentheses.

1. Every boy and girl in the contest (has have) prepared diligently for the spelling bee.

2. Many a child and parent (has have) studied long lists of words together.

3. Many an afternoon and evening (has have) been spent in preparation.

4. Every teacher and student (is are) in the auditorium.

5. Every chair and bench (is are) filled.

6. Spectators and participants (feels feel) the tension.

7. Each word, definition, and context sentence (has have) been checked carefully by the judges.

8. Each word and letter (is are) pronounced clearly by the participants.

9. No questioning or respelling (is are) allowed.

10. Many a participant and audience member (was were) surprised when Frederica spelled *poinsettia* correctly and won the contest.

B. Complete each sentence with the correct present tense form of the verb at the left.

need   1. Every writer and peer editor _____[needs]_____ to work carefully.

catch   2. Computer spell checkers and grammar checkers _____[catch]_____ some problems.

require   3. Each word and sentence _____[requires]_____ careful checking by a person.

be   4. All commas and periods _____[are]_____ important.

need   5. Each question or comment from a peer editor _____[needs]_____ to be taken into account.

get   6. Many a dictionary and grammar book _____[gets]_____ consulted.

take   7. Many an essay or report _____[takes]_____ hours of work.

require   8. Many a spelling rule or grammar point _____[requires]_____ review.

like   9. No teacher or reader _____[likes]_____ to see a lot of spelling errors.

be   10. Students, editors, and teachers _____[are]_____ right to be proud of an error-free report.

Verbs

Name _____

88. Making Subjects Connected by Or or Nor and Verbs Agree

> When compound subjects are connected by *or* or *nor*, the verb agrees with the subject closer to the verb.
>
> **Either hamburgers or hot dogs are served in the cafeteria every day.**
> **Hamburgers or chicken is served in many fast food restaurants.**

A. Circle the correct verb form in parentheses.

1. Neither squash nor cucumbers (is (are)) really fruits.

2. Also, neither pumpkins nor eggplant ((belongs) belong) to the fruit family.

3. Either a dunker or a doorknob ((refers) refer) to a doughnut.

4. Sausage or mushrooms often (sits (sit)) on the top of a pizza.

5. Neither cheese nor tomatoes (tops (top)) all pizza in Italy.

6. Either potato pizza or just vegetable pizza ((is) are) available.

7. Cucumber sandwiches or ham sandwiches (is (are)) often served for tea in England.

8. Neither apples nor wheat ((was) were) native to the Americas.

9. Neither lettuce nor carrots (was (were)) grown in the Americas before the arrival of Europeans.

10. Either a hoagie or a sub ((means) mean) a large sandwich.

11. Soup or salad ((is) are) a common appetizer in the United States.

12. Bread, cheese, or olives (is (are)) sometimes eaten for breakfast in Turkey.

13. Rice porridge or dried pork ((is) are) sometimes eaten for breakfast in China.

14. Neither corn nor potatoes (was (were)) known in Europe until the 1500s.

15. Strawberries or grapes (is (are)) often made into jellies or jams.

B. Complete each sentence. Use verbs in the present tense.

1. Neither the firefighter nor the residents ___[know how the fire started.]___

2. Neither the boys nor the girls ___[are at the fire scene.]___

3. Either the smoke or the flames ___[cause considerable damage.]___

4. Neither the door nor the stairs ___[are safe exits.]___

5. Either the photos or the report ___[is ready for review.]___

[Answers will vary. Samples are given.]

Verbs

Name _____

89. Making Collective Nouns and Verbs Agree

> A collective noun usually requires a singular verb.
>
> **The school baseball team <u>uses</u> a field in the park.**
>
> Use a plural verb if the idea expressed by the subject denotes separate individuals.
>
> **The baseball team <u>use</u> their own equipment.**

A. Circle the correct verb form in parentheses.

1. The committee (has have) decided to improve park facilities.

2. The orchestra (plays play) in the band shell in the park.

3. The orchestra (needs need) separate backstage facilities for their instrument cases and personal items.

4. The audience for the orchestra (needs need) some overhead structure for the rain.

5. The local soccer team (plays play) its games in the park.

6. The marching band (practices practice) on the basketball court.

7. The school marching band (wants want) individual lockers in which to keep their instruments.

8. A flock of swans in the park (swims swim) in the pond.

9. The dance group (is are) looking for apartments.

10. The Irish dance group (needs need) a bigger outdoor stage for its performances.

11. The troop (meets meet) in the field house.

12. The city council (are is) arguing about new requirements for membership.

13. The quilting group (has have) a meeting every week in the field house.

14. Our teachers union (is are) planning to lobby for more space.

15. The staff (agrees agree) that the field house needs to be remodeled.

B. Write sentences using the collective nouns as subjects. [Sentences will vary. Sample answers are given.]

1. The orchestra [tunes up as the audience is being seated.]

2. A herd of cattle [grazes on the prairie.]

3. The city council [meets once a month.]

4. A deck of cards [is needed to play the game.]

5. A pod of whales [swims near the coastline.]

90. Making Indefinite Pronouns and Verbs Agree

An indefinite pronoun points out no particular person, place, or thing. The indefinite pronouns *each, either, neither, one, anyone, anybody, anything, everyone, everybody, everything, someone, somebody, something, no one, nobody,* and *nothing* are always singular and require singular verbs.

Each of the newspaper issues **has** eight pages.
Somebody has the job of writing headlines.

A. Underline the subject in each sentence. Circle the correct form of the verb in parentheses.

1. Everyone in the school (gets) get) a copy of the school newspaper.

2. Somebody (puts) put) copies of the newspaper in pickup boxes throughout the school.

3. Everybody in the school (waits) wait) eagerly for the next issue.

4. Anyone (is) are) eligible to work on the school newspaper.

5. Each of the issues (contain (contains)) an interview with two students in school.

6. Usually one of the issues (feature (features)) a teacher profile.

7. Each of the featured students (tells) tell) about his or her personal interests and goals.

8. No one (refuses) refuse) an invitation for an interview.

9. Each of the articles (is) are) illustrated with pictures.

10. Neither of the cartoons in the last issue (was) were) very funny.

B. Underline the subject in each sentence. Complete each sentence with the correct form of the present tense of the verb at the left.

have 1. Each of the articles in the newspaper _____[has]_____ a student as an author.

be 2. Everyone _____[is]_____ welcome to suggest topics for articles.

assign 3. In fact, somebody _____[assigns]_____ additional articles.

contain 4. Each of the issues _____[contains]_____ a fictional story.

want 5. Everyone _____[wants]_____ to see one of his or her stories in the newspaper.

have 6. Someone _____[has]_____ a funny story about a magical horse in this issue.

put 7. For each issue someone _____[puts]_____ together a list of upcoming school events.

be 8. Nothing important _____[is]_____ missing.

appear 9. Anything especially interesting _____[appears]_____ on the front page.

work 10. Everybody _____[works]_____ to make the newspaper great.

Verbs

96

91. Making Special Singular and Plural Nouns and Verbs Agree

> Some nouns are plural in form but singular in meaning; they require singular verbs. These nouns include *aerobics, aeronautics, civics, economics, genetics, mathematics, measles, molasses, mumps, news,* and *physics*.
>
> Other nouns are plural in form but refer to one thing; they require plural verbs. These nouns include *ashes, clothes, eaves, goods, pliers, pants, proceeds, scissors, thanks, tongs, trousers,* and *tweezers*.

A. **Circle the correct verb form in parentheses.**

1. The clothes (is (are)) blowing off the clothesline.

2. My pants now (has (have)) a tear from the thorns on the rose bush.

3. The eaves of the house (is (are)) falling, and I tripped over the repairer's ladders.

4. The ashes from the fire (is (are)) spilled all over the carpet, because I dropped the pail.

5. Mathematics ((is) are) a study of more than just numbers.

6. The news on the television ((is) are) very depressing.

7. Measles ((is) are) a disease that causes fever and red spots on the skin.

8. The scissors (is (are)) broken, and I can't get the popcorn package open with my fingers.

9. I used my Dad's pliers to open the package, and now the pliers (is (are)) lost.

10. My thanks (is (are)) to my sister for finding them.

B. **Complete each sentence with the correct present tense form of the verb at the left.**

be   1. Civics ____[is]____ the study of the duties and rights of a citizen.

be   2. Congratulations ____[are]____ due to all who have passed the civics test.

present   3. The news ____[presents]____ a lot of information about civics and government.

be   4. Economics ____[is]____ the study of the production and distribution of goods.

be   5. Goods ____[are]____ important in the study of economics.

be   6. Aerobics ____[is]____ a good type of exercise to develop cardiovascular fitness.

promise   7. Genetics ____[promises]____ to aid in the cure of some diseases.

go   8. The proceeds of this fund-raising drive ____[go]____ to genetic research.

be   9. Thanks ____[are]____ due to researchers who devote their life to its study.

interest 10. Physics ____[interests]____ me—I'm doing a physics project for the science fair.

Verbs

92. Reviewing Subject and Verb Agreement

A. Circle the correct verb in parentheses.

1. A legendary creature supposedly (**lives** live) in the Himalayan Mountains.
2. The name of the creature (**is** are) the Abominable Snowman.
3. Creatures of this type supposedly (is **are**) tall, humanlike creatures covered with hair.
4. The people of the area (calls **call**) the creature the Yeti.
5. There (has **have**) been reports of sightings of the creature for hundreds of years.
6. Illness, bad luck, or death (**follows** follow) a sighting of the creature, according to superstition.
7. The explorer and mountaineer Edmund Hillary (**was** were) involved in a search for the Yeti.
8. Hillary and his team members (was **were**) not able to prove the creature's existence.
9. Large footprints in the snow sometimes (is **are**) found in the mountains.
10. However, a leopard, as well a bear or a wolf, often (**leaves** leave) tracks that can get very large as the snow melts.

B. Complete each sentence with the correct form of the present tense of the verb at the left.

have 　　1. Strange creatures, similar to the Abominable Snowman, supposedly
　　　　　___[have]___ homes in northwestern United States and western Canada.

stand 　2. Each of these creatures ___[stands]___ erect, 6 to 15 feet tall.

give 　　3. The creatures ___[give]___ off a foul odor.

form 　　4. Berries and fruit, as well as an occasional deer, ___[form]___
　　　　　the diet of the creature, which is called a Sasquatch.

measure 5. The footprints of the creature ___[measure]___ up to 24 inches.

be 　　　6. There ___[are]___ often sightings of the creature or of its
　　　　　footprints reported in newspapers or on television.

appear 　7. Photographs of the creature sometimes ___[appear]___ also.

be 　　　8. The Sasquatch and the Abominable Snowman
　　　　　___[are]___ both types of primitive humans,
　　　　　according to some.

have 　　9. The study of "supposed creatures" ___[has]___ the name cryptozoology.

be 　　10. There ___[are]___ some researchers with hopes of proving the existence of
　　　　　these "alleged creatures."

Name _____

93. Reviewing Verbs

A. Write the principal parts of each verb. Write whether the verb is regular or irregular.

	PRESENT	PAST	PAST PARTICIPLE	REGULAR OR IRREGULAR
1. study	[study]	[studied]	[studied]	[regular]
2. lie	[lie]	[lay]	[lain]	[irregular]
3. influence	[influence]	[influenced]	[influenced]	[regular]
4. write	[write]	[wrote]	[written]	[irregular]
5. choose	[choose]	[chose]	[chosen]	[irregular]

B. Underline the verb phrase in each sentence.

1. <u>Have</u> you <u>read</u> any works by Charles Dickens?
2. You <u>should read</u> A Christmas Carol.
3. When <u>was</u> A Christmas Carol <u>written</u>?
4. A movie version of the novel <u>will be</u> on television next week.
5. I <u>might watch</u> the movie again.

C. Underline the verb or verb phrase in each sentence. On the line write **T** if it is transitive, **I** if it is intransitive, or **L** if it is linking.

[T] 1. Four ghosts <u>visit</u> Scrooge in A Christmas Carol.

[L] 2. The ghosts <u>seem</u> very scary to Scrooge.

[I] 3. Scrooge <u>goes</u> to the past, present, and the future.

[L] 4. <u>Will</u> Scrooge <u>be</u> different at the end of the book?

[T] 5. <u>Read</u> the story for the answer.

D. Write the tense and voice of the *italicized* verbs.

	TENSE	VOICE
1. As a boy, Scrooge *had shown* generosity and friendliness.	[past perfect]	[active]
2. As a man, he *changed* into a miser.	[past]	[active]
3. Christmas *was* not *celebrated* by Scrooge.	[past]	[passive]
4. The story *is told* again every Christmas.	[present]	[passive]
5. Film versions of the story *will be shown* again next Christmas.	[future]	[passive]

99

Name _____

E. Draw one line under the subject and two lines under the verb.
Write the tense on the line.

_____[past]_____ 1. Last month the science teacher announced
                                    the date for the science fair.

_____[present]_____ 2. The topic of my project for the fair is solar energy.

_____[past perfect]_____ 3. I had already read many articles on the topic.

_____[future perfect]_____ 4. By next week I will have completed my solar home model.

_____[future]_____ 5. According to Mom, my project will win a prize.

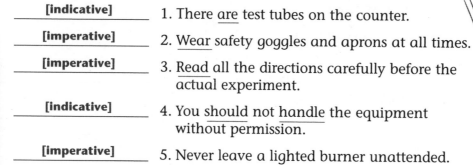

F. Underline the verb. On the line write whether the verb is
in the indicative or the imperative mood.

_____[indicative]_____ 1. There are test tubes on the counter.

_____[imperative]_____ 2. Wear safety goggles and aprons at all times.

_____[imperative]_____ 3. Read all the directions carefully before the
                                    actual experiment.

_____[indicative]_____ 4. You should not handle the equipment
                                    without permission.

_____[imperative]_____ 5. Never leave a lighted burner unattended.

G. Write the correct form of the present tense of the verb at the left to
complete each sentence.

be   1. _____[Are]_____ you going to the mall, Teddy?

need   2. Lila and Serena _____[need]_____ a few things for their science project.

want   3. Each of them _____[wants]_____ a notebook to record results.

have   4. Every project _____[has]_____ a space at the science fair.

be   5. The winning project _____[is]_____ the one that is the most scholarly.

Try It Yourself

On a separate sheet of paper, write a paragraph about a book that you've read
or a movie that you've seen recently. Tell about the plot and give your opinion.
Be sure to use the correct forms of verbs and correct verb agreement.

Check Your Own Work

Choose a piece of writing from your portfolio or journal, a work in progress,
an assignment from another class, or a letter. Revise it, applying the skills
you have reviewed. The checklist will help you.

✔ Are all the verb forms correct?

✔ Are all the past tense and past participle forms correct?

✔ Is the use of verb tenses consistent?

✔ Do all the subjects and verbs agree?

Verbs

Name _____

94. Classifying Adverbs

> An **adverb** is a word that modifies a verb, an adjective, or an adverb.
>
> Adverbs of time answer the question *when* or *how often (then, usually)*.
> Adverbs of place answer the question *where (here, there)*.
> Adverbs of degree answer the question *how much* or *how little (very, rather)*.
> Adverbs of manner answer the question *how* or *in what manner (sincerely, quickly)*.
> Adverbs of affirmation affirm *(yes, indeed)*.
> Adverbs of negation deny *(no, not)*.
>
> **The Wright brothers *worked* <u>diligently</u> on their project.**

Underline the adverb in each sentence. Classify it according to meaning. Write **A** for affirmation, **D** for degree, **M** for manner, **N** for negation, **P** for place, or **T** for time.

__[A]__ 1. The Wright brothers did <u>indeed</u> invent the first successful airplane.

__[T]__ 2. They had experimented <u>previously</u> with a five-foot biplane kite.

__[T]__ 3. <u>Then</u> they had worked with a glider that could carry a person.

__[D]__ 4. The lifting power of their glider was <u>rather</u> disappointing.

__[N]__ 5. Despite many setbacks, they did <u>not</u> give up their dream of flying.

__[M]__ 6. They <u>cleverly</u> developed a better wing design.

__[M]__ 7. They <u>carefully</u> studied books about flight and about birds.

__[T]__ 8. They <u>usually</u> went to North Carolina to test their planes.

__[P]__ 9. The winds <u>there</u> were good for flying.

__[D]__ 10. The first airplane flight on December 17, 1903, was <u>very</u> short.

__[D]__ 11. The airplane <u>barely</u> got off the ground.

__[M]__ 12. Its body seemed to move <u>uncontrollably</u>.

__[P]__ 13. The plane moved <u>forward</u> in the air 120 feet in 12 seconds.

__[M]__ 14. Within two years the Wright brothers' airplane could <u>easily</u> fly 20 miles.

__[M]__ 15. The Wright brothers had <u>actively</u> tested flying machines for four years before their success.

ORVILLE   **WILBUR**

Orville and Wilbur Wright worked cooperatively to achieve their goals. Give an example of how you work cooperatively with others to achieve goals.

95. Identifying Interrogative Adverbs

An adverb modifies a verb, an adjective, or another adverb. An **interrogative adverb** is an adverb used to ask a question.

Did King Arthur <u>really</u> exist?   <u>How</u> did King Arthur become king?

A. Underline each adverb once. Underline each interrogative adverb twice.

1. <u><u>When</u></u> did the story of King Arthur begin?

2. It began <u>originally</u> during the early Middle Ages.

3. According to old writings, a king named Arthur <u>bravely</u> fought the invaders of England.

4. The stories about the king and his knights of the Round Table became <u>very</u> popular.

5. People <u>gradually</u> invented more and more stories about the king.

6. <u>Then</u> the stories were gathered into a poem called *Le Morte d'Arthur.*

7. <u><u>Why</u></u> has the popularity of the stories lasted <u>so</u> long?

8. In the stories Arthur <u>highly</u> values the virtues of peace, duty, and friendship.

9. <u><u>Where</u></u> is Arthur's legendary home?

10. <u>Annually</u> many tourists visit Cadbury Castle, one of several supposed sites of Camelot.

B. Complete each sentence with one of the following adverbs.
Use the clues at the left for the class of adverb. **[Suggested answers are given.]**

| easily | foolishly | how | not | soon |
| speedily | suddenly | unsuccessfully | very | why |

interrogative   1. _____ [How] _____ did King Arthur become king?

negation   2. Arthur was studying to become a knight, and he did _____ [not] _____ know he was the dead king's son.

manner   3. One day Sir Kay, his companion, _____ [foolishly] _____ forgot to bring his sword to a tournament.

manner   4. Arthur rode _____ [speedily] _____ back to town for the sword.

manner   5. Along the way he _____ [suddenly] _____ noticed a sword in a stone.

manner   6. He _____ [easily] _____ pulled it from the stone and returned with it.

interrogative   7. _____ [Why] _____ did the knights at the tournament look in amazement at Arthur and the sword?

degree   8. According to legend, whoever pulled the sword from the stone would be a _____ [very] _____ great king.

manner   9. Many knights had tried _____ [unsuccessfully] _____ to remove the sword.

time   10. _____ [Soon] _____ Arthur was declared king.

96. Identifying Adverbial Nouns

An adverbial noun is a noun that performs the function of an adverb by modifying a verb. An adverbial noun expresses time, distance, measure, weight, value, or direction.

Lewis and Clark spent several <u>years</u> on an expedition to the Northwest.

A. Underline the adverbial noun in each sentence. Write what it expresses. Use **DIS** for distance, **DIR** for direction, **M** for measure, **T** for time, **V** for value, or **W** for weight.

[V] 1. The United States paid France 15 million <u>dollars</u> for the Louisiana Territory.

[DIS/M] 2. The territory covered more than 800,000 square <u>miles</u>.

[V] 3. The United States spent only three <u>cents</u> for each acre!

[V] 4. Thomas Jefferson requested $2,500 <u>dollars</u> for exploration of the territory.

[T] 5. The <u>day</u> after the announcement of the purchase, Meriwether Lewis began to organize an expedition.

[T] 6. It took ten <u>months</u> before the expedition began on May 14, 1804.

[DIS/M] 7. Lewis and William Clark traveled some 7,200 <u>miles</u> to the Pacific coast and back.

[T] 8. The expedition took two and one-half <u>years</u>.

[M] 9. They traveled the Missouri River on a keelboat that measured 55 <u>feet</u>.

[DIS/M] 10. They could travel 14 <u>miles</u> on a good day by the boat.

[T] 11. Did Sacagawea know the journey to the Northwest would take <u>years</u>?

[DIR] 12. She did not guide the expedition <u>west</u>, but she helped deal with the Shoshone people.

[DIR] 13. The expedition pushed <u>west</u> to the Continental Divide and to the Pacific Ocean.

[DIR] 14. The group returned <u>east</u> to St. Louis, September 23, 1806.

[T] 15. The journals of Lewis and Clark make interesting reading <u>today</u>.

B. Complete each sentence with one of the following adverbial nouns.

days   east   hours   miles   today

1. In 1889 a fictional book told of a trip around the world that lasted 80 ____[days]____ .

2. Nellie Bly traveled ____[east]____ , through England, Egypt, Japan, and back to New York.

3. She traveled 23,000 ____[miles]____ by boat, train, rickshaw, and donkey.

4. It took her 72 days and 6 ____[hours]____ for the trip.

5. ____[Today]____ most people don't know of this woman's outstanding feat.

Adverbs

97. Comparing with Adverbs

The comparative degree and superlative degree of most adverbs that end in *-ly* are formed by adding *more/most* or *less/least* before the positive.

slowly, more slowly, most slowly

The comparative degree and superlative degree of adverbs that don't end in *-ly* are formed by adding *-er* or *-est* after the positive.

long, longer, longest

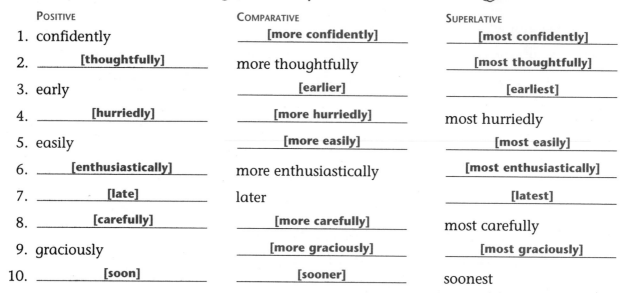

A. Complete the chart with degrees of comparison.

Positive	Comparative	Superlative
1. confidently	[more confidently]	[most confidently]
2. [thoughtfully]	more thoughtfully	[most thoughtfully]
3. early	[earlier]	[earliest]
4. [hurriedly]	[more hurriedly]	most hurriedly
5. easily	[more easily]	[most easily]
6. [enthusiastically]	more enthusiastically	[most enthusiastically]
7. [late]	later	[latest]
8. [carefully]	[more carefully]	most carefully
9. graciously	[more graciously]	[most graciously]
10. [soon]	[sooner]	soonest

B. Underline the adverb in each sentence. On the line write the degree of comparison. Use **P** for positive, **C** for comparative, or **S** for superlative.

___[P]___ 1. Arctic ground squirrels sleep almost <u>continuously</u> for nine months.

___[C]___ 2. Mayflies die <u>sooner</u> than most animals—within a few hours of birth.

___[C]___ 3. The desert locust eats <u>more voraciously</u> than most insects.

___[P]___ 4. Swarms of them <u>quickly</u> devour all the vegetation in their path.

___[S]___ 5. Migrating birds fly <u>most efficiently</u> in a V formation.

___[S]___ 6. The arctic tern travels <u>farthest</u> in its migrations—from the Arctic to the Antarctic.

___[P]___ 7. Elephants <u>affectionately</u> entwine their trunks as a way to communicate.

___[C]___ 8. The Australian kookaburra sings <u>more raucously</u> than most other birds.

___[S]___ 9. Cheetahs run <u>most rapidly</u> of all animals.

___[C]___ 10. Hares can run <u>faster</u> than horses.

Adverbs

98. Identifying Words Used as Adjectives and Adverbs

Adjectives modify nouns and pronouns.

The <u>first</u> *performers* in the circus parade were the trapeze artists.

Adverbs modify verbs, adjectives, and other adverbs.

The trapeze artists <u>first</u> *climbed* up the rope ladders very gracefully.

A. On the line write whether each *italicized* word is an adjective or an adverb.

[adverb]	1. We arrived at the circus *early*.
[adjective]	2. We took the *early* train because we didn't want to miss any of the excitement.
[adjective]	3. I was excited because it was my *first* time at a three-ring circus.
[adjective]	4. Suddenly someone appeared in the *far* corner of the ring.
[adverb]	5. The ringmaster *first* introduced himself— and then the circus acts.
[adverb]	6. The tightrope walker walked *high* above the circus ring.
[adjective]	7. She worked on the *high* wire as easily as if she were walking on the sidewalk.
[adjective]	8. The trapeze artists did very *hard* somersaults in mid-air.
[adverb]	9. I tried *hard* to see everything.
[adverb]	10. We waited really *long* for the lion to jump through the fiery hoop.
[adjective]	11. There was a lot of tension in the air during the *long* wait.
[adverb]	12. Circus animals can be dangerous, so no one should get too *near*.
[adverb]	13. The acrobats juggled balls *far* up into the air—with their feet.
[adjective]	14. They performed the tumbling routines *daily*.
[adjective]	15. *Daily* practice is necessary for all circus performers.
[adjective]	16. There are sometimes *near* misses on the dangerous acts.

Adverbs

B. Write sentences using each word as an adverb and as an adjective.

1. last (adverb)   [The lion tamer performed last.] [Sentences will vary. Samples are given.]

2. last (adjective)   [Uncle Dave bought the last ticket.]

3. back (adverb)   [The lions ran back into the cage.]

4. back (adjective)   [We sat in the back row of seats.]

105

99. Distinguishing Between Adjectives and Adverbs

> Adjectives modify nouns.
> **An earthquake is a violent *shaking* of the land.**
> Adverbs modify verbs, adjectives, and other adverbs.
> **During a quake the earth *shakes* violently.**

A. Circle the correct word in parentheses.

1. Large earthquakes begin as tremors, but they (quick (quickly)) become violent shocks.

2. The ((rapid) rapidly) shaking of the earth sometimes causes major damage.

3. Often the earth shakes only (slight (slightly)).

4. But the ((brief) briefly) shaking can topple buildings.

5. Over time, rocks (gradual (gradually)) move because of pressure from within the earth.

6. At the time of an earthquake, the ((gradual) gradually) pressure becomes too great, and the rocks slip into a new position.

7. The point (direct (directly)) above the center of an earthquake is called the epicenter.

8. Right now scientists have no (real (really)) good way to predict earthquakes.

9. Earthquakes occur (regular (regularly))—there are thousands each day.

10. However, there is no ((regular) regularly) pattern to when they occur.

B. On the line write whether the *italicized* word is used as an adjective or an adverb. Underline the word it modifies.

_____[adverb]_____ 1. Animals may <u>behave</u> *unusually* before an earthquake.

_____[adjective]_____ 2. One fish in California exhibited *unusual* <u>behavior</u> before several earthquakes: it swam on its side.

_____[adjective]_____ 3. Some <u>dogs</u> become *excited* before earthquakes.

_____[adverb]_____ 4. They <u>bark</u> or <u>jump</u> around *excitedly*.

_____[adverb]_____ 5. Most scientists *firmly* <u>deny</u> that animal behavior predicts earthquakes.

_____[adjective]_____ 6. They say there is no *firm* <u>evidence</u> to link the behavior to the earthquakes.

_____[adjective]_____ 7. Experts have advice for people who experience earthquakes in *real* <u>life</u>.

_____[adverb]_____ 8. It can be *really* <u>dangerous</u> to run into the street because of the <u>danger</u> of falling rubble from buildings.

_____[adjective]_____ 9. You should stay *calm*.

_____[adverb]_____ 10. <u>Move</u> *calmly* and get under a table away from windows.

Name _____

100. Using **Farther** and **Further** Correctly

> *Farther* refers to distance. *Further* means "in addition to."
> Both words are used as adjectives and adverbs.
>
> **Spacecraft allow humans to see <u>farther</u> into space.**
> **Scientists continue to encourage <u>further</u> space missions.**

A. Circle the correct word in parentheses.

1. Mathematicians discovered the planet Neptune in the 1840s, and (farther (further)) events proved them right.

2. Because of changes in Uranus's orbit, they concluded that there was a planet ((farther) further) out in space than Uranus.

3. After the time of Galileo, (farther (further)) scientific studies produced better telescopes.

4. The telescopes of the 1800s could see ((farther) further) than earlier ones.

5. In the 1840s, (farther (further)) efforts by astronomers confirmed Neptune's existence through direct observation.

6. Usually Pluto is ((farther) further) from the sun than any other planet.

7. Sometimes Neptune's orbit takes it ((farther) further) from the sun than Pluto.

8. Some scientists think that Pluto should not be called a planet, but (farther (further)) discussion will be needed to decide the issue.

9. Scientists have found many small bodies ((farther) further) out in space than Neptune in what is known as the Kuiper Belt.

10. (Farther (Further)) research and exploration may reveal even more.

B. Complete each sentence with *farther* or *further*.

1. Since people landed on the moon, there has been _____[further]_____ space exploration.

2. Space probes have gone _____[farther]_____ and _____[farther]_____ into space.

3. They have discovered _____[further]_____ details about nearly all the planets.

4. New information has spurred _____[further]_____ discoveries from scientists.

5. *Voyager 1* and *2* explored planets _____[farther]_____ from the sun than Earth.

6. *Voyager 1* traveled _____[farther]_____ into space than any other spacecraft.

7. Scientists expect to get _____[further]_____ information from it about the atmosphere on the outskirts of the solar system.

8. *Pioneer 10* once traveled _____[farther]_____ into space than any other human object.

9. _____[Further]_____ missions are planned—including one to Jupiter's moon Europa.

10. A spacecraft will go _____[farther]_____ than Jupiter to explore the nature of Pluto.

101. Using There, Their, and They're Correctly

There is used as an adverb when it refers to a place.

The heart is a major organ of the human body; blood is pumped <u>there</u>.

There is sometimes an introductory word, usually before the verb *be*.

<u>There</u> are two main types of blood vessels—veins and arteries.

Their is a possessive adjective. *They're* is a contraction for *they are*.

**Veins are blood vessels. <u>They're</u> filled with dark red blood.
<u>Their</u> role is to carry blood toward the heart.**

A. Write **A** if *there* is used as an adverb or **I** if it is used as an introductory word.

___[I]___ 1. There are 206 bones in the human body.

___[A]___ 2. Bones support the human body and blood cells are produced there.

___[I]___ 3. In the human body there are 12 pairs of ribs.

___[I]___ 4. There is a small worm-shaped pouch at the beginning
of the large intestine called the appendix.

___[A]___ 5. There, according to scientists, very little useful happens.

___[I]___ 6. Within the cerebrum there are gray cells.

___[A]___ 7. There in the cerebrum is where thinking takes place.

___[I]___ 8. There is white nerve fiber in the brain that carries signals.

___[A]___ 9. The forebrain includes the diencephalon and the cerebrum;
heartbeat and body temperature are controlled there.

___[A]___ 10. The cerebellum is an important part of the brain because balance
and movement are controlled there.

B. Complete each sentence with *there, their,* or *they're.*

1. ____[There]____ are four chambers in the human heart.

2. ____[Their]____ function is to pump the blood through the body.

3. Deoxygenated blood is pumped from the right atrium and ventricle to the lungs,
and it obtains fresh oxygen ____[there]____.

4. Oxygenated blood goes to the left atrium and ventricle: ____[they're]____
partners in the next step of the process.

5. Blood cells carry food and oxygen to the body; without ____[their]____
services all the other body cells would die.

Name _____

102. Reviewing Adverbs

A. Underline each adverb. On the line write whether it is an adverb of manner, degree, time, or affirmation.

___[degree]___ 1. Annie Oakley was an <u>extremely</u> talented sharpshooter of the Old West.

___[manner]___ 2. At 15, she <u>confidently</u> took part in a shooting match and defeated Frank Butler.

___[time]___ 3. Annie joined Buffalo Bill's Wild West Show where she spent 17 <u>years</u>.

___[manner]___ 4. During the show Frank <u>courageously</u> held a dime in his hand for Annie to shoot.

___[affirmation]___ 5. Annie did <u>indeed</u> have an adventurous life.

B. Complete each sentence with an appropriate interrogative adverb.

1. ___[When]___ was the era of the cowboy?
2. ___[Why]___ was the age of the cowboy so short?
3. ___[Where]___ did cowboys come from?
4. ___[Where]___ was the Chisholm Trail located?
5. ___[How]___ did cowboys prevent stampedes?

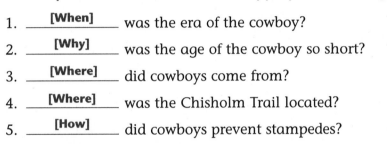

C. Underline each adverbial noun. Write whether it expresses time, measure, distance, value, or direction.

___[time]___ 1. The era of the cattle drive lasted only 20 <u>years</u>.

___[dist/meas]___ 2. The drive could cover only 10 to 20 <u>miles</u> in a day.

___[time]___ 3. The drive took several <u>months</u> to complete.

___[direction]___ 4. The Chisholm Trail went <u>north</u>, from Texas to Abilene, Kansas, which was a rail center.

___[value]___ 5. Ranchers earned more <u>dollars</u> by selling their cattle to markets in the East.

D. Complete the chart with the missing adverbs.

POSITIVE	COMPARATIVE	SUPERLATIVE
1. energetically	[more energetically]	[most energetically]
2. [cautiously]	[more cautiously]	most cautiously
3. [badly]	[worse]	worst
4. [far]	farther	[farthest]
5. late	[later]	[latest]

CONTINUED

Adverbs

Name _____

E. Circle the correct word in parentheses. Write whether it
is used as an adverb or an adjective.

_____[adverb]_____ 1. Clipper ships moved (graceful (gracefully)) across ocean waters.

_____[adverb]_____ 2. They also moved (speedy (speedily)).

_____[adjective]_____ 3. Clipper ships had slim, ((graceful) gracefully) bodies.

_____[adverb]_____ 4. They had an (exceptional (exceptionally)) large spread
of sails on three masts.

_____[adjective]_____ 5. They became ((popular) popularly) in the 1850s.

F. Complete each sentence with *farther* or *further*.

1. In the 1800s people wanted ships that traveled _____[farther]_____ and faster.

2. The first steamships traveled _____[farther]_____ in a day than sailing sloops.

3. However, early steamships had paddle wheels, and _____[further]_____
development was needed before they were suitable for ocean travel.

4. _____[Further]_____ improvements made the first solely steam-powered
crossing of the Atlantic possible in 1838.

5. Eventually there was no _____[further]_____ need for vessels with sails.

G. Complete each sentence with *there*, *their*, or *they're*.

1. _____[There]_____ is a replica of a clipper ship in the museum.

2. I first saw one _____[there]_____.

3. _____[Their]_____ speeds were up to 20 knots per hour.

4. _____[Their]_____ days of glory were over fast.

5. _____[They're]_____ still remembered as beautiful vessels.

Try It Yourself
On a separate sheet of paper, write a paragraph related to a means
of transportation—for example, a train or an airplane trip. Be sure to use
the correct forms of adverbs.

Check Your Own Work
Choose a sheet of writing from your portfolio or journal, a work in progress,
an assignment from another class, or a letter. Revise it, applying the skills
you have reviewed. The checklist will help you.

✔ Have you included appropriate adverbs of time, place, degree, and manner?

✔ Have you used the correct adverbial forms for comparisons?

✔ Have you chosen correct adverb forms—and not confused them with adjective forms?

✔ Have you used *there*, *their*, and *they're* correctly?

Name _____

103. Identifying Prepositions

A **preposition** is a word that shows a relation of a noun, pronoun, or phrase to some other word in a sentence. The object of a preposition is a noun, a pronoun, or a group of words used as a noun. A preposition usually precedes its object.

The samurai were members of the warrior *caste* in *Japan*.

In each sentence circle the prepositions and underline the objects of the prepositions.

1. Samurai were knights (in) feudal Japan.

2. They defended the estates (of) the aristocrats (in) the provinces.

3. The samurai fought (with) two sharp, curved swords.

4. They were equipped (with) special armor made (of) pieces (of) iron.

5. The armor was effective protection (against) thrusts (from) swords.

6. (In) the damp climate, iron would rust, so the coats (of) armor were lacquered (in) black.

7. (During) the 11th and 12th centuries, the samurai developed a code (of) values.

8. They showed unfailing loyalty (to) their overlords and indifference (to) pain.

9. The code (of) honor was called *bushido* (by) the samurai.

10. (In) defeat, some samurai would kill themselves (for) the sake (of) their honor.

11. The samurai were the dominant group (in) Japan (for) centuries.

12. (During) the 15th and 16th centuries their culture produced several traditional customs (of) Japan.

13. (Among) these traditions were the tea ceremony and the art (of) floral arrangement.

14. *Ronin,* who were samurai (without) masters, were a social problem (in) feudal Japan.

15. Needed (in) times (of) war, the *ronin* were a burden (on) society (in) times (of) peace.

16. (In) the 17th century samurai were removed (from) direct control (of) villages.

17. (Until) that time, they lived (in) villages, but then they were moved (into) towns.

18. (After) that, they took up jobs (as) bureaucrats.

19. A result (of) this change was the loss (of) their martial ability.

20. (At) the end (of) the 19th century, feudalism was abolished, and the class (of) samurai went out (of) existence.

111

104. Using Prepositions

Complete each set of sentences with the prepositions given above it.
Use each preposition in a set once.

among   at   during   from   of

1. William Tell was a hero _____[of]_____ the Swiss _____[during]_____ the 14th century.

2. _____[At]_____ the time, the Austrians were trying to take independence _____[from]_____ the Swiss.

3. _____[Among]_____ the Swiss leaders was William Tell.

into   on   over   through   of   with

4. A tyrant named Gessler ruled _____[over]_____ Tell's territory.

5. Gessler placed a cap _____[on]_____ top _____[of]_____ a pole.

6. Gessler threatened to put anyone who did not salute the cap _____[into]_____ jail.

7. One day William Tell was walking _____[through]_____ the town _____[with]_____ his son.

about   as   before   off   without

8. Tell passed the pole _____[without]_____ a glance, and so soldiers captured Tell and brought him _____[before]_____ Gessler.

9. Gessler knew _____[about]_____ Tell's skills _____[as]_____ an archer.

10. He said, "I'll let you go free if you shoot this apple _____[off]_____ your son's head."

at   from   in   of   with

11. Tell looked _____[at]_____ Gessler _____[with/in]_____ considerable contempt.

12. Tell took two arrows _____[from]_____ his quiver _____[of]_____ arrows.

13. The crowd looked _____[in/with]_____ horror as Tell prepared to shoot the arrow.

from   in   to   with   until

14. The apple split _____[in]_____ half and fell _____[to]_____ the ground, and Tell's son was safe.

15. Tell later shot the tyrant _____[with]_____ the second arrow, and so _____[until]_____ the present day the Swiss have kept their independence _____[from]_____ other countries.

105. Using Troublesome Prepositions Correctly

> Some prepositions are often used incorrectly.
> You are *angry at* a person and you are *angry with* a thing.
> Use *between* with groups of two, *among* with groups of three or more.
> *Beside* means "at the side of"; *besides* means "in addition to."
> Use *borrow from*, not *borrow off of*.
> You *differ with* a person and you *differ on* a question.
> Use *different from* usually, not *different than*.
> *In* means "inside of"; *into* is for motion from the outside to the inside.
> Use *off*, not *off of* for movement from.

A. Circle the correct preposition in parentheses.

1. Kathy and her sister Betty always differ (*on* with) the issue of borrowing.

2. Betty often borrows clothes (*from* off of) Kathy, and she doesn't ask in advance.

3. (Beside *Besides*) that, Betty also uses her sister's CDs and CD player.

4. Kathy is different (*from* than) her sister and asks for things in advance.

5. Yesterday Kathy walked (in *into*) Betty's room and asked to have her CDs back.

6. Kathy was really angry (*at* with) Betty.

7. Betty said that this was different (*from* than) other times—she didn't have the CDs.

8. There was a big fight (*between* among) Betty and Kathy.

9. Mom had the CDs, and she was angry (at *with*) the girls' inability to get along.

10. Mom divided Kathy's CDs (*among* between) the three of them to share.

B. Complete each sentence with the correct preposition.

1. I usually differ _____[with]_____ my brother over musical taste.

2. My taste is different _____[from]_____ my brother's—he likes only classical music.

3. He sometimes has difficulty choosing _____[between]_____ an opera and a symphony.

4. _____[Beside]_____ his bed he has a bust of Bach.

5. He makes the cat jump _____[off]_____ the bed so that it won't knock the statue over.

6. My musical choices are usually _____[among]_____ rap, heavy metal, and rock.

7. I was surprised when my brother wanted to borrow a CD _____[from]_____ me.

8. He usually doesn't listen to anything _____[besides]_____ classical music and opera.

9. I didn't want him to be angry _____[at]_____ me, so I said OK.

10. _____[Among]_____ the songs he borrowed was an updated version of a Bach motet!

106. Identifying Words Used as Adverbs and Prepositions

> An adverb tells how, when, or where. A preposition shows the relation
> between an object and some other word in a sentence.
>
> PREPOSITION: **Don't take the top off the container.**
>
> ADVERB: **If you need to take it off, do so carefully.**

A. On the line write **A** if the *italicized* word is an adverb or **P** if it is used as a preposition.

__[A]__ 1. Have you made a terrarium *before*?

__[P]__ 2. A terrarium basically consists of plants grown *inside* a container.

__[A]__ 3. The water cycle occurs on a small scale *inside*.

__[A]__ 4. Here are the steps to go *through*.

__[P]__ 5. *Before* starting, get what you need: a plastic container
with a cover, charcoal, soil, and plants.

__[A]__ 6. Look *around* in garden stores for soil and plants.

__[A]__ 7. Pick *out* plants of different heights and colors for visual effect.

__[A]__ 8. Inside the container, place the charcoal, mentioned *above*.

__[P]__ 9. *Above* this, place a layer of potting soil.

__[A]__ 10. Push the plants *down* carefully into the soil.

__[P]__ 11. Put the smaller plants *around* the edges, and then place the cover.

__[P]__ 12. After a few days check that no water is coming *down* the sides.

__[P]__ 13. If there is, take the cover *off* the terrarium.

__[A]__ 14. Then let the terrarium dry *out* for a short time.

__[P]__ 15. Enjoy looking *through* the clear sides at your plants.

B. Complete each sentence with one of the following words. Write how it is used.

above   into   off   on   up

__[A]__ 1. You can set ____[up]____ a terrarium inside a plastic soda bottle.

__[P]__ 2. Take the black bottom ____[off]____ the bottle.

__[A]__ 3. Place a layer of charcoal and then a layer of soil ____[above]____ .

__[P]__ 4. Put the plants ____[into]____ the soil carefully.

__[A]__ 5. Put the top back ____[on]____ .

107. Identifying Coordinate and Correlative Conjunctions

A **conjunction** is a word used to connect words, phrases, or clauses in a sentence. **Coordinate conjunctions** are used to connect similar words or groups of words; they connect words that have the same use in a sentence. Coordinate conjunctions are *and, but, for, or, nor, so,* and *yet.*

Many instruments are used to study the sea, <u>and</u> new ones are being developed.

Correlative conjunctions are coordinate conjunctions used in pairs. Correlative conjunctions are *both-and, not only-but also, whether-or, either-or,* and *neither-nor.*

Oceanography is <u>not only</u> an interesting area of study <u>but also</u> a growing one.

A. Circle the conjunctions and underline the words or clauses they connect. On the line write **CO** if the conjunctions are coordinate or **CR** if they are correlative.

[CO] 1. Sea otters are cute, (but) they are also fascinating research subjects.

[CR] 2. (Neither) cold temperatures (nor) salt water harms them.

[CO] 3. Otters were thought to be extinct, (but) in 1938 biologists found a group of them near Carmel, California.

[CR] 4. Otters (neither) give birth (nor) raise their young on land.

[CO] 5. A mother secures her pup in kelp, (and) then she dives for food.

[CO] 6. Sea otters can seem friendly, (yet) to be safe, you should keep your distance from them.

[CO] 7. You have about 100,000 hairs on your head, (but) a 64-pound otter has 170,000 hairs per square inch.

[CR] 8. (Either) overfishing (or) oil spills can destroy an otter's environment.

[CO] 9. Otters eat ocean creatures, (and) they spend much of each day diving for food.

[CO] 10. Sea otters are incredibly agile in water, (yet) they are clumsy on land.

B. Complete the sentences by writing either coordinate or correlative conjunctions.

1. The ocean is well mapped, __[but/yet]__ many areas remain uncharted.

2. Some research may be conducted on land, __[but/yet]__ most is performed at sea.

3. __[Not only]__ do researchers gather specimens at sea, __[but]__ they __[also]__ study them carefully.

4. __[Either]__ plant life __[or]__ animal life reveals important information.

5. The oceans are huge, __[and]__ we may never know all their secrets.

Prepositions, Conjunctions, Interjections

115

108. Using Conjunctive Adverbs

Adverbs used to connect two independent clauses are called **conjunctive adverbs**. Some common conjunctive adverbs are *consequently, furthermore, however, moreover, nevertheless, still, therefore,* and *thus.* Semicolons are used before conjunctive adverbs and commas after them.

People have dreamed of labor-saving devices; furthermore, they have invented many.

A. Circle the conjunctive adverb in each sentence.
Insert semicolons and commas where needed.

1. Humanlike machines have long been envisioned; *nevertheless,* the word *robot* didn't come into use until the 1920s.

2. In 1920 a Czech playwright named Karel Capek first used the word in a play; *furthermore,* the play showed a world filled with robots.

3. In the play, robots did most of the work; *therefore,* the world seemed a paradise at first.

4. Humans had less to do; *consequently,* there was soon unemployment and social unrest.

5. The robots in the play brought benefits; *nevertheless,* they also brought problems.

6. The science fiction writer Isaac Asimov coined the term *robotics* in 1941; *moreover,* he made up rules for robots, such as "they must obey human commands."

7. Robots were built by this time; *however,* a robot didn't enter industry until the 1960s.

8. Most robots today are really computer-controlled arms and hands; *consequently,* they do not resemble the robots of films.

9. Some early robots were used to mow laws; *moreover,* similar robots that vacuum floors have been in use for a while.

10. Advances in technology are being made; *consequently,* more humanlike robots are possible.

B. Complete each sentence with a conjunctive adverb. **[Answers may vary.]**

1. People are interested in gadgets to do chores; _____**[consequently]**_____, many labor-saving devices are produced.

2. Appliances do much work; _____**[nevertheless]**_____, people want to improve them.

3. A new house with many devices is available; _____**[moreover]**_____, some of the devices are "intelligent."

4. A leaking washing machine with a sensor will phone the owner about the problem; _____**[therefore]**_____, the owner can call a plumber before getting home.

5. On the owner's command a refrigerator orders the groceries via the Internet; _____**[moreover]**_____, it accepts the groceries when they are delivered.

109. Using Subordinate Conjunctions

Subordinate conjunctions connect an independent clause and a dependent clause. A dependent clause does not express a complete thought and cannot stand alone. Some common subordinate conjunctions are *after, although, as, as if, because, before, if, since, so, so that, than, though, unless, until, when,* and *while.*

Because Arachne was proud, she was turned into a spider.

A. Circle the subordinate conjunction and underline the dependent clause in each sentence.

1. (Because) Arachne's weaving was so beautiful, she was famous throughout ancient Greece.

2. Tailors and weavers came from miles around (so that) they could see her at work.

3. Her hands moved over the loom agilely, (as if) she were making music.

4. (Although) Arachne was skillful, she was also boastful.

5. (If) anyone challenged her to a spinning contest, Arachne was confident of winning.

6. (When) Arachne boasted of this one day, the goddess Athene appeared before her.

7. Arachne challenged the goddess to a contest, (although) this was disrespectful.

8. (After) Athene had woven a picture of the gods, she examined Arachne's work.

9. Arachne was weaving (while) Athene was weaving.

10. (Before) Arachne put her shuttle down, she had woven a comical picture of the gods.

11. Arachne wove and wove more and more beautifully, (until) she was exhausted.

12. (When) Athene saw Arachne's work, she realized Arachne was the winner.

13. Athene decided to punish Arachne, (since) she had made fun of the gods in her picture.

14. (While) the crowd looked on, Athene turned Arachne into the first spider.

15. (As) Athene's command went into effect, Arachne's body shrunk and turned black, her head grew smaller, and her fingers turned into legs.

B. Begin each sentence with a dependent clause introduced by a subordinate conjunction. **[Answers will vary.]**

1. _____, you will never make it up the mountain.

2. _____, many eat right and exercise regularly.

3. _____, he ran around the track at the high school.

4. _____, she lifted weights.

5. _____, both were exhausted but proud.

Prepositions, Conjunctions, Interjections

117

110. Reviewing Conjunctions

A. On the lines identify how the *italicized* words are used. Write
CO for coordinate conjunction, **CR** for correlative conjunction,
SC for subordinate conjunction, or **CA** for conjunctive adverb.

[CR] 1. Jackie Robinson was *both* a great baseball player *and* a great role model.

[SC] 2. *When* he took the field in Brooklyn on April 15, 1947, he made history.

[SC] 3. *Before* Robinson entered baseball, African-American players played in a separate league.

[SC] 4. Jackie Robinson is remembered today *because* he was the first African American in major league baseball in the 20th century.

[CO] 5. Many people know his name from this special role, *but* others remember him as a superb baseball player.

[CR] 6. They recall *either* his exciting base running *or* his daring sliding.

[CR] 7. In school Jackie excelled *not only* in baseball *but also* in football, basketball, and track.

[CA]] 8. In the army, his refusal to move to the back of a bus got him into trouble; *however*, he was cleared of all charges after an investigation.

[CO] 9. The war was over, *and* Robinson began to play baseball professionally.

[SC] 10. *While* Robinson was playing, Branch Rickey, a baseball executive, was looking for a special player to break baseball's race barrier.

B. Circle the correct word in parentheses.

1. Jackie Robinson was Rickey's choice for many reasons: his baseball skills, his intelligence, (and) or) his courage.

2. He could neither show anger (nor) and) act out in the face of insults.

3. Robinson knew the challenge was difficult; (however) furthermore), he accepted it.

7. (Although) Because) he was subjected to verbal abuse, Robinson maintained his composure.

5. Robinson played ten seasons, (and) yet) he was named to the Hall of Fame in 1962.

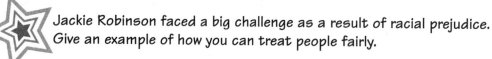

Jackie Robinson faced a big challenge as a result of racial prejudice. Give an example of how you can treat people fairly.

Prepositions, Conjunctions, Interjections

Name _____

III. Using Without and Unless, Like, As and As If Correctly

> *Without* is a preposition and introduces a word or a phrase.
>
> **Without the right sunlight, a garden won't grow.**
>
> *Unless* is a conjunction and introduces a clause.
>
> **Unless you know the growing requirements for a plant, don't plant it.**
>
> *Like* is a preposition and introduces a word or a phrase.
>
> **This flower looks like a rose.**
>
> *As* can be used as a preposition to introduce a word or phrase or as a conjunction to introduce a clause. *As if* is a conjunction and introduces a clause.
>
> **That plant looks as if it needs some water.**

A. Complete each sentence with *without* or *unless*.

1. _____[Without]_____ good care a garden won't grow.

2. So don't start a garden _____[unless]_____ you're prepared to do a lot of hard work.

3. _____[Unless]_____ a space with plenty of sunlight is available, it is not a good idea to start a vegetable garden.

4. _____[Without]_____ a lot of sun, plants like tomatoes won't grow well.

5. _____[Without]_____ nutrients plants won't grow.

6. _____[Unless]_____ the soil is dark and spongy, you might want to add compost, mulch, or fertilizer.

7. Plants of course will die _____[without]_____ enough water.

8. Water them often _____[unless]_____ the soil is moist when you touch it.

9. No gardens grow _____[without]_____ weeds, so you'll have to weed often.

10. Don't pull out anything, however, _____[unless]_____ you are sure that it is not one of your plants!

B. Circle the correct word or words in parentheses.

1. The garden looked (like (as if)) no one had tended it for a while.

2. The gigantic sunflower looked ((like) as) a scarecrow.

3. The old fence looked (like (as if)) it hadn't been painted in years.

4. The old gate swung back and forth (like (as)) the wind blew.

5. The scent of the roses was ((like) as) a sweet but subtle perfume.

Prepositions, Conjunctions, Interjections

119

112. Identifying Interjections

An **interjection** is a word that expresses strong and sudden emotion. Some common emotions are annoyance, delight, disagreement, disappointment, disgust, assent, joy, impatience, pain, surprise, relief, wonder, and warning.

What! The new science fiction movie is opening today?

A. Underline each interjection, and write on the line the emotion it expresses. **[Answers may vary.]**

[joy]	1. <u>Hooray</u>! I'm going to be able to go to the movie today.
[delight]	2. <u>Good</u>! We're all here at the movies early!
[disappointment]	3. <u>Ah</u>! Look at the long ticket line.
[impatience]	4. <u>Hurry</u>! Let's get our tickets.
[surprise]	5. <u>Oops</u>! I dropped my ticket.
[delight]	6. <u>Great</u>! Thanks for getting the popcorn.
[disgust]	7. <u>Yuck</u>! There's butter on the popcorn.
[surprise]	8. <u>What</u>! You can't find your ticket!
[delight]	9. <u>Good</u>! You found it in your pocket!
[pain]	10. <u>Ouch</u>! I bumped my knee on the side of the chair in the dark!
[disagreement]	11. <u>Oh</u>! Let's not sit here. Let's sit closer to the screen.
[warning]	12. <u>Shh</u>! Don't talk while the movie is on.
[surprise]	13. <u>Wow</u>! Look at that wonderful city of the future.
[disgust]	14. <u>Ugh</u>! What a repulsive, slimy villain.
[delight]	15. <u>Wow</u>! What a great chase scene.

B. Use interjections in sentences to express each emotion.

surprise	1.	[Sentences will vary.]
sorrow	2.	_____
disgust	3.	_____
pain	4.	_____
impatience	5.	_____

Name _____

113. Reviewing Prepositions, Conjunctions, and Interjections

A. Underline each preposition. Circle its object.

1. Pecos Bill is a legendary cowboy with great skills.

2. Many stories about his amazing powers were told.

3. He was even the inventor of the lasso.

4. The lasso was very important to cowboys.

5. They threw the lasso around cattle and caught them.

B. Circle the correct word or words in parentheses.

1. Pecos Bill was always different (from than) other cowboys: he was faster and stronger.

2. (Besides Beside) his amazing strength, Bill was also very intelligent and daring.

3. One summer all the cattle stood (beside besides) the dry waterholes with their tongues hanging out.

4. Bill lassoed and jumped on a rain cloud—which made the rain cloud very angry (with at) Bill.

5. Bill jumped (off off of) the rain cloud only after it released its water on the dry land.

C. Underline the conjunction in each sentence. On the line write **CO** if it is a coordinate conjunction, **CR** if it is a correlative conjunction, **CA** if it is a conjunctive adverb, or **SC** if it is a subordinate conjunction.

[CA] 1. Young Pecos Bill wanted to become a cowboy; therefore, he went to the nearest cowboy camp.

[SC] 2. After he had walked several miles, he saw a huge mountain lion on a hill.

[CA] 3. Bill was a bit scared; nevertheless, he walked on.

[CO] 4. He tried to ignore the lion, but the lion didn't leave him alone.

[CO] 5. Suddenly the lion jumped on Bill's back, and it started to wrestle him.

[CR] 6. Neither Bill nor the lion was going to give in first.

[CA] 7. Both were stubborn; consequently, they kept fighting for two hours.

[SC] 8. They fought until they were both exhausted.

[CO] 9. The mountain lion finally surrendered, and Bill said, "OK. Give me a ride."

[SC] 10. Everyone knew Bill was special when he rode into the cowboy camp on a mountain lion.

Name _____

D. Circle the subordinate conjunction and underline
the dependent clause in each sentence.

1. The military uses codes during a war (so that) secret information can be transmitted.

2. Many battles can be lost (if) an enemy breaks the code.

3. (While) World War II was raging, someone had an idea for a code no one could break.

4. (Since) few people knew the Navajo language, it was used to send messages.

5. (Although) they did not fight, the Navajo code talkers contributed to the Allied victory.

E. Circle the correct word(s) in parentheses.

1. At the time of its discovery, the writing on the Rosetta Stone looked (like (as if))
   it would provide the key to hieroglyphics.

2. The writing looked (like (as if)) it repeated the same message in three languages,
   one of which was hieroglyphics.

3. Decipherers first searched for characters that looked ((like) as if) rulers' names.

4. As scientists studied hieroglyphics, it looked (like (as if)) some characters
   represented sounds.

5. So the strange scratchings that looked ((like) as) nonsense at last become decipherable!

F. Underline the interjection in each sentence.
On the line write the emotion it expresses.

[surprise]	1. Wow! It's a thousand-piece puzzle.
[disappointment]	2. Oh! It must be hard to complete!
[surprise]	3. Oops! I dropped a piece.
[relief]	4. Whew! I worked on it day and night.
[joy]	5. Bravo! I put it together myself!

Try It Yourself
On a separate sheet of paper, write a paragraph about a hero—whether real
or legendary. Be sure to use the correct forms of prepositions and conjunctions.

Check Your Own Work
Choose a piece of writing from your portfolio or journal, a work in progress,
an assignment from another class, or a letter. Revise it, applying the skills
you have reviewed. The checklist will help you.

✔ Have you used prepositions correctly?

✔ Have you used appropriate coordinate conjunctions or conjunctive adverbs?

✔ Have you used subordinate conjunctions correctly?

✔ Have you used *without, unless, like, as,* and *as if* correctly?

Prepositions, Conjunctions, Interjections

114. Identifying Phrases

A **phrase** is a group of words without a subject and verb that is used as a single part of speech. A **prepositional phrase** begins with a preposition. It can be used as an adjective or an adverb.

> **The role of insects is very important.** (The phrase *of insects* modifies *role*.)
>
> **Many creatures eat insects for food.** (The phrase *for food* modifies *eat*.)

A. The prepositional phrase in each sentence is *italicized*. Circle the word it modifies. On the line write whether it is used as an adjective or an adverb.

[adjective]   1. The most abundant (creatures) *in the world* are insects.

[adjective]   2. Scientists have named only (one-third) *of them.*

[adverb]   3. Insects (belong) *to the phylum Arthropoda.*

[adverb]   4. The first insects probably (evolved) *from primitive sea worms.*

[adjective]   5. The (body) *of the typical adult insect* has three parts: head, thorax, and abdomen.

[adverb]   6. Most insects (feed) *on plants.*

[adjective]   7. (Insects) *with chewing mouth parts* are the most destructive.

[adjective]   8. Some can destroy large (areas) *of vegetation* quickly.

[adjective]   9. They are an important food (source) *for many creatures.*

[adverb]   10. Many plants (need) insects *for pollination.*

B. Find the prepositional phrase(s) in each sentence. Underline those used as an adjective and circle those used as an adverb.

1. Cockroaches are considered pests (by people).

2. They invade food supplies in homes.

3. They can increase rapidly (in hospitable conditions.)

4. Most species of cockroaches live (in the tropics.)

5. Many cockroaches in the tropics have wings and fly.

6. Most roaches are brown or black, but yellows and reds occur (on some tropical species.)

7. Little claws on their feet allow cockroaches to climb walls.

8. Cockroaches can live a week (without a head.)

9. Eventually they die (of thirst.)

10. Some fossils of cockroaches are about 350 million years old.

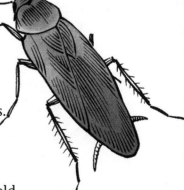

115.   Identifying Adjectival Clauses

A **clause** is a part of a sentence that has a subject and a predicate. An independent clause expresses a complete thought and can stand on its own as a sentence. A dependent clause does not express a complete thought and cannot stand alone.

An **adjectival clause** is a dependent clause used as an adjective. It usually begins with a relative pronoun (*who, whom, whose, which, that*) or a conjunction (*where, when*).

Spain, **which is on Mediterranean Sea**, **is part of the European Union.**

Underline the adjectival clause in each sentence. Circle the word it modifies.

1. Spain, which is in southwestern Europe, shares the Iberian peninsula with Portugal.

2. Famous Spanish cities that tourists visit are Madrid and Barcelona.

3. The main geographical feature of Spain is the central plateau, which lies an average of 2,000 feet above sea level.

4. Spain is separated by only a few miles from Africa, whose culture has had a strong influence on the nation.

5. Spain is ruled by a constitutional monarch, who can propose candidates for prime minister.

6. The Cortes, which is Spain's legislature, consists of a chamber of deputies and a senate.

7. The members, who are elected every four years, have legislative power.

8. Spain, which was under Arab rule during the Middle Ages, has many lovely mosques.

9. The Alhambra, which is in Granada, was a palace of Moorish kings.

10. The reconquista, which refers to the reconquest of the Iberian peninsula by Christian kingdoms, took centuries to complete.

11. Spain, which traditionally has been an agricultural country, is the world's largest producer of olive oil.

12. Crops that Spain produces include wheat, sugar beets, tomatoes, cork, and citrus fruit.

13. Among the products that Spain manufactures are textiles, steel, and chemicals.

14. Don Quixote, whom Cervantes created, is a famous figure in Spanish literature.

15. The work tells about a simple-minded knight who tries to right the world's wrongs.

16. The flamenco, which is a dance with fancy footwork and finger snapping with castanets, originated in southern Spain.

17. Bullfighting, for which Spain is well known, is called an art and not a sport.

18. A popular dish that includes saffron and bits of seafood or meat is known as *paella*.

19. Tapas, which are bite-sized snacks, are also popular in Spain.

20. Gazpacho is a cold vegetable soup that is also popular in Spain.

116. Identifying Restrictive and Nonrestrictive Clauses

> A **restrictive clause** helps identify a certain person or object and is a necessary part of the sentence.
>
> **The person <u>who founded the Round Table</u> was King Arthur.**
>
> **The sword <u>that Arthur found</u> was called Excalibur.**
>
> A **nonrestrictive clause** merely adds information about the word it modifies and is not necessary to the sentence. It is separated from the rest of the sentence by commas.
>
> **King Arthur, <u>who founded the Round Table</u>, had many knights in his court.**
>
> **Excalibur, <u>which Arthur found</u>, was stuck in a stone.**

Underline the adjectival clause. Circle the word to which it refers.
On the line write **R** if it is restrictive or **N** if it is nonrestrictive.

__[R]__ 1. There were many famous (characters) that appeared in the stories of the Round Table.

__[R]__ 2. The (knight) who was the bravest of the knights was Lancelot.

__[N]__ 3. Lancelot fell in love with (Guinevere,) who was King Arthur's wife.

__[R]__ 4. The (character) who was an evil force had the name of Mordred.

__[N]__ 5. (Merlin,) who was a sorcerer and a prophet, was King Arthur's advisor.

__[N]__ 6. (Sir Galahad,) who was one of King Arthur's knights, was perhaps the noblest of all knights of the Round Table.

__[R]__ 7. He came to fill the (seat) that was the most famous of all at the Round Table.

__[R]__ 8. According to belief, any unworthy (person) who sat in the seat would be destroyed.

__[N]__ 9. Miraculously, at Galahad's arrival at court, the seat's (label,) which had read "Seat Perilous," changed to "This is the seat of Galahad, the high prince."

__[N]__ 10. That same year the knights saw a vision of the (Holy Grail,) which was Jesus' holy cup from the Last Supper.

__[R]__ 11. All the (knights) who were present promised to search for the Holy Grail.

__[R]__ 12. The (journeys) that the knights undertook were long and difficult.

__[R]__ 13. It was the noblest and purest (knight) who would find the Grail.

__[R]__ 14. Finally a (vision) that appeared to Galahad led him to a castle.

__[N]__ 15. There he found the (Grail,) which spiritual forces carried up to the heavens along with the noble Galahad himself.

117. Writing Adjectival Clauses

Combine each set of sentences into one sentence with
an adjectival clause. **[Suggested sentences are given.]**

1. There are many different holidays. You may not know these holidays.
   [There are many different holidays that you may not know.]

2. Pulaski Day honors a Polish-American hero. It is a state holiday in Illinois.
   [Pulaski Day, which is a state holiday in Illinois, honors a Polish-American hero.]

3. Susan B. Anthony has her day on February 15. She was a leader in the
   women's movement.
   [Susan B. Anthony, who was a leader in the women's movement, has her day on February 15.]

   _____

4. March 3 in Japan is Dolls Festival. Dolls Festival is celebrated by displaying toys.
   [March 3 in Japan is Dolls Festival, which is celebrated by displaying toys.]

5. On National Gripers' Day in April, people are happy. Those people like to complain.
   [On National Gripers' Day in April, people who like to complain are happy.]

6. National Nothing Day is a day not to honor anything! This day occurs on January 16.
   [National Nothing Day, which occurs on January 16, is a day not to honor anything!]

   _____

7. Cinco de Mayo celebrates a battle. In that battle the Mexicans defeated the French.
   [Cinco de Mayo celebrates a battle in which the Mexicans defeated the French.]

   _____

8. On National Fink Day people gather in Fink, Texas. These people
   have the last name Fink
   [On National Fink Day people who have the last name Fink gather in Fink, Texas.]

   _____

9. National Left-Handers Day gives special attention to this group. The day is on August 13.
   [National Left-Handers Day, which is on August 13, gives special attention to this group.]

   _____

10. World Food Day occurs on October 16. The day's purpose is to make
    people aware of the fight against hunger.
    [World Food Day, the purpose of which is to make people aware of the fight against hunger, occurs

    on October 16.]

118. Identifying Adverbial Clauses

An **adverbial clause** is a dependent clause used as an adverb. It modifies a verb, an adjective, or an adverb. It is introduced by a subordinate conjunction.

Tornadoes occur when certain atmospheric conditions are present.

A. Underline the adverbial clause. Circle the word(s) it modifies.

1. Tornadoes (frighten) us, because they can cause sudden violent destruction.

2. Although there are tornadoes all over the world, they (occur) most often in North America.

3. Unless there is a thunderstorm, a tornado (does) not (occur.)

4. Thunderstorms (are produced) when warm, moist air meets cold, dry air.

5. A tornado (occurs) after warm, moist air gets trapped below a layer of stable cold, dry air.

6. If conditions are right, the warm, moist air (spins) its way through the stable air.

7. The warm air (spirals) upward as its heat is released.

8. The rotating air (gains) speed when it moves up.

9. If tornadoes hit the ground, they can (travel) huge distances.

10. Some tornadoes (darken) after they pick up dust and debris.

11. If this happens, you (can see) the twisting spiral of the tornado.

12. Since there are so many tornadoes in Texas, Oklahoma, and Kansas, this area (is called) Tornado Alley.

13. Although tornadoes can strike any time of the day, they (happen) most frequently in the afternoon.

14. While tornadoes whirl counterclockwise in the Northern Hemisphere, they (turn) clockwise in the Southern Hemisphere.

15. Before tornadoes hit, scientists (can predict) dangerous weather conditions.

B. Complete each sentence with an independent clause. **[Answers will vary. Sample clauses are given.]**

1. Before you leave the house, ___[check the weather conditions.]___

2. After the storm ended, ___[a beautiful rainbow appeared in the sky.]___

3. While I was swimming, ___[my swimming suit fell off.]___

4. ___[Our team has not lost a game]___ since she became the goalie on our team.

5. ___[I usually go to sleep at 10 o'clock]___ unless the next day is a school holiday.

119. Writing Adverbial Clauses

When an adverbial clause begins a sentence, it is usually followed by a comma. When an adverbial clause is at the end of a sentence, it is not usually separated from the rest of the sentence by a comma.

Combine the following sentences into one sentence with an adverbial clause. The subordinate conjunction is given.

1. Bananas are a common food today in the United States. They used to be a rare commodity.

    although [Although bananas are a common food today in the United States, they used to be a rare commodity.]

2. Bananas are a common food in the United States. Refrigerated transportation was invented.

    since [Bananas are a common food in the United States since refrigerated transportation was invented.]

3. Bananas provide vitamin C, fiber, and potassium. They are a healthful food.

    because [Because bananas provide vitamin C, fiber, and potassium, they are a healthful food.]

4. Bananas probably originated in Malaysia. Many varieties of bananas are found there.

    because [Bananas probably originated in Malaysia, because many varieties of bananas are found there.]

5. Alexander the Great conquered India. He supposedly saw bananas there.

    when [When Alexander the Great conquered India, he supposedly saw bananas there.]

6. Spanish explorers brought the banana to the Americas. It became a popular fruit in South America.

    after [After Spanish explorers brought the banana to the Americas, it became a popular fruit in South America.]

7. Much of Central America has a rich soil and a tropical climate. Bananas grow well there.

    as [As much of Central America has a rich soil and a tropical climate, bananas grow well there.]

8. Banana plants bear fruit only once. The plants are cut down to harvest the fruit.

    since [Since banana plants bear fruit only once, the plants are cut down to harvest the fruit.]

9. Bananas were introduced to the United States officially at an 1876 exhibition. They were wrapped in foil and sold for 10 cents each.

    when [When bananas were introduced to the United States officially at an 1876 exhibition, they were wrapped in foil and sold for 10 cents each.]

10. You want a good snack. Try a banana.

    if [If you want a good snack, try a banana.]

120. Distinguishing Between Adjectival and Adverbial Clauses

Underline the dependent clause in each sentence. On the line
write whether it is an adjectival or an adverbial clause.

_____[adverbial]_____ 1. Parachutes actually were invented before people flew.

_____[adjectival]_____ 2. The idea of a parachute, which would break one's fall,
was a simple one.

_____[adjectival]_____ 3. Leonardo da Vinci, who was an inventor, sketched a
cloth parachute in the 1500s.

_____[adjectival]_____ 4. Later an Italian book contained a picture that showed a rectangular
cloth parachute over a wooden frame.

_____[adjectival]_____ 5. The principles that would make a parachute work were clear.

_____[adverbial]_____ 6. Although the scientific ideas were clear, someone had to test them.

_____[adverbial]_____ 7. One French daredevil successfully leaped from the top of a high
tower because he wanted to test his parachute.

_____[adjectival]_____ 8. Parachute jumps, which were considered daring at the time,
soon became popular acts in fairs.

_____[adverbial]_____ 9. After hot-air balloons were invented, there were
more chances to test parachutes.

_____[adjectival]_____ 10. In the 1790s a large crowd watched André Jacques Garnerin,
who jumped 3,000 feet from a hot-air balloon.

_____[adjectival]_____ 11. He used a parachute that resembled an oversized umbrella.

_____[adverbial]_____ 12. After balloons, gliders, and airplanes were invented,
the parachute became practical.

_____[adjectival]_____ 13. According to record, the first person who jumped from a plane with
a parachute was Captain Albert Berry of the U.S. Army in 1912.

_____[adverbial]_____ 14. Although early parachutes are like those in use today,
there are some differences.

_____[adjectival]_____ 15. Canvas, which was used in early parachutes,
has been replaced by nylon.

_____[adverbial]_____ 16. While early parachutes were made of one piece of cloth,
modern ones come in several sections.

_____[adjectival]_____ 17. A tear, which sometimes happens, can be repaired.

_____[adjectival]_____ 18. Now parachutes have ripcords that open them automatically.

_____[adverbial]_____ 19. Parachutes were in the news when giant ones
were used to help space capsules land.

_____[adverbial]_____ 20. Before you jump, think of the history behind the parachute.

Phrases, Clauses, Sentences

129

121. Reviewing Phrases and Clauses

A. Underline the prepositional phrase(s) in each sentence.
Write whether it is used as an adjective or an adverb.

___[adverb]___ 1. A fable is a story that points <u>to a moral</u>.

___[adjective/adjective]___ 2. The setting <u>in a fable</u> is the background <u>for the action</u>.

___[adjective]___ 3. A fable is a very brief story <u>with animal characters</u>.

___[adjective]___ 4. "The Tortoise and the Hare" teaches a lesson <u>about being steady</u>.

___[adverb]___ 5. The moral is included <u>at the end</u>.

B. Rewrite the following sentences, inserting first a nonrestrictive adjectival clause and then a restrictive adjectival clause after the *italicized* word. **[Sentences will vary.]**

The poetry *assignment* was due yesterday.

   1. nonrestrictive [The poetry assignment, which I didn't complete, was due yesterday.]

   2. restrictive [The poetry assignment that I worked on all night was due yesterday.]

Our class *play* was a complete success.

   3. nonrestrictive [Our class play, which was a musical, was a complete success.]

   4. restrictive [Our class play that we performed Friday and Saturday night was a complete success.]

The next *book report* is due in two weeks.

   5. nonrestrictive [The next book report, which I have already completed, is due in two weeks.]

   6. restrictive [The next book report that must be on a biography is due in two weeks.]

C. Combine each pair of simple sentences to write a complex sentence that contains an adjectival or an adverbial clause. Punctuate the sentences correctly.

   1. The first little pig built a house of straw. The wolf blew it down.   **[Sample sentences**
      [The first little pig built a house of straw, which the wolf blew down.]   **are given.]**

   2. The third little pig had bricks. The little pig built a strong house.
      [Because the third little pig had bricks, he built a strong house.]

   3. The bricks were heavy. The little pig carried them home.
      [Although the bricks were heavy, the little pig carried them home.]

   4. The wolf came. The wolf could not blow down the house.
      [When the wolf came, he could not blow down the house.]

122. Recognizing Sentences

A **sentence** is a group of words that expresses a complete thought.
Every sentence has a subject and a predicate.

SENTENCE: **Plants make their own food.**

NOT A SENTENCE: **Soft, delicate petals dropping to the ground**

A. For each group of words write **S** if it is a sentence or **NS** if it is not a sentence.

__[S]__   1. I was distracted while I was doing my homework.

__[NS]__   2. A blast of warm air.

__[S]__   3. Two cardinals were nesting in a bush nearby.

__[NS]__   4. Rabbits in the backyard.

__[S]__   5. My cat watches them warily.

__[NS]__   6. A long, lazy afternoon watching the birds.

__[NS]__   7. Creeping toward the garage door.

__[S]__   8. All of a sudden the squirrel came out of nowhere.

__[NS]__   9. The biggest one landing in the birdbath.

__[S]__   10. My eyes were as wide as saucers.

__[S]__   11. Get up slowly.

__[NS]__   12. Unhooking the cat's claws from the screen.

__[S]__   13. I diverted her attention with a kitty treat.

__[NS]__   14. Brightly colored butterflies.

__[S]__   15. There could be a short story here.

B. Write sentences using each group of words. **[Sentences will vary. Sample sentences are given.]**

1. my two friends
   [My Dad took my two friends and me to the baseball game.]

2. during these hot summer nights
   [I have been sleeping on the back porch during these hot summer nights.]

3. through hill country
   [Our family took a long, tiresome train ride through hill country.]

4. gathering shells along the sandy beach
   [My sister enjoys gathering shells along the sandy beach.]

5. tree at the end of the path
   [My brother likes to sit and read under the tree at the end of the path.]

Phrases, Clauses, Sentences

123. Identifying Natural and Inverted Order

A sentence is in **natural order** when the verb follows the subject.

> Nobles *lived* in castles during the Middle Ages.

A sentence is in **inverted order** when the main verb or an auxiliary verb precedes the subject.

> Above the castle often *rose* large towers.

A. Underline the complete subject. Write **N** if the sentence is in natural order or **I** if it is in inverted order.

[N] 1. The castle was the fortified home of a lord during the Middle Ages.

[I] 2. Around the castle stood rings of stone walls.

[N] 3. Each thick wall acted as a separate defense against an attacking enemy.

[I] 4. How did enemies attack castles?

[N] 5. Attackers shot rocks and fiery arrows at the castle with special machines.

[I] 6. Outside the walls often was a moat.

[I] 7. Inside the moat flowed water.

[I] 8. Did all moats have water?

[N] 9. Some moats were just deep holes in the ground.

[N] 10. An enemy had to cross the difficult barrier.

B. Rewrite each sentence in the order indicated.

1. Inside the castle were the living quarters of the lord.

   Natural: **[The living quarters of the lord were inside the castle.]**

2. The dining room was inside the great hall.

   Inverted: **[Inside the great hall was the dining room.]**

3. Bread, peacock, and eels might lie on a lord's table.

   Inverted: **[On a lord's table might lie bread, peacock, and eels.]**

4. A fireplace stood in the middle of the room or against a wall.

   Inverted: **[In the middle of the room or against a wall stood a fireplace.]**

5. In a separate building was placed the kitchen because of fear of fire.

   Natural: **[The kitchen was placed in a separate building because of fear of fire.]**

Name _____

124. Understanding Simple Sentences

A **simple sentence** contains one subject and one predicate, either or both of which may be compound.

SUBJECT   COMPOUND VERB

Muraski Shikibu *lived* and *wrote* in medieval Japan.

Underline each simple subject once and each simple predicate twice.

1. Murasaki Shikibu lived about 1,000 years ago in Japan.

2. Many experts consider her book *The Tale of Genji* the first novel.

3. The book tells the story of Prince Genji, the "Shining One."

4. Murasaki's novel and diary are still read today.

5. She described and analyzed human emotions with great insight.

6. Murasaki was unusual for her time.

7. She had been well educated.

8. Unlike many women of her time, she read and wrote.

9. At the time in Japan, men and women used different writing systems and writing styles.

10. Women were allowed a freer, less formal style of writing.

11. Murasaki used lovely images from nature in her work.

12. Few facts are known about Murasaki's life, outside of her writings.

13. According to some sources, Murasaki married and had a daughter.

14. After her husband's death, she went to live at the Japanese court.

15. Music, poetry, and gossip were pastimes of the court.

16. Women lived in separate quarters and hid behind screens.

17. Murasaki's writings give great insight into the life of the court.

18. Her long novel about Genji was written over a period of many years.

19. Prince Genji's life and loves are described in the book.

20. According to some, the end of the novel shows Murasaki's increasing belief in Buddhism and in the vanity of the world.

Murasaki lived in a narrow world with many restrictions, yet she used her ability to create. Give an example of a special ability that you have.

Phrases, Clauses, Sentences

133

125. Identifying Compound Sentences

A **compound sentence** has two or more independent clauses. Compound sentences are connected by coordinate conjunctions, conjunctive adverbs, or semicolons.

The Colosseum is an ancient Roman ruin, but it is the most famous of all.

The Colosseum is an ancient Roman ruin; nevertheless, it is the most famous of all.

The Colosseum is an ancient Roman ruin; it is the most famous of all.

Underline the independent clauses in each sentence and insert the proper punctuation.

1. The Colosseum was built 2,000 years ago, but it still stands in the center of modern Rome.

2. The Colosseum is a famous ruin; thousands of tourists visit it every day.

3. The Colosseum was the largest amphitheater built by the ancient Romans; nevertheless, it was built in less than ten years.

4. The Colosseum could seat more than 45,000 spectators, and it was four stories high.

5. The huge structure is about 600 feet long and 500 feet wide; furthermore, it rises over 187 feet into the air.

6. The Colosseum had approximately eighty entrances; therefore, crowds could enter and leave quickly.

7. Under the floor of the Colosseum were passages; wild animals were kept there.

8. Entertainment was provided by the Roman emperors, and it was free to the public.

9. One of the main spectacles was combat between gladiators; another was hunting wild animals.

10. These events were for entertainment; however, the sports often ended in death.

11. Originally the victor determined the fate of the loser, but later the emperor gave the life-or-death signal—thumbs up or thumbs down.

12. The rewards for victors were considerable; they included precious gifts and gold coins.

13. The Colosseum has been damaged by earthquakes; moreover, in the past people stole stones and marble seats.

14. In the past pieces of stone have fallen from the Colosseum, and the structure had to be closed to tourists and reinforced.

15. Today tourists can visit parts of the Colosseum; they can imagine it with 45,000 spectators!

126. Writing Compound Sentences

Combine each pair of simple sentences, to write a compound sentence. Use a coordinate conjunction, a conjunctive adverb, or just a semicolon. **[Suggested answers are given.]**

1. Gold is a precious metal. People have valued it throughout history.
   [Gold is a precious metal, and people have valued it throughout history.]

2. Gold does not rust. Gold objects from ancient tombs often still shine.
   [Gold does not rust; therefore, gold objects from ancient tombs often still shine.]

3. Gold is a soft metal. It can be shaped into a variety of forms.
   [Gold is a soft metal; it can be shaped into a variety of forms.]

4. Gold conducts electricity well. Silver and copper are better conductors.
   [Gold conducts electricity well; however, silver and copper are better conductors.]

5. Jewelry has long been made from gold. Coins also have been made from gold.
   [Jewelry has long been made from gold, and coins also have been made from gold.]

6. The gold in jewelry is measured in karats. Pure gold is 24-karat gold.
   [The gold in jewelry is measured in karats; pure gold is 24-karat gold.]

7. About two-thirds of all gold is made into jewelry. It is also used in electronic devices.
   [About two-thirds of all gold is made into jewelry; furthermore, it is also used in electronic devices.]

8. Gold is found in many places on earth. It usually occurs with other metals.
   [Gold is found in many places on earth, and it usually occurs with other metals.]

9. There is gold in seawater. The cost of extracting it is too expensive.
   [There is gold in seawater; however, the cost of extracting it is too expensive.]

10. The largest gold field is in South Africa. Gold is mined in many places.
    [The largest gold field is in South Africa, but gold is mined in many places.]

11. A gold strike was in Nevada in the 1960s. An open pit mine still operates there.
    [A gold strike was in Nevada in the 1960s, and an open pit mine still operates there.]

12. In the Middle Ages people tried to turn other metals into gold. They were alchemists.
    [In the Middle Ages people tried to turn other metals into gold; they were alchemists.]

13. The Spanish sought gold in the Americas. They had heard of a land rich in gold.
    [The Spanish sought gold in the Americas; they had heard of a land rich in gold.]

14. There have been many gold rushes. Most people don't strike it rich.
    [There have been many gold rushes; nevertheless, most people don't strike it rich.]

15. There was a gold rush to California in 1849. Alaska had a gold rush in the 1890s.
    [There was a gold rush to California in 1849, and Alaska had a gold rush in the 1890s.]

Phrases, Clauses, Sentences

Name _____

127. Identifying Complex Sentences

> A **complex sentence** contains at least one independent clause and one or more dependent clauses.
>
> **The Inca civilization, which was centered in Peru, was conquered by the Spanish.**

A. Underline each independent clause once and each dependent clause twice. Circle the relative pronoun or subordinate conjunction.

1. The Inca Empire, (which) controlled the Andes Mountains, survived fewer than 100 years.

2. The term *Inca* was the name of the group's ruler, (whom) the Incas worshipped as a god.

3. (Before) the Incas expanded in the 15th century, they were a small tribe near Cuzco in Peru.

4. (After) they were attacked by their neighbors, they began a series of conquests.

5. They started attacks (that) established Inca rule from Colombia to Chile.

6. The rulers were worshipped (after) they died.

7. Their mummified bodies were carried into the main square every day (so that) people could worship them.

8. (Because) they didn't have written numbers, the Incas developed a clever counting system with knotted cords.

9. (Since) there was no writing system, oral communication was very important.

10. Messages were memorized and carried by runners, (who) could cover 150 miles a day.

B. Underline each dependent clause. Identify each dependent clause as adjectival or adverbial.

[adjectival] 1. In 1532 the Inca empire was defeated by the Spanish, who were led by Francisco Pizarro.

[adverbial] 2. Although there were fewer than 200 soldiers in Pizarro's group, they defeated an empire of about 12 million.

[adverbial] 3. Before the Spanish arrived, a bloody civil war had occurred.

[adjectival] 4. Atahualpa, who won the civil war, had a greatly weakened army.

[adjectival] 5. The Spanish had guns and horses, which were unknown to the Inca.

[adverbial] 6. When the Spanish used them in a surprise attack, Atahualpa was captured.

[adjectival] 7. Atahualpa offered the Spanish a room that was filled with gold.

[adverbial] 8. Although the Spanish accepted at first, they changed their minds.

[adverbial] 9. If Altahualpa lived, he might start a rebellion.

[adverbial] 10. The Inca empire ended soon after Atahualpa was killed in 1533.

Phrases, Clauses, Sentences

128. Writing Complex Sentences

Combine each pair of simple sentences to write one complex sentence.

[Sample sentences are given.]

1. Coins and bills were invented. People bartered goods.

   [Before coins and bills were invented, people bartered goods.]

2. The Chinese introduced paper money. It was first used in the eighth century A.D.

   [The Chinese introduced paper money, which was first used in the eighth century A.D.]

3. The Lydians began the use of money in 700 B.C. They invented coins.

   [The Lydians, who invented coins, began the use of money in 700 B.C.]

4. Much currency in history has been made of paper or metal. People have used other items.

   [Although much currency in history has been made of paper or

   metal, people have used other items.]

5. Seashell beads were used by European settlers in the Americas. They saw the beads used by Native Americans.

   [Seashell beads were used by European settlers in the Americas

   after they saw the beads used by Native Americans.]

6. In history, coins were stamped with a distinctive mark. This was often the image of a ruler.

   [In history, coins were stamped with a distinctive mark,

   which was often the image of a ruler.]

7. The first woman on a U.S. bill was Martha Washington. She appeared on a one-dollar bill in 1886.

   [The first woman on a U.S. bill was Martha Washington, who

   appeared on a one-dollar bill in 1886.]

8. A new penny was introduced in 1906. It was called the Lincoln penny.

   [A new penny that was called the Lincoln penny was introduced in 1906.]

9. Credit cards were introduced in 1950. They gradually began replacing cash.

   [After credit cards were introduced in 1950, they gradually began replacing cash.]

10. In 1999 the European Union created a new currency. It was called the euro.

    [In 1999 the European Union created a new currency, which was called the euro.]

129. Reviewing Sentence Forms

A. On the line write whether each sentence is simple, compound, or complex.

_____[complex]_____ 1. Because people from various places want to communicate, there has long been a desire for a universal language.

_____[complex]_____ 2. Esperanto is a universal language that has been invented.

_____[complex]_____ 3. Esperanto was invented by Ludwig Zamenhof, who was a Polish doctor.

_____[simple]_____ 4. Zamenhof presented his language to the public in 1887.

_____[compound]_____ 5. People in his town spoke four different native languages, and they could not understand one another.

_____[complex]_____ 6. They sometimes quarreled, since they could not understand each other.

_____[simple]_____ 7. Zamenhof took words from many other languages and put them together.

_____[complex]_____ 8. The rules of Esperanto were simple so that people could learn them easily.

_____[complex]_____ 9. The words are spelled as they are pronounced.

_____[simple]_____ 10. Zamenhof wanted his new language to benefit all of humanity.

_____[complex]_____ 11. Esperanto, whose name comes from the Latin word for *hope*, is still used.

_____[compound]_____ 12. Esperanto hasn't became a universal language, but it has many speakers.

_____[simple]_____ 13. People in 80 countries speak Esperanto.

_____[compound]_____ 14. There are more than 100,000 speakers of Esperanto, and, according to some people, there may be up to 2 million.

ABCĈDEF
GĜHĤIJĴK
LMNOPR
SŜTUŬVZ

B. Write three sentences, one simple, one compound, one complex, about each topic.

Social studies

simple sentence   1. **[Sentences will vary.]** _____

compound sentence 2. _____

complex sentence   3. _____

Science

simple sentence   4. **[Sentences will vary.]** _____

compound sentence 5. _____

complex sentence   6. _____

130. Reviewing Phrases, Clauses, and Sentences

A. On the line write whether each *italicized* prepositional phrase is adjectival or adverbial.

_____[adjectival]_____ 1. The age *of the Vikings* lasted for about three hundred years.

_____[adverbial]_____ 2. It began *in the eighth century* A.D.

_____[adverbial]_____ 3. The Vikings came *from the present-day Scandinavian countries.*

_____[adverbial]_____ 4. They traveled *in long boats.*

_____[adjectival]_____ 5. They conquered many places *in Europe.*

B. Underline the simple subject once and simple predicate twice in each sentence. On the line write **N** if the sentence is in natural order or **I** if it is in inverted order.

___[N]___ 1. Viking <u>society</u> <u><u>had</u></u> a number of classes.

___[N]___ 2. <u>Wealth</u> and <u>land ownership</u> <u><u>determined</u></u> one's class.

___[N]___ 3. A <u>king</u> <u><u>ruled</u></u> and <u><u>had</u></u> much power over his community.

___[I]___ 4. Below him <u><u>ranked</u></u> rich <u>noblemen</u> and <u>freemen</u>.

___[I]___ 5. At the bottom of the social ladder <u><u>were</u></u> <u>slaves</u>.

C. Underline the adjectival clause in each sentence and circle the word to which it refers.

1. The Vikings are most famous as fierce (warriors) <u>who raided many parts of Europe.</u>

2. The Vikings were at first (farmers) <u>who produced their own goods.</u>

3. Rapid population (growth,) <u>which caused overcrowding,</u> led them to turn to the sea.

4. Some (boats) <u>that the Vikings built</u> can be seen in museums.

5. They built fast, maneuverable (ships,) <u>which were known as long boats.</u>

D. Underline the adverbial clause in each sentence and circle the word to which it refers.

1. <u>After the Vikings developed wonderful boats,</u> they (became) great sea traders.

2. The wood hull of Viking ships (was painted) colorfully <u>while the ship's square sails were woven with strips of bright colors.</u>

3. <u>Because the Vikings had such advanced boats,</u> they (could cross) the Atlantic.

4. <u>Although they were the first Europeans in the Americas,</u> they (did) not (establish) a permanent settlement.

5. The Viking raids on Europe (ended) <u>as feudal kingdoms arose and gained strength.</u>

E. For any compound sentences underline the independent clauses.

1. <u>Aluminum is an abundant metal in the earth's crust,</u> but <u>it always occurs in compounds.</u>

2. <u>The lead in a pencil is not lead;</u> <u>it is really graphite.</u>

3. Aquamarines and emeralds are gemstones from beryllium.

4. <u>The ruby is the rarest of gems,</u> and <u>it has a blood-red color.</u>

5. The diamond is the hardest and most lustrous of all gems.

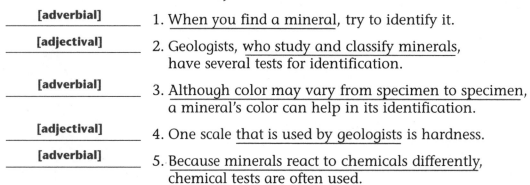

F. Underline the dependent clause in each sentence.
On the line write whether it is adjectival or adverbial.

__[adverbial]__ 1. <u>When you find a mineral,</u> try to identify it.

__[adjectival]__ 2. Geologists, <u>who study and classify minerals,</u> have several tests for identification.

__[adverbial]__ 3. <u>Although color may vary from specimen to specimen,</u> a mineral's color can help in its identification.

__[adjectival]__ 4. One scale <u>that is used by geologists</u> is hardness.

__[adverbial]__ 5. <u>Because minerals react to chemicals differently,</u> chemical tests are often used.

G. Write on the line whether each sentence is simple, compound, or complex.

__[complex]__ 1. Magnetite, which contains iron and oxygen, is naturally magnetic.

__[compound]__ 2. Sulfur has a characteristic color, and jade has a bell-like ring.

__[simple]__ 3. Halite and borax have distinct tastes.

__[complex]__ 4. Minerals that contain calcite fizz in certain acids.

__[simple]__ 5. Certain minerals such as pyrite and arsenopyrite actually smell.

Try It Yourself

On a separate sheet of paper, write a paragraph about a group of people in history. Be sure to use compound and complex sentences. Use the appropriate punctuation for those sentences.

Check Your Own Work

Choose a piece of writing from your portfolio or journal, a work in progress, an assignment from another class, or a letter. Revise it, applying the skills you have reviewed. The checklist will help you.

✔ Have you used a variety of simple, compound, and complex sentences?

✔ Do all your sentences have a complete subject and predicate?

✔ Have you used appropriate punctuation in compound sentences and in complex sentences?

Name _____

131. Using Periods

> Use a period at the end of a declarative sentence and most imperative sentences.
> **The new office building is a skyscraper.**
> Use a period after an abbreviation and after initials in a name.
> **Mr. Jacob Meriwether, Jr.   H. G. Wells**

Insert periods where needed.

1. Have you been to the new H.M.Stellar Building yet?

2. Come with me and see what it is like.

3. The address of the building is 1300 E.Bristol Ave.

4. The building is next to the U.S.post office at
   Third St.and Bristol.

5. I received an invitation to the grand opening.

6. It read "Grand Opening Jan.31 and Feb.1."

7. "Opening reception: Jan.30 at 5:00 P.M."

8. "Please R.S.V.P.by Dec.31."

9. It was signed, "Gov.S.John Rill."

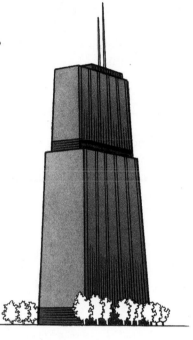

10. I telephoned Ms.Charlene Jones with my acceptance on Dec.30.

11. I went with my neighbor, Mrs.Clement, who also received an invitation.

12. There we met Mr.Roy Smith, Jr., another member of the Urban Renewal Committee.

13. Our local news reporter, C.J.Hoff, was at the reception.

14. I saw a note that said "100 lbs of shrimp, 10 bottles of cocktail sauce."

15. There is a statue of J.P.Morgan, the banker, in the lobby.

16. The cornerstone read "Designed A.D. 2001."

17. My dentist, Dr.Hiromi Tanaka, will have her office on the 35th floor.

18. I saw the line in the building directory that read "Hiromi Tanaka, D.D.S."

19. I also saw a sign for my family lawyer, Michael Morales, L.L.D.

20. My friend's company is called TechoFuture Corp.and will be in the building too.

132. Using Commas—Part 1

Commas are used
1. to separate items in a series   *volcanoes, earthquakes, and tornadoes*
2. to set off parts of dates, addresses, and
   geographical names   *in Naples, Italy, on May 11, 2003*
3. to separate words in direct address   *Keith, do you have a question?*
4. after *yes* or *no* when it begins a sentence   *No, I don't.*

Insert commas where needed. Use the numbers above to identify the use of each comma.

___[1]___ 1. Volcanoes are vents in the earth through which gases, lava,and ash pour out.

___[1]___ 2. Volcanoes are described as active,dormant,or extinct.

___[2]___ 3. Lassen Peak Volcano in California was thought to be dormant until it exploded on May 19,1915.

___[3, 2]___ 4. Joe,you can get information about Lassen Peak Volcano by writing to Lassen Volcanic Park,P.O. Box 100,Mineral,CA 96063.

___[2]___ 5. A famous eruption was of Mount Vesuvius near Naples,Italy, in A.D. 79.

___[1]___ 6. The eruption buried the town of Pompeii with a flow of cinder,ashes,and mud.

___[1]___ 7. The eruption froze in time the city's temples,amphitheaters,and houses.

___[4]___ 8. Yes,much of the excavated town of Pompeii can be visited by tourists.

___[4]___ 9. No,Vesuvius is not an extinct volcano.

___[2]___ 10. It began its last major eruption on March 18,1944.

___[1]___ 11. There are four types of volcanoes: cinder,shield,composite,and lava dome.

___[1]___ 12. Kilauea,Hualalai,and Muana Loa in Hawaii are three shield volcanoes that were formed from lava flows.

___[1]___ 13. Composite volcanoes like Mount Vesuvius,Mount Saint Helens,and Mount Fuji were formed from eruptions of lava and cinders.

___[4, 3]___ 14. Yes,Henry,cinder volcanoes form when rocks shoot out of volcanoes and fall back to earth in small pieces.

___[2]___ 15. A more recent explosive eruption occurred at Mount Saint Helens, Washington,on May 18,1980.

Name _____

133. Using Commas—Part 2

Commas are used
1. to set off an appositive that is not part of a name
   Joan of Arc, the French national hero, died in 1431.
2. to set off a parenthetical expression
   Joan is, I believe, a patron saint of France.
3. to set off an introductory phrase or clause
   When Joan told about her mission, many people followed her.

Insert commas where needed. Use the numbers above to identify the use of each comma.

_____[1]_____ 1. Joan of Arc, the Maid of Orleans, lived in the 15th century.

_____[3]_____ 2. Although she was a simple peasant girl, she helped lead the French to victory in a war.

_____[2]_____ 3. She is, as you may know, a saint of the Catholic religion.

_____[3]_____ 4. When Joan was 13 years old, she claimed she heard voices.

_____[1]_____ 5. These voices told her to assist the dauphin, the heir to the French throne.

_____[1]_____ 6. Joan wore armor and carried a banner with the fleur-de-lis, the French royal emblem.

_____[1]_____ 7. Orleans, a town near Paris, was important to the French cause.

_____[1]_____ 8. She helped the dauphin, later King Charles VII, defend Orleans from the English.

_____[3]_____ 9. When the dauphin was crowned king, Joan was given a place of honor near him.

_____[3]_____ 10. While she was fighting north of Paris, Joan was captured and sold to the English.

_____[1]_____ 11. The English turned her over to a church court that tried her for heresy, a belief that is false.

_____[2]_____ 12. The charges, many think, were made up to get rid of an enemy.

_____[3]_____ 13. After Joan was burned at the stake, her spirit continued to inspire many people.

_____[2]_____ 14. Many, I believe, see Joan as someone committed to a cause.

_____[3]_____ 15. Although many details of Joan's story are unclear, she remains an important figure in French history as a brave fighter for the nation.

Joan of Arc was a source of inspiration to many people because of her courage. Give an example of a person who inspires you. Why does she or he inspire you?

134. Using Commas—Part 3

> Commas are used
> 1. to separate the clauses of a compound sentence connected by *and, or, but, nor,* or *yet*
>   **People have built tunnels throughout history, and they continue to build them.**
> 2. to separate a nonrestrictive clause from the rest of the sentence
>   **The Mont Blanc tunnel, which goes through the Alps, connects France and Italy.**

Insert commas where needed. Use the numbers above to identify the use of each comma.

[2] 1. Tunnels, which are underground passageways, are built under mountains and water.

[1] 2. Tunnels have existed throughout history, and they have had different uses.

[1] 3. Tunnels of the past were often built as burial places, but now they are often used to carry vehicles.

[2] 4. The Pyramids, which were used as tombs, had secret tunnels to burial chambers.

[2] 5. Many tunnels were built by the ancient Romans, who used them to carry water to the city.

[2] 6. Such a tunnel is called an aqueduct, which comes from the Latin words for *water* and *carry*.

[1] 7. Medieval castles were designed to keep invaders out, yet some had secret tunnels for escapes during a siege.

[1] 8. Tunnels today crisscross below large cities, and they are used for transportation and basic services.

[2] 9. Today's most famous tunnel is the Channel Tunnel, which connects England and France.

[2] 10. The tunnel, which is considered a wonder of the modern world, actually consists of three tubes.

[1] 11. Two of the tubes are used for high-speed trains, and the third is used for services and security.

[1] 12. Passengers can ride on the train, or they can stay in their own vehicles on special rail cars.

[2] 13. The tunnel, which has Chunnel as its nickname, is 31 miles long.

[2] 14. The Galera Tunnel, which is in the Andes Mountains of Peru, is the highest tunnel.

[1] 15. The tunnel is about three miles above sea level, and its trains are equipped with oxygen for passengers' breathing.

135. Reviewing Commas

A. Insert commas where needed.

1. Gary Soto,the writer and poet,was born on April 12,1952.

2. He grew up in a Spanish-speaking neighborhood in Fresno,California.

3. Gary's grandparents had come from Mexico,so his family was Mexican American.

4. When Gary was young,his father was killed in a factory accident.

5. His mother had to raise her three children on her own,but she did have the help of Gary's grandparents.

6. When he was growing up,Gary became fascinated with poetry.

7. Gary eventually went to college,and he earned a degree in literature.

8. After Gary finished college,he became a professor at a university in Berkeley,California.

9. He began to publish poetry,and soon his works gained recognition.

10. Gary has written award-winning poetry,novels,short stories, and essays for both young people and adults.

11. He often writes about the ordinary lives of children and teens: playing sports,running through a lawn sprinkler,or a first date.

12. *The Pool Party*,which is one of Soto's novels,is about a teen who brings a huge inner tube to a pool party.

13. Because he describes his experiences while growing up so well,he brings to others the sights and sounds of the barrio.

14. Have you read any works by Gary Soto,Michael?

15. Yes,I've read *Living up the Street*,*The Pool Party*,and *Neighborhood Odes*.

B. There is one comma error in each sentence. Cross out unnecessary commas or add commas were needed.

1. *Taking Sides*,one of Gary Soto's novels, has Lincoln Mendoza as its main character.

2. Lincoln's family, which is Mexican American, moves from the barrio of San Francisco to Sycamore,California.

3. Lincoln, who is in a new school, has to decide whether to show or hide his heritage.

4. Because he is uncertain of his place,he has conflicts with his basketball coach and teammates.

5. *Pacific Crossing*, which is another of Gary's novels,continues Lincoln's story.

136. Using Semicolons and Colons

> A semicolon is used
> - to separate the clauses of a compound sentence that are not joined by a conjunction or that are joined by a conjunctive adverb (for example, *however, therefore, moreover, nevertheless*)
> - before *as* and *namely* when they are used to introduce examples
>
> A colon is used
> - before a list or a long direct quotation
> - after the salutation of a business letter

Insert semicolons and colons were needed.

1. Dear Mr. President:

2. President Theodore Roosevelt enjoyed many sports: walking, wrestling, judo, and polo.

3. President Ulysses S. Grant was given a ticket for speeding in a carriage; therefore, he had to pay a twenty-dollar fine.

4. What presidents' pictures are on these coins: the nickel, the dime, and the quarter?

5. The tallest president was Abraham Lincoln; the shortest president was James Madison.

6. President Andrew Jackson loved horses; consequently, he kept a stable of thoroughbreds on the White House grounds.

7. Two men were bachelors when they were elected president; namely, James Buchanan and Grover Cleveland.

8. Dear President Bush:

9. President Lincoln began the Gettysburg address with these words: "Four score and seven years ago our fathers brought forth on this continent a new nation, conceived in Liberty, and dedicated to the proposition that all men are created equal."

10. The oldest person elected president was Ronald Reagan; the youngest person was John F. Kennedy.

11. Two sets of father and son have been elected president; namely, John Adams and John Quincy Adams, and George H. Bush and George W. Bush.

12. The Twenty-Second Amendment limits presidents to two terms in office; therefore, Franklin D. Roosevelt is likely to remain the president who held office the longest.

13. James Earl Carter, Jr., was his full name; however, he was always called Jimmy.

14. Thomas Jefferson wrote the words that constitute the basis for our nation: "We hold these truths to be self-evident, . . . among these are life, liberty, and the pursuit of happiness."

15. William Henry Harrison died of pneumonia after only a month in office; he was the first president to have died in office.

Name _____

137. Using Quotation Marks and Underlining

Quotation marks are used before and after direct quotations and around every part of divided quotations. For quotations within a quotation, use single quotation marks.

"I am looking for information on the constellations," Rob told the librarian.

Quotation marks set off the titles of stories, poems, songs, magazine and newspaper articles, television shows, and radio programs.

The librarian replied, "The magazine article titled 'Seeing Stars' is a good resource."

Titles of books, magazines, newspapers, movies, and works of art are usually printed in italics. When these titles are handwritten, they are underlined.

My Dad reads the <u>New York Times</u> on his way to work.

Insert quotation marks, punctuation marks, and underlining where needed.

1. Josh said, "I need to find information on mummies for my report."

2. "I have some research to do on astronomy," replied Rob, "and I want to get some information on snowboarding."

3. "So let's go to the library together," answered Josh.

4. Josh found a book on mummies titled <u>Mummies in Ancient Egypt</u>.

5. Rob found an article on snowboarding in a magazine called <u>Sports Illustrated for Kids</u>.

6. He also found an article titled "Extreme Sports" in the magazine <u>Sports Today</u>.

7. Josh noticed that there was a TV show titled "Ancient Mummies" available on video.

8. "May I take out videos?" Josh asked the librarian.

9. "Yes, you may," the librarian answered, "but some videos cost a dollar."

10. Josh noticed a novel called <u>The Egypt Game</u>.

11. "The novel is about two children who get involved in an exciting game," said a librarian.

12. "Where can I check out books?" asked Rob.

13. Rob took out a book of short stories by Gary Soto with a story called "Baseball in April."

14. "Let's watch the baseball game on TV," suggested Rob.

15. Josh answered, "I have to finish my report on Alfred Noyes's poem 'The Highwayman' for English."

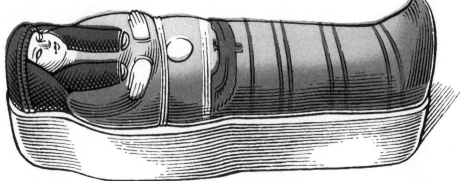

138. Using Apostrophes, Hyphens, and Dashes

An apostrophe is used
- to show possession or a relationship: *my mother's story*
- to show the omission of a letter(s) or numbers: *I'm not in the class of '03.*
- with an *s* to form the plural of a letter: *There are two s's in my name.*

A hyphen is used
- in compound numbers from twenty-one to ninety-nine
- to separate the parts of some compound words: *sister-in-law, forget-me-not*
- to divide words at the end of lines when you are writing

A dash is used to indicate a change in thought.

Blizzards—thankfully they don't happen that often—can cause many problems.

Insert apostrophes, hyphens, and dashes where needed.

1. Do you remember the blizzard of '79?

2. I don't remember it.

3. I suppose that's not surprising since I wasn't born yet.

4. My parents met at least they tell me this at a dance in 1984.

5. I hear my parent's recollections of that blizzard sometimes.

6. Apparently twenty-six inches of snow fell in less than twenty-four hours.

7. After the storm almost everyone's electricity was off.

8. It was really cold cold enough to see your breath inside before the heat returned.

9. My mother's story about the blizzard was in a journal in my grandmother's attic.

10. My grandmother looked for it, because she wanted to read it to her son-in-law.

11. The dust-covered folder with the story had Mom's maiden name on it.

12. There were twenty-nine handwritten pages!

13. It's going to be boring, I thought.

14. I couldn't put the story down; the problems can you imagine no electricity for two days? were so real and were described so well.

15. "Mom, it's a great story," I said.

16. Well, last week's blizzard was bad.

17. My parents' suggestion was that I write about it so that I don't forget.

18. It's an idea that seems OK to me.

19. I'll be able to use it for my personal writing assignment in Mr. Wright's class.

20. How many *z*'s are in *blizzard*?

139. Working with Punctuation

Insert punctuation where needed in each sentence.

1. There was a thick envelope in the mail for me, and my name was written on it in large letters.

2. "Come to a holiday party," read the invitation.

3. It will be on Dec. 14 at 4 P.M., it continued.

4. The address on the invitation was 145 Castle Lane, Knightsville, New Jersey.

5. The signature was Mr. Thomas Smith.

6. Mr. Smith, who is my mother's second cousin, was going to have a holiday party for children in the family.

7. "May I go, Mom?" I asked.

8. She replied, "Yes, you may go, but you must be on your best behavior."

9. What does R.S.V.P. on the envelope mean?

10. When I arrived at Mr. Smith's house, there were a lot of children.

11. I soon met some nice kids my age; namely, Peter, Edna, and Wanda.

12. We had cookies, cake, juice, and soda.

13. After we had some refreshments, Mr. and Mrs. Smith announced a treasure hunt.

14. I was excited; I had never been on a treasure hunt before.

15. Each of us got a piece of paper; there was a clue on the paper.

16. After we read our clues, Peter, Edna, Wanda, and I decided to search in different places.

17. I was told to look under the source of knowledge; therefore, I thought I'd look in the library for the treasure.

18. There was a piece of paper under the <u>Dictionary of American Biography</u>.

19. Because I found the paper, I was the winner of a prize.

20. My prize, which was a CD with holiday songs, was great!

Name _____

140. Using Capital Letters Correctly

Use a capital letter for the following:
1. the first word in a sentence, a direct quotation, and most lines of poetry
2. proper nouns and adjectives and the pronoun *I*
3. a title when it precedes a person's name
4. *north, south, east,* and *west* when they refer to sections of the country
5. names of deities and sacred books
6. words in titles except for articles, prepositions, and coordinate conjunctions (when they aren't the first or last word)
7. abbreviations of words that would normally be capitalized

A. Use the proofreading symbol (≡) to show which letters should be capitalized. Use the numbers above to identify the use of each capital letter.

[1, 2, 4]   1. in social studies class we're studying about the american west.

[1, 4]   2. hoping to find gold, many easterners settled in the west.

[1, 2]   3. during the gold rush to california in 1849, people came from europe, china, and mexico.

[1, 2]   4. a railroad across north america was completed in 1869.

[1, 2]   5. on may 10, 1869, the union pacific railway and the central pacific railroad linked up in utah.

[1, 2]   6. there was a big rush to alaska in the 1890s.

[1, 2, 7]   7. gold was found by george w. carmack near the klondike river.

[1, 2]   8. the find was near the border between alaska and canada.

[1, 2, 6]   9. this event is described in donna walsh shepherd's book *the klondike gold rush.*

[1]   10. the author writes, "people from over fifty countries came with dreams of gold but with little knowledge about the difficulties."

B. Write each phrase, using capital letters where necessary.

1. the grand canyon   [the Grand Canyon]

2. jack london's the call of the wild   [Jack London's The Call of the Wild]

3. the battles of gen. ulysses s. grant   [the battles of Gen. Ulysses S. Grant]

4. robert service's spell of the yukon   [Robert Service's Spell of the Yukon]

5. the short story "to build a fire"   [the short story "To Build a Fire"]

141. Reviewing Punctuation and Capitalization

A. Insert commas and periods where needed.

1. We traveled through three states: Pennsylvania, Delaware, and Maryland.

2. After we went through those states, we visited Washington, D.C.

3. We stopped at Gettysburg, Pennsylvania.

4. Gettysburg, which is in the southern part of the state, was the site of a great Civil War battle.

5. Gen. Meade, I believe, defeated Gen. Robert E. Lee in the battle.

6. Abraham Lincoln, the president during the Civil War, delivered a speech there.

7. Yes, it is called the Gettysburg Address.

8. Lincoln talked about the meaning of the war, and he made one of his greatest speeches there.

9. Pres. Abraham Lincoln said, "The world will little note, nor long remember what we say here, but it will never forget what they did here."

10. Although Lincoln said this years ago, we still remember his words today.

B. Insert colons, semicolons, and quotation marks where needed.

1. In Washington we went inside these sites: the Capitol Building, the White House, and the Lincoln Memorial.

2. "It's really gigantic," I said, when I saw Lincoln's statue.

3. We also visited the Smithsonian Institution; it has many different museums.

4. In the National History Museum we saw many things: dinosaurs, diamonds, insects' nests, and a copper mine.

5. In the Air and Space Museum I asked, "What's that odd-looking thing?"

6. "It's an early rocket ship," a guide answered.

7. On the trip I took photos with a digital camera; Dad used a video camera.

8. In her guidebook to Washington, Lori Perkins writes the following: "Washington, D.C., is so much more than just a living history lesson. It is also one of the top art centers of the country and world, with as many museums as New York City and fascinating architecture."

9. One of the most moving sites was the Vietnam Memorial; it is a wall with the names of dead soldiers.

10. I said, "Let's come back next year."

CONTINUED

Punctuation & Capitalization

Name _____

C. Insert apostrophes, hyphens, and dashes where needed.

1. There were fifty-five people at my Dad's family reunion.

2. Some of them—can you imagine?—hadn't seen one another in years.

3. The last reunion was in '99.

4. My Dad's sister-in-law was one of the few people who couldn't make it.

5. We spell our name Welles, with two e's.

D. Circle the correct example of capitalization in each row.

1. (the Guggenheim Museum)   Fifth avenue   St. Patrick's cathedral
2. House Of Representatives   (the *Washington Post*)   the Potomac river
3. (the Civil War)   general Sherman   Appomattox courthouse
4. (*To Kill a Mockingbird*)   Elizabeth g. Speare   the american colonies
5. the renaissance   pope Leo X   (St. Peter's Square)
6. king Richard   the middle ages   (*The Tales of Robin Hood*)
7. (Microsoft Company)   Redmond, washington   the pacific northwest
8. thursday   french club   (Lincoln High School)
9. Labor day   Summer   (Silver Lake)
10. *Sports illustrated*   (the World Series)   Fenway park
11. (the Alamo)   Austin, texas   the Rio grande

Try It Yourself
On a separate piece of paper, write a paragraph about a trip you've taken. Be sure to use punctuation and capitalization correctly.

Check Your Own Work
Choose a piece of writing from your portfolio or journal, a work in progress, an assignment from another class, or a letter. Revise it, applying the skills you have reviewed. The checklist will help you.

✔ Do your sentences end with the correct punctuation marks?

✔ Have you inserted commas where needed and not used them where they aren't needed?

✔ Have you used quotation marks around direct quotations?

✔ Have you used commas and semicolons correctly in compound sentences?

✔ Have you used apostrophes where needed?

✔ Have you capitalized all proper nouns and adjectives?

✔ Have you used correct capitalization and punctuation (quotation marks or underlining) for titles of works?

Punctuation & Capitalization

152

142. Using Information from the Internet

Just as you have to give information about a book or newspaper source that you use for a report, you have to cite the source for any information that you get on the Internet. These sources could be Web sites or online databases.

If you use information from an online database such as the *Encyclopædia Britannica* or the Web site of an educational institution, a business, or a department of the government, you must cite the following information:

- author's name, last name first
- title of the document or article
- title of the complete publication if the article is from a larger work such as a magazine or book
- date of publication of the larger work if it was a printed publication
- name of the online source you used (this is whatever search engine you used, if you used one)
- document date

The document date could be the day, month, and year when it was posted or the date when you downloaded the document. Sometimes there is no date for the posting of a particular piece on a Web site. The only date may be the date on which the site was last changed. Whether you use the posting/update date or the date you accessed the information will depend on what you can find on the site.

While you do not have to include the Web address in your bibliography, it is useful to have in case you want to go back to the site or if your teacher wants to check your data. Be sure to include the complete Web address in your notes.

A complete citation would look like this:

> Jones, Lia. "The San Andreas Fault Heaves a Sigh and Los Angeles Trembles." *The New York Times*. April 4, 1999. Online. November 22, 2000.

If you used an online search engine to find the same information, the citation would look like this:

> Jones, Lia. "The San Andreas Fault Heaves a Sigh and Los Angeles Trembles." *The New York Times*. April 4, 1999. Online. Yahoo. November 22, 2000.

Suppose you visit the National Park Service site for Valley Forge. No author is cited, and the only date is the last time the site was updated. Your citation would look like this:

> "Washington at Valley Forge." Valley Forge National Historical Park. Online. March 12, 2001.

Put the following information into the proper form for citations from the Internet.

1. An article entitled "Japanese Art Wows Museum-Goers" from the *Dallas Morning News* written by Esperanza Martinez. It was published originally in the newspaper on March 1, 2001, and went up on the paper's Web site the same day. You downloaded it on May 2, 2001.

   [Martinez, Esperanza. "Japanese Art Wows Museum-Goers." Dallas Morning News. March 1, 2001. Online. May 2, 2001.]

2. Two pages from the Web site of Standard Electric Utility, a utility company, about the ways it is protecting the environment by cooling the water it discharges into the river. The article has no title, and no author is given. The last time the site was changed was January 2, 2001. You found it by using the search engine Google on January 16, 2001.

   [Untitled article about its environmental protection efforts. Standard Electric Utility Company Home Page. January 2, 2001. Online. Google. January 16, 2001.]

3. "Geological Fault Lines in Funding Research," an article signed by Drs. C. Elizabeth Patterson and L. Mott that appeared on the National Academy of Sciences Web site. The article is dated March 2000, and you downloaded it on December 8, 2000.

   [Patterson, Dr. C. Elizabeth, and Dr. L. Mott. "Geological Fault Lines in Funding Research." National Academy of Sciences. March 2000. Online. December 8, 2000.]

4. An unsigned article entitled "The Economic Causes of World War I," which you found in the online *Encyclopædia Britannica.* You used the search engine AltaVista to find it and downloaded it on February 25, 2001.

   ["The Economic Causes of World War I." Encyclopædia Britannica. Online. AltaVista. February 25, 2001.]

143. Using Books of Quotations

Can you imagine an entire book of quotations by people from ancient times to the present? The use of quotations can be helpful in setting a mood, emphasizing a point, or just adding interest to what you are writing. There are several books of quotations, but the most familiar is probably *Bartlett's Familiar Quotations*. You can find this online at http://www.columbia.edu/acis/bartleby/bartlett/

Books of quotations are generally organized in the same way, and you can find what you want in several ways.

- If you want to find a particular quotation or a quotation about a certain subject, choose one or more keywords and look them up in the Index. The Index is arranged in alphabetical order by the first word of the quotation.

  For example, you want to find a quotation that refers to candles or candlelight, so you look under the keyword *candle*. There you will find page references to 20 or more quotations. Now you have to read and decide which quotation fits your need.

- If you want to find something that a notable person such as Abraham Lincoln said, you look in the alphabetical Index of Authors under the person's last name. There you will be given the pages on which his quotations appear. Depending on the book, you may find just a single index; the author index is incorporated into the index of quotations.

  Authors appear in the book chronologically in birth-date order. Their quotations also are arranged chronologically within the person's entry. All of Abraham Lincoln's quotes will be in that part of the book. When known, information following a quotation tells the origin of the quotation (date, place, etc.).

Name _____

Use a copy of *Bartlett's Familiar Quotations* or another book of quotations to locate quotations about the following subjects or by the following people.

In each case, copy one quotation that you particularly like. State the subject area for which you might use the quotation if you are writing a report. Be sure to include the name of the person who said or wrote it.

1. mountains _____ **[Answers will vary. Quotations should include the author or speaker and in** _____

which subject area a student might consider using the quotation in a report.] _____

_____

_____

2. rocks _____

_____

_____

_____

3. Napoleon _____

_____

_____

_____

4. Shakespeare _____

_____

_____

_____

5. music _____

_____

_____

_____

CONTINUED

6. nature _____

_____

_____

_____

7. Mark Twain _____

_____

_____

_____

8. Thomas Jefferson _____

_____

_____

_____

9. culture _____

_____

_____

_____

10. books _____

_____

_____

_____

144. Identifying Books in Print

There are several ways to find out if a book you might need for your research is still being published even if it is not in your library. You can use reference works such as *Children's Books in Print, Books in Print,* or *Subject Guide to Books in Print* to see if a publisher still prints the book. Updated each year, these references come in book form and online on computers in some libraries.

Children's Books in Print is an author, title, and illustrator index to books for young adults and children. It is organized in two sections—one is arranged alphabetically by the author's last name and the other is arranged alphabetically by the illustrator's last name.

If you are looking for a book by a particular author, you simply look under the author's name. For example, you want to check the exact title of a book by Charles Dickens. You look for *Dickens, Charles,* and then note the titles listed below his name. There may be more than one version or edition listed for some titles. If a book is not listed, it usually means the book is no longer being printed.

The information given about a book title is shown below:

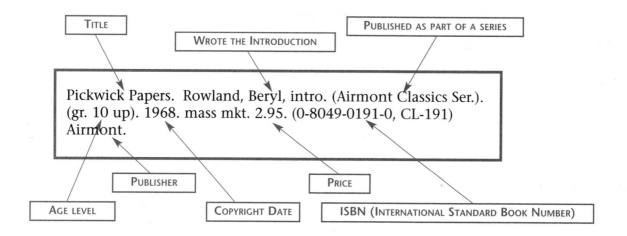

You can also use a books-in-print entry to check the information needed for a bibliography.

Use the *Children's Books in Print* sample on page 160 to answer these questions.

1. For what age group is *Bleak House* appropriate?

   [grades 9 and up] _____

2. What is the copyright date of the *Dombey & Sons* listed here?

   [1990] _____

3. How many pages long is Dial Bks Young's edition of *Oliver Twist?*

   [144 pages] _____

4. What is the cost of *Pickwick Papers* published by NAL-Dutton?

   [$5.95] _____

5. Is the Dutton version listed as a hardbound book or a paperback book?

   [paperback] _____

6. How many different book versions of *A Christmas Carol* are listed as being in print?

   [28] _____

7. *The Bagman's Story* is a part of what series?

   [Creative's Classic Short Stories Series] _____

8. What is the ISBN number for *Nicholas Nickleby?*

   [0-553-21265-6] _____

9. Who wrote the introduction for the edition of *Nicholas Nickleby* listed?

   [Edgar Johnson] _____

10. Who illustrated the version of *The Baron of Grogzwig* published by Whispering Coyote Press?

    [Barnes-Murphy, Rowan] _____

11. Who are the publishers of the two listings for *Great Expectations?*

    [Cambridge University Press and Puffin Books] _____

12. Which version of *Great Expectations* is less expensive?

    [The abbreviated version published by Puffin Books] _____

13. Who wrote the introduction for *Mystery of Edwin Drood?*

    [N. F. Budgey] _____

14. Who illustrated the version of *A Tale of Two Cities* published by Raintree Steck-V?

    [Charles Shaw] _____

15. Why are two versions listed for *A Tale of Two Cities* published by Bantam?

    [One version is a teacher edition.] _____

Research Skills

Dickens, Charles. The Bagman's Story. (Creative Classic Short Stories Ser.) 48p. (gr. 4 up). 1983. lib. bdg. 13.95 (0-87191-922-2) Creative Ed.

— The Baron of Grogzwig. Greenway, Shirley, ed. Barnes-Murphy, Rowan, illus. LC 93-18627. 32p. 1993. 14.95 (1-879085-81-X) Whsprng Coyote Pr.

— Bleak House. Zabel, Morton D., ed. LC 84-25543. (gr. 9 up). 1956. pap. 11.16 (0-395-05104-5, RivEd) HM.

— Charles Dickens' A Christmas Carol. Richardson, I. M., ed. Kendall, Jane F., illus. LC 87-11270. 32p. (gr. 2-6). 1988. lib. bdg. 10.50 (0-8167-1053-8); pap. 2.50 (0-8167-1054-6) Troll Communs.

— Christmas Books. Glancy, Ruth, intro. (World's Classics Ser.). 520p. 1989. pap. 7.95 (0-19-281790-6) OUP.

— A Christmas Carol. Benson, Patrick, illus. French, Vivian, abr. LC 93-54577. 48p. (ps up). 1993. 15.95 (1-56402-204-8) Candlewick Pr.

— Christmas Carol. 1992. pap. 10.95 (0-395-60726-4) HM.

— Christmas Carol. Date not set. pap. 2.95 (0-8167-2883-6) Troll Communs.

— A Christmas Carol. Imsand, Marcel, illus. LC 85-15815. (Creative's Christmas Stories Ser.). 78p. (gr. 4. up). 1984. lib. bdg. 13.95 (0-87191-955-9) Creative Ed.

— A Christmas Carol. Innocenti, Roberto, illus. (Creative Editions Ser.). 152p. (gr. 1-12). 1990. 35.00 (0-88682-327-7, 97200-098) Creative Ed.

— A Christmas Carol. Staton, Joe, adapted by. (Classics Illustrated Ser.). (Illus.). 52p. 1990. pap. 4.95 (1-57209-016-2) First Classics.

— A Christmas Carol. Heyer, Carol, illus. Kennedy, Pamela, retold by. L 95-9990. 32p. 1995. 14.95 (1-57102-047-0, Ideals Child) Hambleton-Hill.

— A Christmas Carol. Jones, Kristy, illus. Montgomery, Tama M., retold by. 24p. (gr. k-4). 1996. 5.95 (1-57102-097-7, Ideals Child); pap. 2.49 (1-57102-074-8, Ideals Child) Hambleton-Hill.

— A Christmas Carol. Hyman, Trina S., illus. LC 85-15815. 128p. (gr. 4-6). 1983. 18.95 (0-8234-0486-2) Holiday.

— A Christmas Carol. Rice, James, illus. Rice, James, retold by. 48p. 14.95 (0-88289-812-4) Pelican.

— A Christmas Carol. Fagan, Tom, ed. LoFamia, Jun, illus. (Now Age Illustrated IV Ser.). (gr. 4-12). 1978. student ed 1.25 (0-88301-337-1) Pendulum Pr.

— A Christmas Carol. Holder, John, illus. Collins, Joan, as told by. (Classics Ser.). 52p. 1994. 3.50 (0-7214-1729-9), Ladybrd) Penguin.

— A Christmas Carol. LC 85-15815. 240p. 1983. mass mkt. 3.99 (0-671-47369-7, WSP) PB.

— A Christmas Carol. 128p. (gr. 4-7). 1987. pap. 3.50 (0-590-43527-2) Scholastic Inc.

— A Christmas Carol. Zwerger, Lisbeth, illus. LC 88-15161. 60p. (gr. 5 up). 1991. pap. 19.95 (0-88708-069-3, Picture Book Studio) S&S Childrens.

— A Christmas Carol. 1990. pap. 2.50 (0-8125-0434-8) Tor Bks.

— A Christmas Carol. 1995. pap. 16.95 (0-14-086178-5) Viking Penguin.

— A Christmas Carol. Goodrich, Carter, illus. Glassman, Peter, afterword by. (Books of Wonder). 64p. 1996. 18.00 (0-688-13606-0, Morrow Junior) Morrow.

— A Christmas Carol. Blake, Quentin, illus. LC 94-48346. 144p. 1995. 19.95 (0-689-80213-7, McElderry) S&S Childrens.

— A Christmas Carol. (Puffin Classics Ser.). (gr. 5 up). 1995. pap. 3.99 (0-14-036723-3) Puffin Bks.

— A Christmas Carol. Innocenti, Roberto, illus. 152p. 1995. 19.95 (0-15-100200-2, Red Wagon Bks) HarBrace.

— A Christmas Carol. 2.99p. (gr. 2-4). 1996. pap. 2.99 (0-7214-5677-4, Ladybrd) Penguin.

— A Christmas Carol. Colombo, Ruth, intro. (gr. 7 up). 1963. mass mkt. 2.95 (0-8049-0026-4, CL-26) Airmont.

— A Christmas Carol. LC 85-15815. 191p. 1981. reprint ed. lib. bdg. 15.95 (0-89966-344-3) Buccaneer Bks.

— A Christmas Carol. Benson, Patrick, illus. French, Vivian, abr. LC 92-54577. 48p. (gr. 3-7). 1996. reprint ed. pap. 6.99 (1-56402-977-8) Candlewick Pr.

— A Christmas Carol. LC 85-15815. 150p. 1980. reprint ed. lib. bdg. 15.95 (0-89967-017-2) Harmony Raine.

— A Christmas Carol & Other Christmas Stories. Busch, Frederick, into. 224p. 1984. pap. 3.95 (0-451-52283-4, Sig Classics) NAL-Dutton.

— Dombey & Sons. (ps-8). 1990. reprint ed. lib. bdg. 29.95 (0-89966-678-7) Buccaneer Bks.

— Great Expectations. Seward, Tim, ed. (Literature Ser.). (Illus.). 512p. (gr. 9 up). 1996. pap. 6.95 (0-521-48472-3) Cambridge U Pr.

— Great Expectations. abr. ed. (Classics Ser.). 432p. (gr. 5 up). 1995. pap. 3.99 (0-14-036681-4) Puffin Bks.

— The Life of Our Lord. 128p. 1991. 15.99 (0-8407-9126-7) Nelson.

— Mystery of Edwin Drood. Budgey, N. F., intro. (Airmont Classics Ser.). (gr. 10 up). 1966. mass mkt. 1.50 (0-8049-0114-7, CL-114) Airmont.

— Nicholas Nickleby. Johnson, Edgar, intro. 816p. (gr.10-12). 1983. pap. 5.95 (0-553-21265-6, Bantam Classics) Bantam.

— Oliver Twist. Birmingham, Christian, illus. Morpurgo, Michael, intro. Baxter, Lesley, abr. 144p. (gr. 3 up). 1996. pap. 19.99 (0-8037-1995-7) Dial Bks Young.

— Pickwick Papers. Rowland, Beryl, intro. (Airmont Classics Ser.). (gr. 10 up). 1968. mass mkt. 2.95 (0-8049-0191-0, CL-191) Airmont.

— Pickwick Papers. 1964. pap. 5.95 (0-451-51756-3, CE1756, Sig Classics) NAL-Dutton.

— Senor Scrooge: Charles Dickens' A Christmas Carol adapted for the Bilingual Stage. Alderete, Betty, tr. McDonough, Jerome, adapted by. (Illus.). 32p. (Orig.). 1995. pap. 3.25 (0-88680-404-3, 404-3) I E Clark.

— Tale of Two Cities. Pitt, David G., intro. (Airmont Classics Ser.). (gr. 9 up). 1964. mass mkt. 4.95 (0-8049-0021-3, CL-21) Airmont.

— Tale of Two Cities. Hutchinson, Emily, adapted by. LC 95-77835. (Classroom Reading Plays Ser.). 32p. (gr. 6-12). 1995. pap. 2.40 (1-56103-107-0) Am Guidance.

— Tale of Two Cities. 384p. (gr. 7). 1960. pap. 3.95 (0-451-52441-1, Sig Classics) NAL-Dutton.

— Tale of Two Cities. 384p. 1989. pap. 2.50 (0-8125-0506-9) Tor Bks.

— A Tale of Two Cities. 368p. (gr. 9-12). 1989. pap. 3.95 (0-553-21176-5, Bantam Classics) Bantam.

— A Tale of Two Cities. 368p. (gr. 9-12). 1989. teacher ed write for info. (0-318-51005-7, Bantam Classics) Bantam.

— A Tale of Two Cities. Shaw, Charles, illus. Krapesh, Patti, adapted by. LC 79-24746. (Short Classics Ser.). (gr. 4 up). 1983. lib. bdg. 22.83 (0-8172-1658-8) Raintree Steck-V.

— A Tale of Two Cities. LC 95-77835. 384p. (gr. 5 up). 1996. pap. 3.99 (0-14-037336-5) Puffin Bks.

145. Using an Atlas

To find information about a particular country or a continent such as Africa, you can read books, use encyclopedias, view videos, and so on. However, some atlases will provide much of the information you need through maps and pictures, charts, and informative text blocks.

Physical maps show the general physical features of an area, such as mountains, plateaus, grasslands, deserts, rivers, and other bodies of water. Text blocks with these maps may provide facts about the highest and lowest elevations, longest river, total area in square miles, and other information.

Political maps show the borders and names of countries and sometimes the states or provinces within the countries. The larger cities are noted, and a special symbol is used to show the capital. Some physical features such as national parks, lakes, and rivers may be shown. Text blocks with these maps give information about such things as population and economy.

Atlases also have special purpose maps, or thematic maps, that show specific kinds of information for countries and continents. An atlas may have maps that show geographical features such as vegetation, natural resources, land use, climate, and population distribution. An atlas may also have maps that show cultural features such as languages spoken within a country, distribution of ethnic groups, and areas where certain religions predominate.

Informational text blocks in these large atlases list such information as the capital of a country, the size of its population, and the languages spoken there. They may also show the design of the country's flag. This information may be found in other resources such as an almanac, but an atlas pulls it together in one place and often in a more interesting way.

Name _____

Use an atlas to find answers to as many of these questions as you can about the continent of Africa.
[Area and population figures may vary depending on the atlas and the edition used.]

1. What is the total number of square miles in Africa?

   [About 11,700,000 square miles] _____

2. What is the total number of square miles in Nigeria?

   [About 356,668 square miles] _____

3. What is the estimated total population of Africa?

   [About 778,000,000 people] _____

4. What is the population of Botswana?

   [About 1,500,000 people] _____

5. What is the capital of Zimbabwe?

   [Harare] _____

6. What type of economic development or work is important in South Africa?

   [Mining of gold, diamonds, and coal; textiles; cotton] _____

   _____

7. What language is spoken in Angola?

   [Portuguese and African languages] _____

8. Describe the flag of Malawi.

   [The flag of Malawi has three horizontal stripes—black, red, and green—from top to bottom. The

   top half of a red sun surrounded by a halo of red appears in the black stripe.] _____

   _____

   _____

9. What African countries border Egypt?

   [Libya, Sudan] _____

10. Name at least two African countries that the Equator passes through.

   [Gabon, Congo, Zaïre, Uganda, Kenya, Somalia] _____

   _____

Sentence Diagrams

A diagram is a visual outline of a sentence. It shows the essential parts of the sentence *(subject, verb, object, complement)* and the relationship of the other words and constructions to those essentials.

Diagramming a Simple Sentence

A. A simple sentence has one complete thought. This simple sentence has one subject noun, one verb, and one direct object.

Yesterday many excited children played noisy games in the park.

Here's how to diagram it.

The main line of a diagram is a horizontal line.

- The verb is written on the center of the diagram line.

- The subject is written in front of the verb with a vertical line separating it from the verb. This vertical line cuts through the horizontal line.

- The direct object is written after the verb with a vertical line separating it from the verb. This vertical line touches the horizontal line but does not cut through it.

Modifiers of the subject, verb, and direct object are written on slanted lines under the appropriate word. Note the way in which the prepositional phrase is indicated.

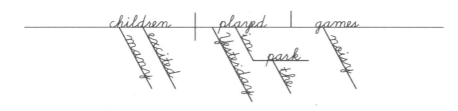

B. These simple sentences have subject complements. Indicate a subject complement by drawing a slanted line pointing back to the subject between the verb and the complement. Remember that the complement can be a noun, a pronoun, or an adjective.

Mrs. Mitchell is a good teacher. She is always very kind.

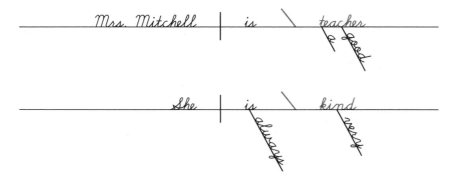

C. This simple sentence has an indirect object. The indirect object is placed under the verb.

The babysitter read the children a scary story.

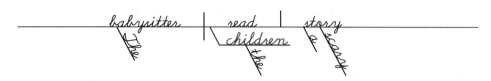

D. This simple sentence has an appositive. The appositive goes in parentheses after the noun it renames or describes.

My family visited Tokyo, the capital of Japan.

E. A simple sentence may have a compound subject, a compound predicate, and/or a compound direct object. These are diagrammed in similar ways—on parallel lines with the conjunction on a broken line between the words it joins. Add modifiers to the appropriate words.

Bob and Joanne designed and built the children's playhouse.

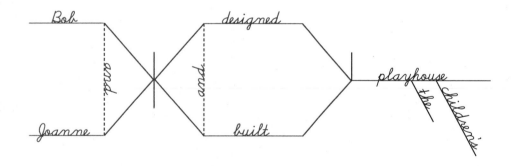

The children and their parents ate chocolate cake and vanilla ice cream.

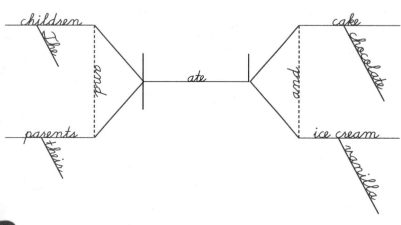

Diagramming a Compound Sentence

A compound sentence contains two or more independent clauses. Each clause is diagrammed according to the form for a simple sentence. When both independent clauses have been diagrammed, place the conjunction on a horizontal line between the verbs and connect it to the main diagram lines with broken vertical lines.

The longest cave in the world is Mammoth Cave, but the deepest cave is in France.

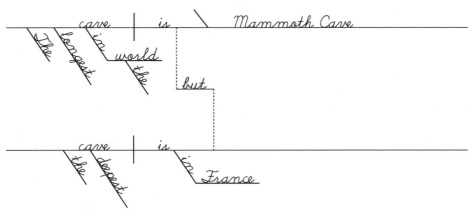

If a semicolon is used instead of a conjunction, place an X on the line between the clauses.

Snow fell during the night; the field lay under a soft, white blanket.

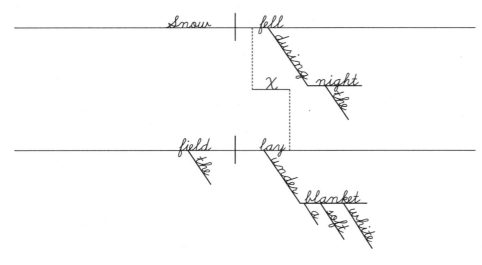

Try It Yourself

Diagram each of these sentences on a sheet of paper. **[Answers are given on next page.]**

1. The quick, brown fox jumped over the lazy dog; the dog never moved.

2. Tom and his friends visited Disneyland, a famous park in California.

3. The old man and the little boy fished in the lake and picnicked on the shore.

4. The cheerleaders from our school were the best team in the contest.

5. The teacher gave the class instructions, but nobody paid attention.

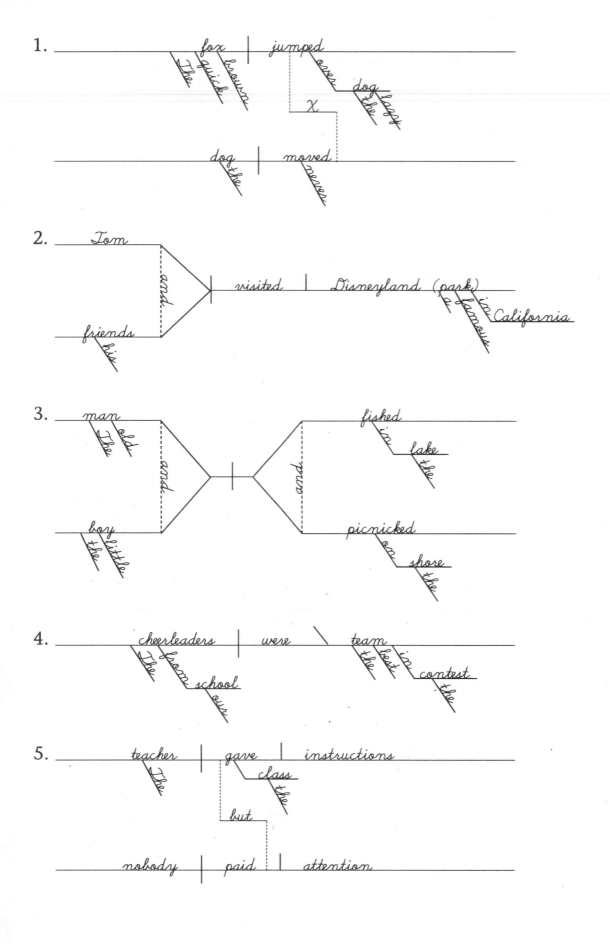

Handbook of Terms

A

adjective A word that describes a noun or pronoun.

Some descriptive adjectives come from proper nouns and are called proper adjectives. A proper adjective begins with a capital letter: *American* history.

The adjectives *a, an,* and *the* point out nouns. They are called articles.

Demonstrative adjectives point out specific persons, places, or things.

- *This* and *that* point out one person, place, or thing.
- *These* and *those* point out more than one person, place, or thing.
- *This* and *these* point out persons, places, or things that are near.
- *That* and *those* point out persons, places, or things, that are far.

Possessive adjectives show possession or ownership. The possessive adjectives are *my, your, his, her, its, our, your,* and *their.*

Numeral adjectives indicate exact numbers: *ten, twenty-five, third, twelfth.*

Some adjectives indicate number but not an exact number: *many, few, several, some.*

An adjective usually comes before the noun it modifies: *sunny* morning, *hot* chocolate.

An adjective that follows a linking verb is a subject complement. A subject complement completes the meaning of the verb and describes the subject of the sentence: The night was *dark* and *cold.*

Some adjectives may be used as pronouns: There were a *few* cookies on the plate. I ate a *few.*

Some words may function as nouns or adjectives: *drama, drama* class, *property, property* tax.

See also **comparison.**

adverb A word that modifies a verb, an adjective, or another adverb.

An adverb of time answers the question *when* or *how often:* It rained *yesterday.* We *usually* eat lunch at noon.

An adverb of place answers the question *where:* Toshi bent his head *forward.* Sit *here* by the gate.

An adverb of manner answers the question *how* or *in what manner:* Jason draws *well.* She dances the waltz *gracefully.*

(continued on next page)

An adverb of degree answers the question *how much* or *how little:* The boy is *very* tall. Gaelic is *seldom* spoken in that part of Ireland.

An adverb of affirmation asserts something: The music is *certainly* beautiful.

An adverb of negation expresses the negative of an alternative choice or possibility: The door is *not* locked.

A conjunctive adverb is used to connect two independent clauses. The principal conjunctive adverbs are *consequently, however, moreover, nevertheless, therefore,* and *thus:* Jill had studied journalism; *therefore,* the newspaper editor hired her.

Interrogative adverbs are used in asking questions: *Where* was she born?

Nouns that express time, distance, measure, weight, value, or direction can function as adverbs by modifying verbs: Every *Sunday* we attend church. He is six *feet* tall.

Some words may be used as adverbs or as adjectives: He runs *fast.* He is a *fast* runner.

See also **comparison.**

apostrophe A punctuation mark (') used in the following ways:

- to show ownership: the *cook's* hat, the *girls'* horses
- to replace letters left out in a contraction: *wasn't* for *was not; I'm* for *I am*
- with *s* to show the plural of letters: Mind your *p's* and *q's.*

articles The adjectives *a, an,* and *the. A* and *an* are the indefinite articles. An indefinite article refers to any of a class of things: *a* banana, *an* elephant. *The* is the definite article. The definite article refers to one or more specific things: *the* bananas in the bowl, *the* elephants in the zoo.

C

capitalization The use of capital letters. Capital letters are used for many purposes, including the following:

- the first word of a sentence: *T*he bell rang.
- proper nouns and proper adjectives: *Betsy Ross' American* flag
- an abbreviation if the word it stands for begins with a capital letter: *Rev.* for *Reverend.*
- the first word and the name of a person addressed in the salutation of a letter: *Dear Marie,*
- the first word in the complimentary close of a letter: *Yours* truly,
- the principal words in the titles of books, plays, pictures, and most poems: A T*ale of Two Cities, Romeo and Juliet, Mona Lisa,* "*Fire and Ice*"
- the first word of a direct quotation: Mother said, "*It's* time for my favorite television program."

- proper nouns and proper adjectives: *China, Chinese* checkers
- titles when used in direct address as substitutes for the names of persons: Thank you, *Professor.*
- North, East, South, West when they refer to a section of the country or the world: the old *West.* They are not capitalized when they refer to direction: He drove *west* on Main Street.
- the pronoun *I,* the interjection *O*
- names referring to deities or to sacred books: *God,* the *Bible*
- two-letter state postal abbreviations: *MA, NY, CA*

clause A group of related words that contain a subject and predicate and is used as part of a sentence.

An independent clause expresses a complete thought.

A dependent clause does not express a complete thought and cannot stand alone. A dependent clause, together with an independent clause, forms a complex sentence.

- An adjectival clause is a dependent clause used as an adjective: The roses *that he bought* were yellow. Adjectival clauses are usually introduced by relative pronouns: *who, whom, which, whose, that.*
- An adverbial clause is a dependent clause used as an adverb: *After we had canoed down the river,* we went to a clambake on the beach. Adverbial clauses are usually introduced by conjunctions such as *after, although, as, because, before, for, since, that, though, unless, until, when, where,* and *while.*

A restrictive clause points out or identifies a certain person, place, or thing. A restrictive clause cannot be omitted without changing the meaning of a sentence: The girl *who runs the fastest* will win the prize.

A nonrestrictive clause adds to the information about a person, place, or thing, but it is not necessary to the meaning of the sentence: New York, *which is located on the eastern seaboard,* contains many museums. A nonrestrictive clause is separated from the rest of the sentence by commas.

colon A punctuation mark (:) used after the salutation in a business letter: Dear Sir:

A colon is also used before a list or an enumeration of items: We bought the following: eggs, limes, bread.

comma A punctuation mark (,) used to make reading clearer. Among its many uses are the following:

- to separate words or groups of words in a series: elephants, giraffes, hyenas, and monkeys
- to set off parts of dates, addresses, or geographical names: June 1, 2003; 321 Spring Road, Atlanta, Georgia; Paris, France
- to set off words in direct address: Josie, I'm so pleased that you called me this morning.
- after the words *yes* and *no* when they introduce sentences: Yes, I agree with you completely.

(continued on next page)

- to set off direct quotations, unless a question mark or exclamation point is required: "We have only vanilla and chocolate today," he said in an apologetic tone.
- to separate simple sentences connected by the conjunctions *and, but,* and *or:* She called his name, but he didn't answer her.
- after the salutation and closing in a social or friendly letter: Dear Mrs. Porter, Dear Ben, Sincerely yours,
- to set off parenthetical expressions—words or groups of words that are inserted in a sentence as comments or explanatory remarks that are not necessary to the thought of the sentence: The time, I think, is up.
- after long introductory phrases and clauses: As the band marched down the street, the class cheered and applauded.
- to separate nonrestrictive phrases and clauses from the rest of the sentence: Chicago, which is the biggest city in Illinois, is not the state capital.

comparison The act of comparing. Many adjectives and adverbs can be used to compare two or more persons, places, or things.

Adjectives

- An adjective in the *positive* degree describes one or more persons, places, or things: The cat is *quiet.* The dogs are *powerful.*
- An adjective in the comparative degree compares two persons, places, or things. Form comparative adjectives by adding *-er* to the positive degree or by putting *more* before the positive degree: *quieter, more powerful.*
- An adjective in the superlative degree compares three or more persons, places, or things. Form superlative adjectives by adding *-est* to the positive degree or by putting *most* before the positive degree: *quietest, most powerful.*

Adverbs

- Form the comparative degree by adding *-er* to the positive degree or by putting *more* before the positive degree: *faster, more carefully.*
- Form the superlative degree by adding *-est* to the positive degree or by putting *most* before the positive degree: *faster, most carefully.*

Farther refers to distance: She went *farther* into the forest. *Further* denotes an addition: *Further* research is necessary. Both *farther* and *further* are used as nouns and as adjectives.

complex sentence A sentence that contains one independent clause and one or more dependent clauses: *If you want to win, you must jump higher.*

- An independent clause expresses a complete thought: *You must jump higher.*
- A dependent clauses does not express a complete thought and cannot stand alone: *If you want to win.*

- A dependent clause may precede, follow, or be contained within an independent clause.

compound sentence A sentence that contains two or more independent clauses: *Usually Jane drives to work, but today she took the train.*

- The clauses in a compound sentence are usually connected by a conjunction or by a conjunctive adverb.
- A semicolon may be used to separate the clauses in a compound sentence.

compound subjects, predicates, objects In a simple sentence, the subject, the predicate, and the direct object may be compound: *Ivan* and *John* argued with the grocer. The baby *walks* and *talks* well. Wear your *hat, scarf,* and *gloves.*

conjunction A word used to connect words, phrases, or clauses in a sentence. The most common conjunctions are *and, but,* and *or.*

Coordinate conjunctions connect subjects, predicates, direct objects, and clauses of the same rank and function: Joshua *and* Leanne cut *and* pasted the words *and* pictures on the posters. It poured all day, *and* a cold wind blew.

Correlative conjunctions are coordinate conjunctions used in pairs: *Neither* Tom *nor* Laurie left the party early.

Conjunctive adverbs connect two independent clauses: The meal was expensive; *however,* I wasn't surprised.

Subordinate conjunctions connect an independent and a dependent clause: He missed gym class *because* he was sick.

contraction Two words written as one with one or more letters omitted: *doesn't* for *does not, I've* for *I have.* An apostrophe is used to show the omission of a letter or letters.

D

dash A punctuation mark (—) used to indicate a sudden change of thought: The boy jumped—indeed soared—over the hurdle.

demonstrative pronoun A pronoun that points out a definite person, place, or thing. *This* and *these* are used for objects that are nearby; *that* and *those* are used for objects that are distant.

A demonstrative pronoun may be used as an adjective to modify a noun or as a pronoun to take the place of a noun: Is *this* book yours? Is *this* yours?

direct object The receiver of the action of a verb: Nathaniel gave the *baby* to her mother. An object pronoun can be used as a direct object: Nathaniel gave *her* to her mother.

E

exclamation point A punctuation mark (!) used after an exclamatory word, phrase, or sentence: More than one thousand people attended the wedding! Wonderful! What a celebration!

H

hyphen A punctuation mark (-) used to divide a word at the end of a line whenever one or more syllables are carried to the next line.

The hyphen is also used in the words for compound numbers from twenty-one to ninety-nine and to separate the parts of some compound words: *soldier-statesman, half-baked plan.*

I

indefinite pronoun An indefinite pronoun refers to any or all of a group of persons, places, or things.

Indefinite pronouns such as *anyone, anything, everybody, no one, nobody, nothing, one, somebody, something, each, either,* and *neither* are always singular and require a singular verb. Possessive adjectives and pronouns that refer to these pronouns must be singular: Somebody left *her* coat on the bus. Everyone in this class works hard for *his* or *her* grades.

Indefinite pronouns such as *all, both, few, many, several,* and *some* are generally plural. Possessive adjectives and pronouns that refer to these pronouns must be plural: *Few* look to *their* left before turning.

indirect object The noun or pronoun that tells to whom or for whom the action in a sentence is done: I gave *him* a present. He baked *Martha* a cake.

intensive pronouns The pronouns ending in *-self* or *-selves* (*myself, yourself, himself, herself, itself, ourselves, yourselves,* and *themselves*) can be used to show emphasis: I *myself* cooked the entire dinner.

interjection A word that expresses a strong or sudden emotion. An interjection may express delight, disgust, pain, agreement, impatience, surprise, sorrow, wonder, etc. An interjection is grammatically distinct from the rest of the sentence: *Oh! Shh! Ouch! Wow!*

interrogative pronoun A pronoun that is used to ask a question.

- *Who* and *whom* are used to ask about persons. *Who* is used when the pronoun is the subject of the sentence. *Whom* is used when the pronoun is the object of a verb or of a preposition.
- *Which* is used to ask about persons, places, or things.
- *What* is used to ask about places or things and to seek information.
- *Whose* is used to ask about possession.

N

noun The name of a person, place, or thing.

There are two main kinds of nouns: proper nouns and common nouns.

- A common noun names any one member of a group of persons, places, or things: *queen, city, church.*
- A proper noun names a particular person, place, or thing. A proper noun is capitalized: *Queen Elizabeth, London, Westminster Abbey.*

- A collective noun names a group of persons, places, or things considered as a unit. A collective noun usually takes a singular verb: The *crew* is tired. The *herd* is resting.
- A concrete noun names something that can be seen or touched: *brother, river, tree.* Most nouns are concrete.
- An abstract noun names a quality, a condition, or a state of mind. It names something that cannot be seen or touched: *anger, idea, spirit.*

A noun can be singular or plural.
- A singular noun names one person, place, or thing: *boy, river, berry.*
- A plural noun names more than one person, place, or thing: *boys, rivers, berries.*

The possessive form of a noun expresses possession, ownership, or connection. The apostrophe (') is the sign of a possessive noun.
- To form the possessive of a singular noun, add *'s* to the singular form: *architect's.*
- To form the possessive of a plural noun that ends in s, add an apostrophe (') to the plural form: *farmers'.*
- To form the possessive of a plural noun that does not end in *s,* add *'s* to the plural form: *children's.*

An appositive is a noun that follows another noun. It renames or describes the noun it follows: Kanisha Taylor, the *president* of our class, will make the first speech.

A noun used in direct address names the person spoken to: *Tyrone,* would you help me?

Some words can function as nouns or as verbs: Rudy needs *help.* After school we *help* him clean up the store.

O

order in a sentence The sequence of the subject and verb in a sentence expresses its order.

- When the verb in a sentence follows the subject, the sentence is in natural order: The *settlers planted* the seeds.
- When the main verb or the helping verb in a sentence comes before the subject, the sentence is in inverted order: Across the plain *marched* the tired *soldiers.*

P

period A punctuation mark (.) used at the end of a declarative or an imperative sentence and after initials and some abbreviations.

phrase A group of related words that forms a single unit within a sentence: *beside the sofa; before the storm.*

- An adjectival phrase is used as an adjective and modifies a noun: The book *on the table* is mine.

(continued on next page)

- An adverbial phrase is used as an adverb and modifies a verb, an adjective, or an adverb: The children played *in the park*.

  See also **prepositional phrase.**

possessive adjective *See* **adjective.**

possessive pronoun A pronoun that shows possession or ownership by the speaker; the person spoken to; or the person, place, or thing spoken about: *mine, yours, his, hers, its, ours,* and *theirs*. A possessive pronoun takes the place of a noun and its possessive adjective.

Although possessive pronouns show ownership, they do not contain apostrophes: The new skates are *hers*.

predicate The part of a sentence that tells something about the subject. The predicate consists of a verb and its modifiers, objects, and complements, if any: Jason *laughed*. Nikki *ate breakfast*. They *have run through the tall grass*.

preposition A preposition is a word that relates a noun or a pronoun to some other word in the sentence. The noun or pronoun that follows the preposition is the object of the proposition: The huge mountain lion leaped *through* (preposition) the tall *grass* (object of the preposition).

Some words may function as prepositions or as adverbs:

- A preposition shows the relationship between its object and some other word in the sentence: Megan sat *near* the door.
- An adverb tells how, when, or where: My friend is always *near*.

prepositional phrase A phrase that is introduced by a preposition. A prepositional phrase contains a preposition and an object: *off* (preposition) the *grass* (object of the preposition).

- An adjectival phrase is used as an adjective and modifies a noun: The cabin *in the woods* burned down.
- An adverbial phrase is used as an adverb and modifies a verb: The river flows *into the sea*.

pronoun A word that takes the place of a noun or nouns.

A personal pronoun names

- the speaker (first person): *I, mine, me, we, ours, us*
- the person spoken to (second person): *you, yours*
- the person, place, or thing spoken about (third person): *he, she, it, his, hers, its, him, her, they, theirs, them*

A personal pronoun is singular when it refers to one person, place, or thing. A personal pronoun is plural when it refers to more than one person, place, or thing.

The third person singular pronoun can be masculine, feminine, or neuter.

A pronoun may be used as the subject of a sentence. The subject pronouns are *I, you, he, she, it, we,* and *they*.

A subject pronoun can replace a noun used as a subject complement.

A pronoun may be used as the direct object of a verb. The object pronouns are *me, you, him, her, it, us,* and *them.*

An object pronoun may be used as the object of a preposition.

A pronoun that follows the conjunction *than* or *as* must be a subject pronoun if the word with which it is compared is a subject: *John* is happier than *I.* It must be an object pronoun if the word with which it is compared is an object pronoun: The loud music bothered *John* more than *her.*

When a sentence contains a negative, such as *not* or *never,* use *anyone* or *anything* rather than *no one* or *nothing.*

See also **contraction, possessive pronoun,** *and* **reflexive pronoun.**

Q

question mark A punctuation mark (?) used at the end of a question: What time is it?

quotation marks Punctuation marks (" ") used before and after every direct quotation and every part of a divided quotation: "Let's go shopping," said Michiko. "I can go with you," Father said, "after I have eaten lunch."

Quotation marks enclose titles of short stories, poems, magazine articles, television shows, and radio programs. Titles of books, magazines, newspapers, movies, and works of art are usually printed in *italics* or are underlined.

R

reflexive pronoun A reflexive pronoun ends in *-self* or *-selves.* The reflexive pronouns are *myself, yourself, himself, herself, itself, ourselves, yourselves,* and *themselves.* A reflexive pronoun often refers to the subject of the sentence: She saw *herself* in the mirror.

relative pronoun A pronoun that connects a dependent clause to the person, place, or thing it modifies: Hal, *who* grew up in Indonesia, now lives in Boston.

The relative pronouns are *who, whom, whose, which,* and *that.* Use *who* if the pronoun is the subject of the dependent clause: Sue, *who* helped me, is my cousin. Use *whom* if the pronoun is the object of the dependent clause: Sue, *whom* you know, helps me study.

S

semicolon A punctuation mark (;) used as follows:

- to separate the clauses of a compound sentence when they are not separated by a conjunction: The bicycle was broken; the wheel was damaged.
- to separate the clauses of a compound sentence that are connected by a conjunctive adverb: Helga plays the violin; however, she can barely read music.

(continued on next page)

- before *as* and *namely* when these words introduce an example or an illustration: Three famous composers of classical music are called the three B's; namely, Bach, Beethoven, and Brahms.

sentence A group of words that expresses a complete thought.

A declarative sentence makes a statement; it is followed by a period: *The sun is shining.*

An interrogative sentence asks a question; it is followed by a question mark: *Where is my pen?*

An imperative sentence gives a command or makes a request; it is followed by a period: *Go to the store. Please pick up the papers.*

An exclamatory sentence expresses strong or sudden emotion; it is followed by an exclamation point: *What a loud noise that was!*

A sentence is made up of a subject and a predicate.

- The subject names a person, a place, or a thing about which a statement is made. The simple subject is a noun or pronoun without any of its modifiers: The *man* is riding his bike.
- The complete subject is the simple subject with all its modifiers: *The tall, athletic young man* is riding his bike.
- The predicate tells something about the subject. The simple predicate is a verb without any of its modifiers, objects, and complements: Teresa *waved.*
- The complete predicate is the verb with all its modifiers, objects, and complements: Teresa *waved to the child from the window.*

A simple sentence contains one subject and one predicate. Either or both may be compound. *See also* **compound subjects, predicates, objects.**

See also **complex sentence, compound sentence, order in a sentence.**

subject The person, place, or thing that a sentence is about: *Daniel* spoke. The *prairie* was dry. The *cup* broke into pieces.

subject complement A word that completes the meaning of a linking verb in a sentence. A subject complement may be a noun, a pronoun, or an adjective: Broccoli is a green *vegetable.* The prettiest one was *she.* The sea will be *cold.*

V

verb A word that expresses action or state of being.

A verb has four principal parts: the present, the present participle, the past, and the past participle.

- The present participle is formed by adding *-ing* to the present.
- The simple past and past participle of regular verbs are formed by adding *-ed* to the present.
- The simple past and past participle of irregular verbs are not formed by adding *-ed* to the present.

The tense of a verb shows the time of its action.

- The simple present tense tells about an action that happens again and again: I *play* the piano every afternoon.
- The simple past tense tells about an action that happened in the past: I *played* the piano yesterday afternoon.
- The future tense tells about an action that will happen in the future; the future is formed with the present and the auxiliary verb *will:* I *will play* in the piano recital next Sunday.
- The present progressive tense tells what is happening now; the present progressive tense is formed with the present participle and a form of the verb *be:* He *is eating* his lunch now.
- The past progressive tense tells what was happening in the past; the past progressive tense is formed with the past participle and a past form of the verb *be:* He *was eating* his lunch when I saw him.
- The present perfect tense tells about a past action that is relevant to the present: I *have lived* here for six years now.
- The past perfect tense tells about a past action that happened before another past action: I *had lived* in Memphis for a year before I moved here.
- The future perfect tense tells about an action that will be completed by a specific time in the future: I *will have finished* dinner by the time you get here.

A transitive verb expresses an action that passes from a doer to a receiver. The receiver is the direct object of the verb: The dog *ate* the bone.

An intransitive verb has no receiver of the action. It does not have a direct object: The sun *shone* on the lake.

Some verbs may be transitive or intransitive according to their use in the sentence: Chita *played* the harp. Joel *played* at Notre Dame.

A linking verb links a subject with a subject complement (a noun, a pronoun, or an adjective).

- The verb *be* in its many forms (*is, are, was, will be, have been, etc.*) is the most common linking verb.
- The verbs *appear, become, continue, feel, grow, look, remain, seem, smell, sound, stay,* and *taste* are also considered to be linking verbs.

In the active voice, the subject is the doer of the action: Betty *wrote* a poem. In the passive voice, the subject is the receiver of the action: The poem *was written* by Betty.

The modal auxiliary verbs *may, might, can, could, must, should,* and *would* are used to express permission, possibility, ability, necessity, and obligation.

A verb phrase is a group of words that does the work of a single verb. A verb phrase contains one or more auxiliary or helping verbs (*is, are, has, have, will, can, could, would, should, etc.*) and a main verb: She *had forgotten* her hat.

(continued on next page)

A subject and a verb must always agree.

- Singular subjects must have singular verbs. The third person singular of the simple present tense ends in -*s* or -*es:* I *run.* You *run.* He *runs.*

- Plural subjects must have plural verbs. A plural verb does not end in -*s* or -*es:* We *run.* You *run.* They *run.*

- Use *am* with the first person singular subject pronoun: I *am* a soccer player.

- Use *is* with a singular noun or a third person singular subject pronoun: Paris *is* a city. She *is* a pianist. It *is* a truck.

- Use *are* with a plural noun, the second person subject pronoun, or a third person plural pronoun: Dogs *are* good pets. You *are* the winner. We *are* happy. They *are* my neighbors.

- Use *was* with a singular noun or a first or third person singular subject pronoun: The boy *was* sad. I *was* lucky. It *was* a hard job.

- Use *were* with a plural noun, a second person subject pronoun, or a third person plural subject pronoun: The babies *were* crying. You *were* a good friend.

- A phrase or a parenthetical expression between the subject and the verb does not affect the verb: A *crate* of bananas *was* hoisted off the boat.

A collective noun requires a singular verb if the idea expressed by the subject is thought of as a unit: The orchestra *plays* tomorrow. A collective noun requires a plural verb if the idea expressed by the subject is throught of as individuals: The family *are* living in Georgia, Virginia, and the Carolinas.

In sentences beginning with *there,* use *there is* or *there was* when the subject that follows is singular: *There is* no cause for alarm. Use *there are* or *there were* when the subject is plural: *There were* many passengers on the bus.